D1235606

THE KING JAMES BIBLE

The King James Bible (KJB) was the result of an extraordinary effort over nearly a century to take many good English translations and turn them into what the translators called 'one principal good one, not justly to be excepted against'. David Norton traces the work of Tyndale and his successors, analysing the translation and revisions of two representative passages. His fascinating new account follows in detail the creation of the KJB, including attention to the translators' manuscript work. He also examines previously unknown evidence such as the diary of John Bois, the only man who made notes on the translation. At the centre of the book is a thorough discussion of the first edition. The latter part of the book traces the printing and textual history of the KJB and provides a concise account of its changing scholarly and literary reputations.

DAVID NORTON is Professor of English at Victoria University of Wellington. His previous publications include *A History of the Bible as Literature*, 2 volumes (Cambridge, 1993), and *The New Cambridge Paragraph Bible* (Cambridge, 2005).

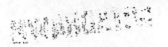

THE KING JAMES BIBLE

A Short History from Tyndale to Today

DAVID NORTON

CAMBRIDGE
UNIVERSITY PRESS

CAMBRIDGE
UNIVERSITY PRESS

University Printing House, Cambridge CB2 8BS, United Kingdom

Cambridge University Press is part of the University of Cambridge.

It furthers the University's mission by disseminating knowledge in the pursuit of
education, learning and research at the highest international levels of excellence.

www.cambridge.org
Information on this title: www.cambridge.org/9780521616881

© David Norton 2011

First published 2011
6th printing 2014

A catalogue record for this publication is available from the British Library

Library of Congress Cataloguing in Publication data
Norton, David.
The King James Bible : a short history from Tyndale to today / David Norton.
p. cm.
Includes bibliographical references and index.
ISBN 978-0-521-85149-7 – ISBN 978-0-521-61688-1 (pbk.)
1. Bible. English. Authorized – History.   I. Title.
BS186.N66   2010
220.5´203 – dc22   2010041513

ISBN 978-0-521-85149-7 Hardback
ISBN 978-0-521-61688-1 Paperback

Contents

Illustrations

D.N. unto the reader

This heading is homage to William Tyndale, who used the same form for his prologue to his 1534 New Testament. It was Tyndale who began the writing in English of what became the King James Bible and did most to make it what it is. Of course he had to have a Bible to translate, so I begin with the Bible itself and a selective look at the resources available to the Reformation translators. The English story of the King James Bible starts with Tyndale, and I explore how he and his successors collectively created it. In part this is done through the history of their work, in part through showing how they developed two brief passages. Then I trace the history of the work on the King James Bible itself, and examine the translators' scholarship particularly through the library of one of the translators and the previously unknown diary of another. At the heart of the story is the first edition of 1611, explored from title page through to minute details of the text. Then comes a survey of the printing history of the King James Bible through to the establishment of the standard text in 1769, followed by a more selective look at later editions. The King James Bible was not always admired as it has been over the last two and a half centuries of its life, so I conclude with a sketch of its changing reputation. It is a story that I hope will increase understanding and appreciation of the prime Bible in English.

There have been accounts of the English Bible, many of them excellent, from as early as 1645. Like the creation of the KJB, gathering information has been a collaborative process over centuries, so some of what is offered here can be found in many other books, and I have been glad to draw on them. I have not made this into a colourful picture of the time of the translators: translation is above all a matter of weighing the finest details of words, and I have attempted to give as genuine an impression of this as possible, hoping that the reader is willing to share the attention to detail that made the King James Bible what it is. I have also drawn on some of my earlier work on the Bible, and occasionally repeated myself, for which I hope to be forgiven.

The availability of digital images of early books, notably in *Early English Books Online* (Chadwyck-Healey) and *Eighteenth-Century Collections Online* (Gale), besides making so much more available, has allowed me to cite original editions in most cases, but I have used modern spelling for the quotations.

Besides the indebtedness to other writers on the English Bible in general and the King James Bible in particular, I owe debts of thanks to Ward Allen, pioneering scholar of the King James Bible, Jim Urry, self-appointed indefatigable research assistant, Art Pomeroy and Peter Gainsford, who have given me invaluable help in understanding John Bois's diary, Tatjana Schaefer and Jack Thiessen, who have helped me understand Luther's German, Paul Morris, Kathryn Walls, Glyn Parry, Michael Wheeler, Laurence M. Vance, and many Cambridge librarians and scholars, including Alan Jesson and Rosemary Matthews (Bible Society), Nicholas Rogers (Sidney Sussex), David McKitterick (Trinity), Scott Mandelbrote (Peterhouse), Helen Carron (Emmanuel), and the staff of Gonville and Caius library.

This is also an opportunity to thank correspondents who helped me to find the errors in *The New Cambridge Paragraph Bible*: their interest was helpful and heartening. I am especially grateful to Raoul Comninos, who sent detailed notes and suggestions on the entire text, and to Thomas L. Hubeart.

Reflecting on what long seemed a curious moment in my career that led to my working on the Bible, it seems now to have a kind of inevitability, so I come to my greatest debt of gratitude, to my mother and her ongoing love of the Bible. Her Welsh Methodist heritage, going back to one of the founders of Methodism, Daniel Rowland, influenced me more than I knew. The presence of a variety of Bibles in our house, including J.B. Phillips and James Moffatt's translations, and E.S. Bates's *The Bible Designed to be Read as Literature*, helped shape my consciousness of the Bible. That she had read from *The New Cambridge Paragraph Bible*, sometimes aloud to my father, was a strange, deep-felt pleasure for me. This book was originally dedicated to her, but now I must inscribe it thus:

In memory of my mother, Margaret Norton,
whose loving kindness taught us all how to live

Abbreviations

CHAPTER I

Predecessors

ORIGINALS AND TEXTS

THE ORIGINALS

The most important book in English religion and culture, the King James Bible, began to be created at some unknown moment nearer three than two thousand years before 1604, the year in which James VI and I, king of Scotland, now also king of England, assembled the religious leaders of the land at Hampton Court and, seemingly by chance, ordered the making of a new translation of the Bible. That unknown original moment of creation came when the descendants of Abraham moved beyond telling to writing down their beliefs and the stories of their heritage. It was a crucial moment in civilisation. The ancient Hebrews began to be the people of the written word. Their writings became the collection of books we know as the Old Testament. It enshrined their knowledge of themselves and of their relationship to their God. Without it they might not have survived as a people, and without it the Christian world – perhaps also the Islamic world – would have been something unimaginably different from what it is.

The word of God was all in all to the religious Jews. In the beginning God talked with Adam and Eve as a lord to his tenants, person to person, then to Moses 'face to face, as a man speaketh unto his friend' (Exod. 33:11). The intimacy might have declined and, by the time of the young Samuel, the word of the Lord had become 'precious' (1 Sam. 3:1), that is, both rare and valuable. God still spoke through his prophets, and they could say, 'thus saith the Lord'. But for ordinary people he spoke most surely in the words of the book. These words came to be guarded as the greatest treasure, for God and the word were the same thing: 'the Word was God' (John 1:1). Not the smallest detail, not 'one jot or one tittle' (Matt. 5:18) would go unfulfilled, and nothing in it could be changed. So Moses commanded the children of Israel, 'ye shall not add unto the word which I command you, neither shall you diminish aught from it, that ye may keep the commandments of the LORD your God which I command you' (Deut. 4:2). Perfect obedience to the commandments of God went hand in hand with an immutable text.

Such obedience was only possible if the book was understood. However simple some parts of it such as the Ten Commandments were, there were parts such as the prophetic visions of Ezekiel that were immensely difficult, so that one might say with the disciples, 'What meaneth this?' (Acts 2:12). Even the literal meaning of individual words could be difficult. The Old Testament represents almost all that survives of ancient Hebrew: it is an exceedingly small corpus from which to determine the meaning of all its words and to understand fully how it works as a language. Its vocabulary has little more than 8,000 words, of which nearly 1,000 occur once only, and four-fifths occur less than twenty times. Moreover, the text was defective in places. The enormous effort of preservation had operated on a text that was in places more than a thousand years old: inevitably, whether through editorial work or imperfect copying, it did not always represent what had originally been written. Indeed, sometimes it scarcely made sense.

Reverence for the text and the problems of understanding it are essential background to the story of books, scholarship and men that becomes the story of the King James Bible.

God promised Abraham that he would be 'a father of many nations' (Gen. 17:4), and many non-Hebrew-speaking nations inherited the Hebrew Bible. However much they reverenced the text, they could not in practice treat it as the Jews treated it. One thing mattered more than having the Bible in the language of God: having it in the language of the people. With the greatest reverence, it had to be translated, and the practice began early. Aramaic superseded Hebrew as the everyday language of the Jewish people, so, dating back to the Babylonian exile in the sixth century BC, Aramaic

Targums – translation-interpretations – were made of all the OT except Ezra, Nehemiah and Daniel. The next most important language of Judaism was Greek, as Jewish communities developed outside Israel. Their translation was the Septuagint (*c.* third century BC), notable for giving alternative versions of some books such as Esther, Daniel, Jeremiah, Ezra and Nehemiah, and for including other books that were not part of the Hebrew Bible: Tobit, Susanna, the Wisdom of Solomon, Ecclesiasticus, Baruch and Maccabees (here is the basis of the Apocrypha). This was the version of the Old Testament used for quotations in the New Testament. The Eastern or Orthodox Church, keeping Greek as its primary language, still uses the Septuagint as its standard Old Testament. In due course Latin became the dominant language for western Christianity, and it too acquired a standard version, Jerome's Vulgate, made between 382 and *c.* AD 404. These were the main ancient versions used by the Reformation translators.

The New Testament, the sacred writings of what began as a small sect within Judaism, the followers of Jesus Christ, created on the foundation of the Old Testament a new understanding of the relationship between God and humanity based on the teachings of Jesus and the belief that he was the Messiah, the risen son of God. What became the final and most important part of the KJB was written in Greek, and developed within a much shorter time span than the Old Testament. Its rapid development and dissemination prevented it from reaching as fixed a form as the Old Testament. It came to the Reformation through a small number of manuscripts (far fewer than are now known) that did not always read identically. Also, like the Old Testament, it came through the Vulgate.

TEXTS

As one would expect from the tradition lying behind it, there was little variation among Hebrew texts, and the sixteenth- and seventeenth-century translators probably used whatever printed edition they had to hand without feeling a need to make comparisons. Though not the first, the basic printed text of the Reformation was the work of a Christian scholar-printer working in Venice, Daniel Bomberg, and a Jewish convert, Felix Pratensis, first published 1516–17. These Bomberg or Rabbinic Bibles, most notably the second edition of 1524–5, set the standard. The main editions gave the Targums, printed alongside the Hebrew in smaller type, and medieval rabbinic commentaries on the literal sense, printed round the outside of the text and often completely enclosing it. The commentaries were chiefly by Rashi, highly influential as a preserver of Jewish tradition, the philologist Abraham Ibn Ezra, and the outstanding grammarian, David Kimchi.

The NT text was later to be printed and slower to take something like a standard form. Work to produce the first printed Greek NTs depended primarily on the manuscripts the early editors happened to have access to, then on the way the results of their work were put together by later editors, sometimes using further manuscripts. The first two printed Greek NTs were the result of concurrent, independent work. At Alcala (Complutum) in Spain a text was printed for the Complutensian Polyglot in 1514 but not published until 1522, and then only in an edition of 600 expensive copies. It claimed to have been made from the oldest manuscripts, but we do not know which they were, only that very creditable work went into the text. Urged on by the printer John Froben, Desiderius Erasmus, among the most famous scholars of the time, gazumped the Spaniards with an annotated Greek text accompanied by his new Latin translation, the *Novum Instrumentum* in 1516. The text was, as the errors showed and as Erasmus admitted, 'truly more rushed than edited',[1] prepared in a matter of months principally from two twelfth-century manuscripts, compared with a few others, and a single, incomplete manuscript of Revelation, also from the twelfth century; he used his earliest manuscript, from the tenth century, least because it conformed least with his other texts (it is now thought to be the best of the manuscripts he had available to him).[2] He had hoped to find a manuscript good enough for Froben to use as copy, but some corrections were needed, and these he made directly on the manuscripts.[3] Where his manuscripts had omissions, or where text and commentary were so mixed as to be indistinguishable, he supplied his own Greek translation, based on the Vulgate. Sometimes the results do

---

[1] 'Praecipitatum verius quam editum'; quoted in Greenslade (ed.), *Cambridge History of the Bible*, vol. III, p. 59.
[2] Metzger, *The Text of the New Testament*, p. 102.   [3] Ibid., pp. 99 ff., plate XVI.

not correspond to any Greek manuscripts, yet have remained in the Received Text.

Some 3,300 copies of the first two editions of Erasmus's text, its comparative cheapness and convenience, and Erasmus's own prestige all ensured that this was the preferred text through – and well beyond – the time of the translators. Erasmus and subsequent editors refined it, drawing on the Complutensian text and further work with manuscripts. In 1550 the scholar-printer Robert Estienne (Stephanus or Stephens) published a fine folio that highlighted problems of textual accuracy by giving variant readings in the margin based on the Complutensian text and collation of more than fifteen manuscripts by his son, Henri. Nevertheless, the text itself was little changed from Erasmus's final editions. Without making many alterations to the text, the leading Genevan scholar, Theodore Beza, elaborated the critical work in a succession of editions from 1565 onwards; the KJB translators used his 1588–9 and 1598 editions.[4] In spite of the accumulating knowledge of variant readings, there was a strong sense that the Greek text had attained a similar authenticity to that of the Hebrew. It was sufficiently settled for the Elzevir press, producing relatively cheap, popular editions, to inform the purchaser of its second edition, 1633, that 'you have the text received by everybody'.[5]

'Textus Receptus', Received Text, stuck as the name for this text, and Estienne's 1550 version of Erasmus remained the standard text into the nineteenth century. It represents the general form of the text found in the majority of the manuscripts, the Byzantine text, that is, associated with the Eastern Church in Byzantium (Constantinople). Majority attestation and traditional use have given this, the text that the Reformation translations are based on, special status and importance. It represents what most Christians have understood the truth of the NT to be. Nevertheless, advances in textual criticism and knowledge of many more manuscripts now make it clear that this is not the closest we can get to the lost originals of the NT authors (a complex subject beyond the scope of this book). The choice is between tradition and authenticity: what was believed to be the truth

---

[4] Ibid., p. 105.
[5] 'Textum ergo habes, nunc ab omnibus receptum'; quoted in Greenslade (ed.), *Cambridge History of the Bible*, vol. III, p. 64.

set against something closer to the truth of the NT writers, and, through them, the origins of Christianity.

The Hebrew and Greek were often printed with other versions, notably Latin versions. These were of great use for translators, for Latin was the international vernacular of scholarship. The polyglots, the Complutensian and Plantin's Antwerp polyglot (1569–72), included other ancient versions with sometimes interlinear Latin translations. Erasmus's NT had his Latin translation, the *Novum Instrumentum*, in a parallel column. Sanctes Pagninus's extremely literal Latin translation, *Veteris et Novi Testamenti nova translatio* (1528), was highly influential, not just its literal Latin translation of the OT (other versions superseded its NT), but also because of its extensive use of rabbinic sources. Translators in several languages found their teacher in Pagninus. Coverdale was one such; the Bishops' Bible translators were instructed to follow Pagninus and Münster 'for the verity of the Hebrew', and the KJB drew on Pagninus for some readings.[6] Sebastian Münster had published an annotated Latin version of the OT, printed alongside the Hebrew in 1535 which also drew extensively on rabbinic sources. Though his translation did not have the enduring success of Pagninus's, his annotations were long valued. The Zurich Latin Bible of 1543 included a new translation of the Apocrypha, and a revised version of Erasmus's Latin NT. The latest of these influential, annotated, Jewish-influenced Latin OTs was the work of Immanuel Tremellius and his son-in-law Franciscus Junius. It included translations of the OT, the Peshitta NT and the Apocrypha. The main new Latin version of the NT after Erasmus's was Beza's (1557); both included annotations and were frequently reprinted.

Presentation often enhanced the value of these versions, for they were usually presented as cribs. Ways of highlighting the connections between the Latin and the original languages were developed. The Complutensian Polyglot tied the words of the NT to the Vulgate by using superscript letters: the reader had only to glance from the Greek in the left column to the Latin in the right to see which word represented which.[7] Interlinear texts were even easier to use. After the publication of Pagninus's translation, 1528, few, perhaps none

---

[6] 'Observations respected of the translators', Pollard, *Records of the English Bible*, p. 297; Lloyd Jones, *Discovery of Hebrew in Tudor England*, pp. 41–2.
[7] Metzger, *Text of the New Testament*, p. 97, plate XVI.

of the translators would have found themselves working from the original languages alone, aided by nothing more than grammars and dictionaries, and never would they have found themselves working without an already vast knowledge of the text in their heads: most knew the Vulgate intimately.

From the unknown first Hebrew writer to Beza, all these men contributed, directly or indirectly, to the KJB. Many more, especially continental vernacular translators such as Martin Luther and the makers of dictionaries, grammars and concordances, should be added, but this is sufficient to give a sense of the books the English translators worked from.

THE FIRST DRAFT: WILLIAM TYNDALE

The KJB translators thought of themselves as revisers, not as creators of a new translation. In their preface, 'the translators to the reader', they say:

Truly, good Christian reader, we never thought from the beginning that we should need to make a new translation, nor yet to make of a bad one a good one . . . but to make a good one better, or out of many good ones one principal good one, not justly to be excepted against, that hath been our endeavour, that our mark.[8]

The 'good one' they were to make better was the official Bible of the Church of England, the Bishops' Bible of 1568, the 'many good ones' were the Testaments and Bibles made by William Tyndale and his successors. These many men drafted and re-drafted the KJB. Yet the KJB's immense debt to its English predecessors is different in kind from its debt to the creators of the Bible and the scholars who established the text and showed how it had been and might be understood. The English predecessors contributed to the understanding but their primary contribution was to develop an English way of expressing it. Expression from the English translators, understanding from the continental scholars: this, too crudely, is the formula for the KJB.

This chapter explores the external history of the preceding versions, thinking of them as drafts for the KJB and sometimes looking at ways

[8] *NCPB*, p. xxxi.

they were involved in arguments that influenced the KJB. In the next I turn to the internal history, taking two short passages to indicate how the English translators shaped the version into what we have received as the KJB.[9]

William Tyndale was martyred before he could complete his translation. Printing of his NT was initially thwarted by a raid of the printer's shop in 1525: only a prologue and most of Matthew survive. His complete NT appeared in 1526, with a revised edition in 1534. The first part of the OT, the Pentateuch, was published in 1530, and Jonah a little later. His translation of Joshua to 2 Chronicles appeared posthumously in the Matthew Bible (1537). This was enough to settle the general character of the English Bible through to and beyond the KJB. Without Tyndale, the English Bible would have been a different and, in all likelihood, lesser thing. Reading the KJB, we are for long stretches reading Tyndale, sometimes little revised, sometimes substantially worked over. A single spirit animates the Protestant – even, to a significant extent, the Catholic – English Bible from Tyndale to the KJB, and Tyndale was its first and most important manifestation.

'I had no man to counterfeit [imitate], neither was helped with English of any that had interpreted the same or such like thing in the Scripture beforetime', he declares in the address 'to the reader' in his 1526 NT. He was indeed a pioneer, yet, as this recognises, there had been other translations of the Bible or parts of it into English. Most notable among these was the Wyclif or Lollard Bible which appeared in two versions about 1382 and 1388. This pre-Reformation manuscript Bible was translated from the Vulgate, first with such literalness that it is like a crib for the Latin, then revised towards slightly more idiomatic English. Tyndale may have been familiar with this, but the Latin source, the very dated English and the excessive literalness would have made it a model to avoid.

He did have a very few non-English models, but, of all the English translators, he was the one who came closest to working from the original languages alone. This is suggested in his last surviving letter, written in Latin from prison shortly before his martyrdom, where he

---

[9] 'External history' and 'internal history' are the two main divisions of Westcott's *History of the English Bible*, one of the best works on the subject.

asks for 'the Hebrew bible, Hebrew grammar, and Hebrew dictionary, that I may pass the time in that study'.[10] We should not take this as suggesting that he continued his translation in prison – he would have needed much more for that, paper not least – but it does show what he considered basic for his study: text, grammar and dictionary.

His revised NT points in the same direction. The title proclaims it to be 'diligently corrected and compared with the Greek', and this is the first point he makes in both his prefaces. In 'W.T. unto the reader' he writes that 'I have looked over [it] again (now at the last) with all diligence, and compared it unto the Greek, and have weeded out of it many faults, which lack of help at the beginning, and oversight, did sow therein'. He adds that 'if ought seem changed, or not altogether agreeing with the Greek, let the finder of the fault consider the Hebrew phrase or manner of speech left in the Greek words', and he goes on to explain some of the Hebrew characteristics of NT Greek.[11] Tyndale's first study was the original language text, and his primary effort was to be as true to it as possible, including keeping to its 'phrase or manner of speech'.

He had helps – text, grammar and dictionary were enough for private study but not for translation. For the NT he had Erasmus's Greek text and Latin translation, and the Vulgate; he appears also to have had a general knowledge of other translations, for he writes of 'all the translators that ever I heard of in what tongue soever it be'.[12] And he had Luther. Martin Luther, giant among giants of the Reformation, published the first edition of his German NT in 1522; the Pentateuch followed in 1523, and Joshua to the Song of Solomon in 1524. For the OT, Tyndale had the Vulgate, the Septuagint, Luther and possibly Pagninus.

Estimates of Tyndale's dependence on these aids vary. Westcott and Hammond are most persuasive. Westcott demonstrates that 'both in his first translation and in his two subsequent revisions of the NT, [Tyndale] dealt directly and principally with the Greek text. If he used the Vulgate or Erasmus or Luther it was with the judgment of a scholar' (p. 146). His Greek was proficient, but he probably needed more help with the Hebrew, since he began to learn that

---

[10] As given in Daniell, *William Tyndale*, p. 379.
[11] New Testament, 1534, fol. *v[r].   [12] Ibid., fols *viii[r], **iiii[v].

language late, probably about 1526.[13] Hammond's view of the OT work suggests that Tyndale gave similar primacy to the Hebrew but

> that [he] relied heavily on Luther; that he quite probably made some use of Pagninus' version; that he made as much use of the Vulgate as would be consistent with his automatic familiarity with the established church version; and, most important of all, that his knowledge of the Hebrew original was sufficient for him to respond sensitively and effectively to the peculiarities of Hebrew vocabulary and style.[14]

Tyndale's judicious independence was a model for his successors. Just as he, revising his NT, moved it closer to fidelity to the original texts, so they, completing and revising what he had commenced, moved it towards further fidelity – something which often meant a greater literalness of rendering. Sometimes this work of revision was even, as Daniell points out, at the expense of clarity.[15]

While truth to the original languages was Tyndale's scholarly priority, his motivation was to make the Scriptures comprehensible to his fellow countrymen. The martyrologist John Foxe reports him as saying to a clerical opponent in the heat of an argument, 'if God spare my life, ere many years I will cause a boy that driveth the plough shall know more of the Scripture than thou dost'.[16] There were issues of huge importance involved in this seemingly simple ambition: to give the people a basis on which to come at their own sense of the truth was to challenge the Catholic Church's power and inevitably to split Christendom. For the Church, heresy went hand in hand with translation – an act that placed an unauthorised approximation of one part of truth, shorn of the wisdom and guardianship of the Church, in the hands of the uneducated. Yet the early heretics had been raised in the Church and could not, even if Tyndale wished to, rid themselves of the belief that the Bible was difficult. They had learnt that there were levels of meaning beyond the literal; they had learnt too that every detail of the text was to be pressed for its sacred meaning. The words they chose would not be the whole truth and might perhaps be no more than the beginnings of truth, but they would certainly be

---

[13] Daniell, *William Tyndale*, p. 296.
[14] Hammond, 'William Tyndale's Pentateuch', p. 354. See also Hammond's *Making of the English Bible*, chapters 1 and 2.
[15] Daniell, *William Tyndale*, p. 2.   [16] Foxe, *Acts and Monuments*, p. 514b.

examined minutely: if the scholarly did not dismiss them out of hand, they would examine them for their fidelity to the detail of the text (that is, the Vulgate), and if the unscholarly were to use them as the translators wished, it would be with an equal, though sympathetic, attention. Further, the people Tyndale and then Coverdale worked for would have the translation alone as the key to truth: such people could not use it as a way to the genuinely sacred text, Latin, Greek or Hebrew, nor could they use it side by side with other translations as an approximation to the truth; they could not even use it with a gloss, since vernacular commentary on the text had yet to be created. The translation had to be, as nearly as possible, perfect in itself. So Tyndale laboured to be faithful to the originals.

The Bible in English shaped Protestant English-speaking culture. It was not just that the Bible was read, heard and known: the Bible in English made the individualistic act of reading and understanding primary, creating a culture wedded to the belief that understood words were of the highest importance. Besides this, the Bible, more than any other writing in English, shaped the English language. This was an unlooked-for consequence of Tyndale's work, for he never set out to create a linguistic or literary revolution. Yet this, besides the religious revolution, is what he created. The decisions he made as to the kind of English he should use have affected every speaker and writer of English. Thomas More, his arch-antagonist, mockingly suggested that 'all England list now to go to school with Tyndale to learn English'.[17] His point was the difficulty of Tyndale's language. That we now find it remarkably straightforward and even powerful is precisely because all England went to school with Tyndale and learnt English from him and his successors, most notably from the principal form his work took, the KJB.

In spite of the many English literary achievements we now recognise from times before Tyndale, English had no prestige as a language for literature or scholarship. Not long before Shakespeare began to write, and more than half a century after the publication of Tyndale's NT, the literary translator George Pettie could declare that 'there are some others yet who will set light by my labours, because I write in

---

[17] More, *The Confutation of Tyndale's Answer* (1532, 1533); *Complete Works of St. Thomas More*, vol. VIII, p. 187.

English: and...the worst is, they think [good writing] impossible
to be done in our tongue, for they count it barren, they count it
barbarous, they count it unworthy to be accounted of'.[18] Though
Pettie went on to defend English, the situation is clear: to translate
the Bible into English was both to debase it and to put it into a
language many felt had not the ability to express its meaning.

Here we need to be mindful that language may do more than
mean: it may convey feeling, it may even be magical at the expense of
meaning. Tyndale and his successors did create in English both the
meaning of the Bible and 'the beauty of holiness' (Ps. 29:2 etc.), but
to understand how this happened and something of what it consists
in, we need to set aside modern perspectives and try to think from
the point of view of the 1520s. What choices did Tyndale have as to
how he should write? He had his duty to the text, and we have already
seen that he tried to shape his style to its styles. He also had his duty
to his audience, imagined as the 'boy that driveth the plough' (we
would say, the man in the street): it was a duty to be comprehensible
to an unsophisticated audience, so the unavoidable choice was to
write in a way that approximated to the English he heard spoken all
around him. These two duties were paramount, and the choices seem
inevitable.

He probably had two other choices. One was to make the translation thoroughly literal, following the word order of the original and
imitating its vocabulary wherever possible. This would sometimes
have worked against the duty to be comprehensible. Another was
to try to write appropriately majestic religious English, if only such
a thing existed – but it did not. The nearest he might have come
would have been to try to write majestically by shaping his language
according to the best standards of eloquence he knew, those of classical Latin and Greek. Again the question of comprehensibility would
have arisen, for the audience he had in mind did not know Latin.
Latin was far less assimilated into English then than it is now. The
common people would have heard much of what we take for granted
as English as a foreign language only partly assimilated into their
own, and they would have found Latin sentence structures very alien
to their own way of talking. Any attempt to write with the eloquence

---

[18] Pettie, *Civil Conversation of M. Stephen Guazzo*, fol. ii^{r-v}.

of the classics would have sinned against both comprehensibility and the English language just as much as literal translation would have.

There was a further, political reason for avoiding a Latinate way of writing, either in vocabulary or sentence structure. It would have seemed too close to the language of the Vulgate and the Catholic Church, and so to be supporting the institution he opposed.

Tyndale's choice was to attempt a balance between ordinary English and the ways of writing he found in the original languages. Fortunately, as he observed, the Hebrew (and to some extent the Greek) way of writing, especially in its simple sentence structures and its vocabulary tied to the everyday world, fitted well with English. What he says should be placed alongside the observation already given from Pettie in its sense of attitudes to English as a language:

Saint Jerome also translated the Bible into his mother tongue. Why may not we also? They will say it cannot be translated into our tongue, it is so rude. It is not so rude as they are false liars. For the Greek tongue agreeth more with the English than with the Latin. And the properties of the Hebrew tongue agreeth a thousand times more with the English than with the Latin. The manner of speaking is both one so that in a thousand places thou needest not but to translate it into the English, word for word, when thou must seek a compass in the Latin, and yet shall have much work to translate it well-favouredly, so that it have the same grace and sweetness, sense and pure understanding with it in the Latin, as it hath in the Hebrew. A thousand parts better may it be translated into the English than into the Latin.[19]

This perception of qualities in English that matched the Greek and, especially, the Hebrew is crucial to the way Tyndale translated. He could often translate 'word for word', that is, literally, and still write natural English that would reveal the full meaning of the original. It would be as true to the meaning as the Vulgate, and truer to the way the originals were written. This, in general terms, was to be the method, style and purpose of the KJB.

Nevertheless, these terms are indeed general. The idea of 'natural English' should not be pressed too hard. As More's words suggested, Tyndale's English – and subsequently that of the KJB – did not seem as natural and easy as we are inclined to think it. Nor did it seem grand or majestic. England did learn English from Tyndale. In drafting the

[19] Tyndale, *Obedience of a Christian Man*, fol. xv^v.

KJB he shaped English so that, as the years passed, many came to see the KJB as English perfected. Further, with Cranmer's Prayer Book, it created religious English.

REVISION, COMPLETION OF THE FIRST DRAFT, AND MORE REVISION: MYLES COVERDALE

Myles Coverdale completed and revised the work begun by Tyndale, producing the first complete English printed Bible (OT, Apocrypha and NT) in 1535. He was not a linguist to rank with Tyndale or his continental predecessors, lacking sufficient Hebrew and Greek to work from the primary texts. So this, his first Bible, declares on one version of its title page that it is 'faithfully and truly translated out of Douche [German] and Latin into English'. In the dedication to Henry VIII, he avers that he has 'with a clear conscience purely and faithfully translated this out of five sundry interpreters, having only the manifest truth of scripture before mine eyes'. These 'interpreters' were, in Latin, the Vulgate and Pagninus, and, in German, Luther and the Zurich Bible of 1524–9, all of which have left clear marks on his work. If Coverdale meant his five to be German and Latin only – so tactfully omitting mention of his main source, the proscribed Tyndale – then the fifth was probably Erasmus's NT.

Limited as he was as a scholar, Coverdale had great strengths. He was a very able writer of English; moreover, he had worked as Tyndale's assistant in preparing the Pentateuch, so he was thoroughly familiar both with his style and practice as a translator, and could carry on the work in a way that did not jar with what had already been done. He was also industrious, perhaps even unbelievably so. His prologue to the 1550 edition states that he was asked to produce an English Bible in 1534 and implies that he began work in that year. Moreover, Tyndale's revised NT, which he used as his draft for the NT, was published no earlier than August 1534. Printing of Coverdale's Bible was completed on 4 October 1535. If, as has been strongly argued,[20] he did not *begin* work until the latter half of 1534, this means that he revised Tyndale's work and translated from scratch the OT from Joshua onwards and the Apocrypha, and saw it all through

---

[20] Mozley, *Coverdale*, pp. 71–2.

the press in little more than a year. Save for the legendary making of the Septuagint in seventy-two days, such a feat is unparalleled in the history of Bible making and strains credibility. There are not far short of a million words in the English Bible, including the Apocrypha. Of these, Coverdale revised just over a third, and created nearly two-thirds. Ignoring the time needed for the printing, he was revising or translating nearly 2,400 words a day. But, even if we take the more probable view, that Coverdale had been translating before 1534,[21] still the amount of work accomplished in 1534–5 was enormous: in this period he certainly revised the NT (roughly 180,000 words); he shaped the whole work so that it used Tyndale wherever Tyndale had published, he completed whatever he had not done of the OT and the Apocrypha, and may well have revised what he had done; and at the last he saw everything through the press.

However one solves the mystery of how Coverdale managed to produce a complete Bible in 1535, the fact remains that it was exceedingly quick work. This could only have been possible for someone who did not labour at the original languages, and who regarded translation as no more than an approximation to the meaning. Such indeed was his attitude. He links variety of translation and vocabulary with his use of a variety of sources because he sees both as relating to truth. In effect, he portrays translation as a hit or miss process: more translations will produce more hits, and a range of synonyms will prevent the truth from being limited by single words. In an important passage that is highly applicable to our present times with their extraordinary variety of versions, he writes:

sure I am that there cometh more knowledge and understanding of the Scripture by their sundry translations than by all the glosses of our sophisti-cal doctors. For that one interpreteth something obscurely in one place, the same translateth another, or else he himself, more manifestly by a more plain vocable of the same meaning in another place. Be not thou offended therefore, good reader, though one call a scribe that another calleth a lawyer . . . For if thou be not deceived by men's traditions, thou shalt find

---

[21] Mozley insists that the plain meaning of Coverdale's statements in the dedication and the prologue is that he began translating in 1534 (p. 71), but it may mean that he began to work towards publication in 1534; this may be what 'set forth' means in his statement, 'for the which cause (according as I was desired. Anno 1534.) I took upon me to set forth this special translation' (prologue).

no more diversity between these terms than between four pence and a groat. And this manner have I used in my translation, calling it in some place penance that in another place I call repentance, and that not only because the interpreters have done so before me, but that the adversaries of the truth may see how that we abhor not this word penance, as they untruly report of us. (Prologue)

Ultimately this is an expression of a translator's diffidence, and it directs the reader, if not exactly away from, certainly beyond the words.

The 1535 Bible was no more than a first complete draft, and it was quickly revised as the early history of the KJB ceased to develop in a simple, linear way. First, in 1537, John Rogers (one of the first of the Marian martyrs), using the pseudonym Thomas Matthew, published the Matthew Bible. He contributed a little of his own to the text (he made revisions to Coverdale's work that occasionally, as in the early chapters of Job, amounted to new work, and he added the Prayer of Manasses), but his achievement is to be found in the margins and presentation of this Bible. He also made one editorial decision of real importance to the writing of the KJB: he not only reverted, with variations, to Tyndale in the NT and the Pentateuch,[22] but he also used Tyndale's manuscript translation of Joshua to 2 Chronicles. In this way the draft reverted to being as much by Tyndale as it could be (save that Rogers did not use Tyndale's translation of Jonah). For the rest of the OT and the Apocrypha, he followed Coverdale.

By 1537, then, there were two complete drafts of the KJB, largely identical in about half the work, Coverdale and Matthew. Some parts of these had been revised several times. The NT had been revised once by Tyndale (not counting the occasional changes between 1525 and 1526), and then again by Coverdale. The Pentateuch had been revised by Coverdale. Joshua to 2 Chronicles had been independently translated by both Tyndale and Coverdale. The rest of the OT and the Apocrypha existed as a first draft by Coverdale.

It is also worth noting that by the next year, 1538, there were other drafts of parts of the Bible that were discarded – not because they were worthless but because, until the making of the KJB, translators

---

[22] Daniell notes over 300 variations from Tyndale's 1534 text in Genesis (*Tyndale's Old Testament*, p. xxviii).

generally worked in relation to a single English predecessor, and these particular drafts happened not to be chosen. There were two versions of Psalms (1529, 1534), Isaiah (1531), Jeremiah (1534), Proverbs and Ecclesiastes (?1534), and a revision of Tyndale's NT (1534) by George Joye, a revision of the whole Bible by Richard Taverner (1538), and a revision of the NT by Coverdale based on the Vulgate (1538). This phenomenon of discarded drafts continued in the work of, among others, Sir John Cheke and, at the end of the century, Hugh Broughton.

THE FIRST 'AUTHORISED' VERSION: THE GREAT BIBLE

The next draft, again made by Coverdale, was the Great Bible of 1539, also known as Cranmer's Bible because of the preface by the Archbishop included from the second edition onwards. It was the first major revision done under the auspices of the English Church. As such, it was the official ancestor of the Bishops' Bible, which in its turn was the official ancestor of the Church's third revision, the KJB.

The names by which we know these early Bibles are nicknames rather than official titles. Some Great Bible title pages state 'this is the Bible appointed to the use of the churches'; the fourth and sixth editions (1541) elaborated this to 'the Bible in English of the largest and greatest volume, authorised and appointed by the commandment of our most redoubted prince and sovereign lord, King Henry the VIII'. This is a direct reference to Edward VI's proclamation of 1541 ordering 'the Bible of the largest and greatest volume to be had in every church'.[23] Size or greatness would continue to be a defining characteristic of official church Bibles into the seventeenth century. Retrospect makes 'authorised' seem a key word. The Great Bible only used it twice, and the Bishops' Bible did not have it on its title page until 1584, sixteen years after it first appeared (in 1588 this became 'authorised and appointed'). The KJB did not use 'authorised', only 'appointed to be read in Churches'. 'Authorised' was much less significant than we now consider it.

The draft the Great Bible revised was not, as might have been expected, Coverdale's 1535 Bible but the Matthew Bible. This was because Archbishop Thomas Cranmer, deeming the Matthew Bible

[23] Pollard, *Records of the English Bible*, p. 261.

to be 'better than any other translation heretofore made', had persuaded Henry VIII to authorise it.[24] Whether Coverdale was happy to discard his own work on Joshua to 2 Chronicles we will never know, but he was clearly willing to change his source texts and to revise what he had already done. Now he used Münster's Hebrew and Latin Bible of 1535 as a prime source for his OT work,[25] and Erasmus's *Novum Instrumentum* for the NT work, and he worked over the Matthew Bible intensively. Unlike the Matthew Bible, in which most of the new work developed the margin rather than the text, Coverdale's work on the Great Bible was primarily concerned with the text and work on the annotations was never completed.

Light annotation was to be a characteristic of the official Bibles, perhaps because the Church leaders distrusted it. Annotation removed the task of interpreting the Bible from the Church, and, though one could argue that it was a way of creating orthodoxy, it might also be thought of as encouraging independent thought, and therefore dissent and even heresy. Cranmer's prologue suggests this fear. Though 'the scriptures be the fat pastures of the soul; therein is no venomous meat, no unwholesome thing; they be the very dainty and pure feeding', there are 'idle babblers and talkers of the scripture' in 'every marketplace, every alehouse and tavern, every feast house'. Rather than this dangerous freedom, the doubting reader should go to his clergyman: true understanding belonged to the Church, not to the individual. So Cranmer startlingly declares, 'I forbid not to read, but I forbid to reason'.

As well as being a draft of the KJB, the Great Bible also completed the writing of the version of the Psalms used in the Prayer Book. As a general rule, setting aside the very popular metrical or singing Psalms, Anglicans know the Psalms from this source, whereas nonconformists know them from the KJB.

GENEVA, THE PEOPLE'S BIBLE

Through his reliance on translations by others for his source texts, Coverdale took the drafting of the KJB in a false direction. One of the major contributions of the Geneva Bible (1560) was that it

---

[24] MacCulloch, *Thomas Cranmer*, pp. 196–7.   [25] Berry, Geneva 1560 facsimile, p. 3.

returned to Tyndale's principle of translating from the Hebrew and Greek texts, a move that was particularly important for the poetic and prophetic books which had not yet been translated from the Hebrew. The Geneva Bible was also immensely important for the quality of its scholarship, the extent of its annotations and its popularity. Though not the draft the KJB translators were directed to base their work on, it was the immediate predecessor that had most influence on the KJB.

To view the Geneva Bible simply as a draft of the KJB is, it should go without saying, grossly unfair to it. One could say the same in varying degrees about the other versions, but Geneva was a lasting achievement in its own right. It was by far the most successful English Bible for at least eighty years, going through about 140 editions up to 1644, with a subsequent edition in 1775, and several facsimiles in the twentieth and twenty-first centuries. It was for a long time the official Bible of Scotland, and, even though it was never officially appointed or authorised in England, it was not only the Bible of the people but also the English version most of the clergy used. Much of its popularity was owing to its annotations, print quality and relative cheapness. The annotations were not always theologically neutral and became strongly identified with non-conformity. Nevertheless, the qualities of the Geneva text should not be underestimated. If the KJB had never been made, the Geneva Bible might have held the place in the English consciousness that the KJB gradually achieved. It could well have been the definitive English Bible rather than one more draft on the way to that version.[26]

The Geneva Bible was the first truly collaborative English version. It was the work of a dozen or so Protestant scholars living in exile from an England that had returned to Catholicism under Queen Mary. Their leader was William Whittingham who had produced a remarkable preliminary draft, the 1557 Geneva NT. Anthony Gilby, particularly known for his Hebrew scholarship, seems to have been chiefly responsible for the OT. Coverdale also took part in the work. The whole group possessed considerable scholarship, and it was bolstered by living in Geneva in the late 1550s, where, in their words, 'seeing the great opportunity and occasions which God presented

---

[26] Hammond makes the same point, *Making of the English Bible*, p. 137.

unto us in this Church, by reason of so many godly and learned men, and such diversities of translations in divers tongues, we undertook this great and wonderful work'.[27] Dominant among these 'godly and learned men' were John Calvin (his 'Epistle declaring that Christ is the end of the Law' begins the 1557 NT), Beza and, among the English, John Knox. Geneva was a centre of Protestant thought, described by the 1557 preface as 'the patron and mirror of true religion and godliness' (fol. ii[v]). Biblical scholarship and printing was flourishing, with the Academy (later, University) of Geneva being founded in 1559. At least twenty-two editions of French Bibles, as well as Italian and Spanish Bibles, were published there in the 1550s, many of them in new versions (the close connection of the Geneva Bible with these is blatant in the use of illustrations which have French in them).[28]

The English Geneva translators used the Great Bible as their base text, making most revisions in Coverdale's OT work from Ezra onwards and in the Apocrypha.[29] They made particular use of Münster's Hebrew-Latin Bible, Kimchi's Hebrew commentary, the Zurich Latin Bible, Estienne's revision of Pagninus's Latin OT (1557), and Beza's Latin NT (1556).[30] With justification the translators compared their situation with that of their predecessors: 'yet considering the infancy of those times and imperfect knowledge of the tongues, in respect of this ripe age and clear light which God hath now revealed, the translations required greatly to be perused and reformed'.[31]

'Reformed' seems a strong word, suggesting the translators were attempting something new and different. The Geneva Bible (and the 1557 NT before it) was reformed in this sense in that, as a whole, it was a study Bible. As comprehensively as possible, it gave to 'simple lambs', especially those who could not afford to buy a commentary, all that was needed to understand the sense and doctrinal significance, to note more literal or more idiomatic renderings, possible alternative meanings, and places where there were significant variants in the originals, even to see what the text meant by the use of illustrations

[27] Preface, fol. iiii[r].
[28] For a fuller account of the Genevan context, see, e.g., Daniell, *Bible in English*, pp. 291–3.
[29] Westcott, *History of the English Bible*, p. 214.
[30] Berry, Geneva 1560 facsimile, pp. 10–11; Westcott, *A General View*, pp. 212–13.
[31] Preface, fol. iiii[r].

that are best thought of as diagrams.[32] Never before in English had a Bible given in such equal measure text and understanding.

Along with this use of the margin and other aids such as arguments, headers and appendices, the inclusion of verse numbers enhanced the studiability of the text. This change, so familiar to Bible readers, had a huge effect on the way translators and readers experienced the text. Rather than something to be read continuously, it became a text in bits, each bit numbered and presented like a paragraph. The previous paragraphed presentation did not quite disappear, but the paragraphs became less visible. They are marked with paraphs (or pilcrows): ¶. In some places paraphs are omitted, notably in the Psalms, the Song of Solomon and Job 3–41; they are infrequent to rare in the Apocrypha and the NT (Revelation has only eight). Attention by both translators and readers to the natural structure – or 'principal matters' – of the writing has been substantially lost because of the demands of a reference system and the presentation of verses as if they are paragraphs. Verse numbers and cross-references move the reader and student from continuous reading towards what might be called concordant reading, a verse in one part of the Bible directing the reader not to its surrounding verse but to another some distance away. This is not necessarily a bad thing, but the Geneva Bible does create a sense quite different from that created by its English predecessors of what the Bible is to read. One other aspect of this presentation is perhaps a gain: in the poetry the verses often enhance a sense of the Hebrew parallelism.

'Reformed' also meant revised and corrected: it is this milder sense the translators probably intended. Like Tyndale, they tried to make a version 'faithfully and plainly translated according to the languages wherein they were first written'.[33] The translation is often literal, as they warn the reader:

as we have chiefly observed the sense, and laboured always to restore it to full integrity: so we have most reverently kept the propriety of the words, considering that the Apostles who spoke and wrote to the Gentiles in the Greek tongue rather constrained them to the lively phrase of the Hebrew than enterprised far by mollifying their language to speak as the Gentiles did. And for this and other causes we have in many places reserved the

---

[32] 1557 preface, fols. ii[r], iii[r].   [33] Epistle to the Queen, 1560 Bible, fol. ii[r].

Hebrew phrases, notwithstanding that they may seem somewhat hard in their ears that are not well practised and also delight in the sweet sounding phrases of the holy Scriptures. (fol. iiii^r)

Their aim is not just to give the reader the meaning but also to keep visible the original languages' way of writing. Besides being generally literal, they used italic type to mark where they had added words necessary for English but not present in the original language. Sometimes, though, they judged a literal translation inappropriate for the text: then the reader could find it in the margin.

As time passed the Geneva OT remained largely unchanged, but the NT text was revised once and the margin twice. Laurence Tomson's *The New Testament... translated out of Greek by Theod. Beza* (1576) was a light revision of the Geneva text accompanied by substantial new annotations. It continued the trend towards literalness, as at John 1:1, 'in the beginning was that word, and that word was with God, and that word was God'. This is exactly how Tyndale had first translated this verse. Thomas More reproved him for poor English and suggested the familiar reading, which Tyndale used in his subsequent NTs. In using 'that', Tomson is following Beza's attention to the Greek article at the expense of good English. This NT became part of the Geneva text in 1587 (usually referred to as Geneva-Tomson), but the original text also continued to be printed. Tomson's version appears not to have generated any KJB readings:[34] it is another discarded draft.

Tomson, unlike the original Geneva Bible, left Revelation unannotated. This gap was filled in 1599 by the inclusion of Franciscus Junius's annotations (Geneva-Tomson-Junius). These contained some sharply anti-Catholic notes that fuelled a prejudice against the Geneva notes in some quarters.

THE SECOND 'AUTHORISED' VERSION, THE BISHOPS' BIBLE

Hugh Broughton, a man to whom vituperation was second nature and vilification first, declared that 'our Bishops' Bible might well give

---

[34] There is no detailed collation of the 1560 and Tomson NTs. Westcott (*History of the English Bible*, pp. 223–7) details some of Tomson's readings but does not note any connection with the KJB.

place to the Al-koran, pestered with lies',[35] and vilification has been the general fate of this, the second official Bible of the English Church. Yet, especially in its final form, it is not as bad as sometimes suggested. Westcott is more sympathetic than most: 'the Greek scholarship of the revisers is superior to their Hebrew scholarship'; he judges that the NT 'shows considerable vigour and freshness' (p. 231). Moreover, it is of very particular importance as a draft of the KJB: under instruction, the KJB translators used its final form as their base text. This final form had some revisions in the OT, and it reverted to the Great Bible Psalms; the NT was more thoroughly revised.

Matthew Parker, Archbishop of Canterbury, was the prime mover. He had in 1565 appeared sympathetic to the Geneva Bible, writing that he thought well of it and requesting an extension of John Bodley's privilege to print it in England. Though he already had plans for 'one other special Bible for the churches', he thought it would 'do much good to have diversity of translations and readings'. He made one stipulation, 'that no impression shall pass but by our direction, consent and advice';[36] quite possibly as a consequence, no Geneva Bible was printed in England until the year after his death.

The Bishops' Bible was a revision of the Great Bible, intended to replace it as the official Bible in the churches; Parker presented it to the Queen as a 'new edition', intended not to 'vary much from that translation which was commonly used by public order, except where either the verity of the Hebrew and Greek moved alteration, or where the text was by some negligence mutilated from the original'.[37] He seems to have thought that it would be called the Great English Bible.[38] His emphasis was on continuity ahead

[35] *An Advertisement* (fol. H4ʳ). As usual with Broughton, the particular point is biblical chronology, which, in his view, is absolutely true provided one understands it properly. His quarrel here is with the Bishops' Bible's rendering of Acts 13:20, 'he gave unto them judges, about the space of four hundred and fifty years'. He says that Beza thought this place corrupt in the Greek, and that Paul meant 'after a sort 450 years'. 'About the space' would seem to give this reading, but Broughton will not have it. The consequence is 'that the stories of Joshua, Samuel, Saul and David should be all fables: and no time for David to be in the world'. Numerical errors make the book of truth into lies, hence Broughton's opprobrium. The KJB repeated the 'error' exactly. Few, if any, modern versions would have escaped Broughton's censure here.

[36] Pollard, *Records of the English Bible*, p. 286.   [37] Ibid., p. 294.

[38] Strype uses this term, and writes, 'the Bible called *The Great English Bible*, with the year of the impression (*viz.* 1568) I find in the catalogue of the books the Archbishop gave to the library of Corpus Christi, Cambridge' (*Life and Acts of Matthew Parker*, p. 272).

of innovation, with nothing more done than corrections to bring it closer to the original. He drew up some principles or 'observations respected of the translators'. They make curious reading, especially when set against the instructions given to the KJB translators; they appear to be an after-the-fact statement of things the translators were expected to do:

First, to follow the common English translation used in the churches and not to recede from it but where it varieth manifestly from the Hebrew or Greek original.

Item, to use such sections and divisions in the texts as Pagninus in his translation useth, and for the verity of the Hebrew to follow the said Pagninus and Münster specially, and generally others learned in the tongues.

Item, to make no bitter notes upon any text, or yet to set down any determination in places of controversy.

Item, to note such chapters and places as containeth matter of genealogies or other such places not edifying, with some strike or note that the reader may eschew them in his public reading.

Item, that all such words as soundeth in the old translation to any offence of lightness or obscenity be expressed with more convenient terms or phrases.

The printer hath bestowed his thickest paper in the New Testament because it shall be most occupied.[39]

It was, therefore, a revision of the Great Bible for accurate representation of the originals, using particular editions of the Hebrew but also drawing generally on other scholars, including a source Geneva had not used, Sebastian Castellio's Latin Bible (1551). The annotations were to be unlike what Parker described to the Queen as the 'divers prejudicial notes' of Geneva;[40] rather than aiming to give official interpretation of controversial points, they were to leave them alone. Here one of the problems with annotation from an official point of view is manifest: any notes dealing with contested theological points were asking for trouble. An unusual (but perhaps not unreasonable) sense of the different merits of different parts comes in the idea of marking unedifying parts (not much of Leviticus survived this marking). If there was any real attempt to avoid 'any offence of lightness or obscenity', it is difficult to find.

---

[39] Pollard, *Records of the English Bible*, pp. 297–8.   [40] Ibid., p. 295.

Overall, Parker's notes say very little about how the translators were to work, and they went their own way. The Great Bible was a collective rather than a collaborative version: individual translators did their assigned parts, and most had their initials appended to their parts, something Parker thought politic 'to make them more diligent, as answerable for their doings'.[41] No doubt he recognised the inconsistency in principles and unevenness in quality. The translators were mostly Bishops (or, perhaps, members of their entourage), all to some degree drafters of the KJB: Parker himself, Archbishop of Canterbury, William Alley (Exeter), William Barlow (Chichester), Thomas Bentham (Coventry and Lichfield), Nicholas Bullingham (Lincoln), Richard Cox (Ely), Richard Davies (St David's), Edmund Grindal (London), Robert Horne (Winchester), perhaps Hugh Jones (Llandaff), John Parkhurst (Norwich), Edwin Sandys (Worcester), Edmund Scambler (Peterborough), Thomas Bickley, chaplain to Parker, Gabriel Goodman, Dean of Westminster, Andrew Peerson, Prebendary of Canterbury, and Andrew Perne, Dean of Ely.[42]

A little correspondence survives. Edmund Guest (Rochester) was to have done the Psalms, but it seems from the initials his work was not used. His letter to Parker suggests the freedom some of the translators took, and shows how a translator could go wrong if he departed from the principle of following the literal sense, in particular his statement that 'where in the New Testament one piece of a psalm is reported, I translate it in the Psalms according to the translation thereof in the New Testament, for the avoiding of the offence that may rise to the people upon divers translations'.[43] Such a principle opens the gates to rewriting every parallel passage and to harmonising the Gospels, in short, to creating the Bible as the translator thinks it should have been written. Others give real insight into how the translators thought and worked. Sandys, reviser of Kings and Chronicles, recommended strong oversight of the whole project 'that it may be done in such perfection that the adversaries can have no occasion to quarrel with it. Which thing will require a time.' He offered a translator's judgement on the Great Bible version of his books: it 'followed Münster too much, who doubtless was a very negligent man in his doings, and often swerved very much from

[41] Ibid., p. 293.   [42] Ibid., pp. 30–2.   [43] Strype, *Life and Acts of Matthew Parker*, p. 208.

the Hebrew'.[44] Cox, reviser of Acts and Romans, apparently at the beginning of the project, also hinted that Parker would have a lot of overseeing to do, and offered some thoughts on the language a translator should use: 'I would wish that such usual words as we English people be acquainted with might still remain in their form and sound, so far forth as the Hebrew will well bear; inkhorn terms to be avoided'.[45] It should be common English as far as possible, and should avoid the fashion for Latin-based neologisms such as were to find their way into the Rheims-Douai Bible.

Giles Lawrence, regius professor of Greek at Oxford, not one of the original translators, assisted with the revision of the NT for the second edition, 1572. His notes on twenty-nine readings in the Synoptic Gospels and Colossians are unique in the early history of English Bible translation because he explains exactly why he makes his suggestions. This is the kind of material one would love to have more of, because it shows the attention that had to be given to even the smallest details and what scholarship might be brought to bear. Moreover, it is the only set of notes from a near-contemporary with which we can compare the one set of notes made by a translator of the KJB. All but two of Lawrence's notes are followed either literally or in spirit in the second edition and the readings remain in the 1602 edition, whence most of them were adopted by the KJB translators. Few as they are, Lawrence's notes create and explain the rationale for over twenty KJB readings. In short, here is one of the authors of the KJB explaining exactly what he was doing.[46]

Half the notes come in Lawrence's first category, 'words not aptly translated'. One of his simplest entries, characteristic in its form, is for Luke 6:44, beginning with the words of the Bishops' Bible first edition:

Nor of bushes gather they grapes. ἐκ βάτου; (that is) *of a bramble. Dioscorides,* lib. 4. ca. 37. *Bush* is so general that it may signify a *holly bush*, or *furze-bush*, as well as a *bramble bush*.

Precise knowledge of Greek, backed up with a reference, leads to precise English; it is also more literal, a singular for a singular.

[44] Ibid., p. 208.   [45] Ibid., p. 209.
[46] Ibid., p. 404. All the quotations from Lawrence's notes are from appendix 85, pp. 139–42 (the pagination starts afresh in the appendices).

Consequently the Bishops' Bible reading, identical to Tyndale, the Matthew and Great Bibles and Geneva, is changed in the second edition to 'nor of a bramble bush gather they grapes', and this becomes the KJB reading.

Lawrence argues that 'cast an angle' (Matt. 17:27) should be 'cast an hook' because the Greek is 'an *hook*, and not an *angle*; if the *angle* be cast without the *hook*, there is no hope to catch the fish'. He cites a Greek author distinguishing the Greek noun used here from two others. Hence comes the Bishops' Bible's revised reading and the KJB's reading. All the other versions use 'angle'. The point is pithy and persuasive in its attention to English meaning. 'Angle' had changed from its original sense, a fishhook, to fishing gear.

In terms of what happened to a Bishops' Bible reading and then to a KJB reading, the most curious of these 'words not aptly translated' comes in the parable of the wicked husbandmen. Lawrence argues that 'enjoy' in 'let us kill him, and let us enjoy his inheritance' (Matt. 21:38) is a mistranslation (as usual, he notes what Greek word would have been needed to produce this English word). The meaning is 'let us take possession or seisin upon his inheritance'. Now generally unknown except in legal use, 'seisin' meant, 'in early use, Possession: chiefly in phrases, *to have, take seisin* (*in, of*)' (*OED*). Lawrence adds that 'enjoy' and 'take possession' are 'not all one, for I may take possession and yet not enjoy'. The second edition responds to this with a reading that, in the original spelling, looks very odd: 'and let vs season vpon his inheritance'. 'Seisin' has been used in its now obsolete verbal form (*OED*'s last quotation is from 1623), and given in one of its possible sixteenth-century spellings. 'Season upon' looks to modern eyes like an error for 'seize on' or 'seize upon', and it did cause difficulty in its own time: the 1578 edition changed it to 'let us reason upon', and William Fulke's edition has 'let vs sease vpon' (original spelling). The first of these is certainly, and the second probably, a printer's error. The KJB gives 'let us seize on his inheritance', which seems simple and sensible until one knows this history. It uses Fulke's spelling, 'sease', a possible spelling for 'seize', but one the KJB does not use elsewhere. The KJB's reading may be an accident, either because it copied Fulke's mistake or because the translators (or the printer) independently made the same mistake. Or it may have been deliberate, either because they thought 'season upon' a mistake or because they judged it to be unclear or clumsy. Since one meaning of 'to seisin' is 'to seize', they could have been improving the English. Alternatively, they recognised the meaning of 'season upon', and used 'sease/seize' because it could carry the sense of 'seisin' as a verb. If this last possibility is what happened, the KJB's 'let us seize on his inheritance' carries a sense we have lost. The complexities of a single word are rife, but what is certain is that Lawrence, whether understood or not, again helped to draft the KJB.

Lawrence's second category is omissions of something found in the Greek. Most of these are peculiar to the Bishops' Bible first edition, while one shows the influence of the Textus Receptus. Mark 15:3 normally reads, in the words of the versions from Tyndale to Geneva, 'and the high priests accused him of many things'. Lawrence notes that the Textus Receptus (he does not use this phrase) has some extra words, so the second edition and the KJB add 'but he answered nothing'. Next is 'words superfluous', with two notes ('what needeth *feathered?*' he asks tartly of 'feathered fowls', Mark 13:16); then, also with two notes, 'the sentences changed, and error in doctrine'.

These examples confirm the extent to which the KJB is based on the Bishops' Bible of 1602. They also suggest that its readings tended to take precedence over other readings, for there are instances where earlier translations could have provided as good a solution but were not followed. The man with the unclean spirit cries out to Jesus, in the words of the first edition and the Great Bible, 'saying: Alas, what have we to do with thee' (Mark 1:24). Lawrence points out that 'Alas' represents a Greek imperative, and suggests 'let be, or, let us alone'. The second edition and the KJB choose 'let us alone'. Here the KJB could have followed Tyndale or Matthew, which both have Lawrence's first suggestion, 'let be' (Coverdale and Geneva have exclamations instead, 'Oh' and 'Ah').

THE RHEIMS NEW TESTAMENT

The two final drafts had now been made: officially, the Bishops' Bible, and, in terms of its influence, the Geneva Bible. In 1582, in an attempt to counteract Protestant translation with Catholic truth, the exiled Roman Catholics published the Rheims NT (the OT followed in two volumes, 1609 and 1610, too late to be used in the KJB).

For all their enmity, the two sides drew on each other's scholarship, so Rheims, as a translation, is part of the tradition established by Tyndale; in their turn, the KJB translators drew on words or phrases from Rheims when it suited them: it too was a draft of sorts.

The translator was an Oxford Greek scholar, Gregory Martin, probably assisted by William (later, Cardinal) Allen, Richard Bristow, thought to have been author of the NT notes, William Rainolds or Reynolds (brother of the KJB translator John Rainolds) and Thomas Worthington, annotator of the OT. Somewhat like Coverdale, Martin took the English Bible on the false track of translating from a translation, the Vulgate, and, for the Psalms, a translation of a translation, using Jerome's translation of the Septuagint Psalms. Unlike Coverdale, he could and did refer his work to the Greek. So, in Westcott's words, 'it is to [Rheims] rather than to Coverdale's Testaments [translated from the Latin] that we owe the final and most powerful action of the Vulgate upon our present Version' (p. 245); in places, notably in its treatment of the Greek article, it also takes the English closer to the Greek.

Rheims is the most literal of the early translations. In his preface, Martin castigates the Protestants for their looseness and goes on to explain his literalness. He complains of the Protestants 'most shamefully in all their versions, Latin, English and other tongues, corrupting both the letter and the sense by false translation, adding, detracting, altering, transposing, pointing and all other guileful means'. They 'frame and fine the phrases of Holy Scriptures after the form of profane writers, sticking not for the same to supply, add, alter or diminish as freely as if they translated Livy, Virgil or Terence' (fol. biᵛ). Castellio is his pattern for this general charge of falsifying through failing to be literal, even, through attempting to be literary. He, by contrast, has used

no more license than is sufferable in translating of Holy Scriptures: continually keeping ourselves as near as is possible to our text and to the very words and phrases which by long use are made venerable, though to some profane or delicate ears they may seem more hard or barbarous, as the whole style of Scripture doth lightly to such at the beginning. (fol. biiʳ)

If the original is crudely written or ungrammatical or even incomprehensible, his translation must be also; the reader should not be

shocked by such apparent faults: they are part of the truth of the
original and part of what makes the Bible different from secular literature. His frequent literalism 'may seem to the vulgar reader and
to common English ears not yet acquainted therewith, rudeness or
ignorance', but he appeals to the future: 'all sorts of Catholic readers will in short time think that familiar, which at the first may
seem strange, and will esteem it more when they shall otherwise be
taught to understand it than if it were the common known English'
(fol. ciiiʳ). This reflects More's jibe that 'all England list now to
go to school with Tyndale to learn English' (above, p. 11). English
words and phrases were of course being formed by the language of
the translators, but Martin's work never attained the currency of the
Protestant versions, so failed to make his literalisms familiar (some
of the words he thought difficult have become familiar, but not from
his work).

Martin practised what he preached, and reaped the reward of
mockery. Often he transcribed rather than translated words, as in
'charity of the fraternity' for the Vulgate's 'caritas fraternitatis' (Heb.
13:1) instead of 'brotherly love', or 'detractors, odible to God' (Rom.
1:30), for 'detractores, Deo odibiles'. Sometimes transcription leads
to nonsense: 'beneficence and communication do not forget: for with
such hosts God is promerited' (Heb. 13:16); the Latin reads, 'benefi-
cientiae autem et communionis nolite oblivisci talibus enim hostiis
promeretur Deus'. Here the KJB adopts one word from Rheims,
'communicate' for the earlier versions' 'distribute', using it in its now
obsolete sense, to share; it is arguably no improvement on 'distribute'.
Even when translating badly, Rheims could still suggest the occasional
word to the KJB translators.

The Rheims notes were as important as the text, for it was explicitly
a controversial version; in the words of the title page, they were more
than 'necessary helps for the better understanding of the text': they
were 'specially for the discovery of the corruptions of divers late
translations, and for clearing the controversies in religion of these
days'. They had an indirect effect on the KJB in continually drawing
attention to issues of translation, perhaps also in enhancing the dislike
of 'bitter notes' shown in Parker's instructions for the Bishops' Bible.
The note on 'God is promerited' is characteristic in its length and
contents:

This Latin word *promeretur* cannot be expressed effectually in any one English word. It signifieth God's favour to be procured by the foresaid works of alms and charity, as by the deserts and merits of the doers. Which doctrine and word of merits the adversaries like so ill that they flee both here and elsewhere from the word, translating here for *promeretur Deus, God is pleased*, more near to the Greek, as they pretend. Which indeed maketh no more for them than the Latin, which is agreeable to most ancient copies, as we see by Primasius, St Augustine's scholar. For if God be pleased with good works and show favour for them, then are they meritorious, and then only faith is not the cause of God's favour to men.

Though it suggests Martin could have translated more simply had he chosen to – 'alms and charity' is arguably better than both 'beneficence and communication' and 'to do good and to distribute' – the argument that English cannot always express effectually the word in the text is a real challenge to translators. In general the Protestant translators relied on the expressive power of English and believed that their text could give the reader God's truth, though Geneva's extensive use of annotation had modified this position. Martin makes the margin the primary location of truth. If the KJB was to be an essentially unannotated translation, the pressure to get its words exactly right was increased by his work. Having explained the meaning, Martin then attacks the Protestants for tendentious translation in avoiding 'merit'. Here was one of the great theological divides, whether salvation could come from merit or good works, or whether it depended on the freely given grace of Christ. Tyndale put the issue this way: 'Christ is lord over all, and whatsoever any man will have of God, he must have it given him freely for Christ's sake. Now to have heaven by my own deserving is my own praise, and not Christ's. For I cannot have it by favour and grace in Christ, and by my own merits also: for free giving and deserving cannot stand together.'[47] Martin was right: except for a few places in the Wycliffite versions, the Protestant translators did not use 'merit'. Rather, in the Geneva OT, its later versions of the NT and the Bishops' Bible they give notes such as this to Rom. 11:35: 'this saying overthroweth the doctrine of foreseen works and merits'.[48] The KJB's summary of Psalm 16 seems to do the same thing: 'David in distrust of merits and hatred of idolatry flieth to God for preservation'.

---

[47] Pentateuch, preface to Numbers, fol. A7ᵛ.   [48] Geneva-Tomson, 1587.

Through arguments, translations and annotations, the Rheims NT probably made sharper what was already sharp, the KJB translators' awareness of their inseparable linguistic and theological responsibilities. The Rheims NT, as published by the Catholics, was a rare book, reprinted only four times, 1600, 1621, 1633 and 1738. The translators knew it from a work that highlighted both the controversies and the different translations, William Fulke's *The Text of the New Testament of Jesus Christ, translated out of the vulgar Latin by the Papists of the traitorous Seminary at Rheims* (1589). This gave the Rheims Testament in full, with every argument and annotation confuted, and with the second edition Bishops' Bible text in a parallel column. At the end is 'a table directing the readers to all controversies handled in this work'. There were other confutations besides this, including one by the future KJB translator, Thomas Bilson.

Occasionally it had a colloquial vigour that the KJB drew on, but Rheims's prime contribution to the KJB was an added sprinkle of latinate vocabulary in the NT, though none of it is new to the Protestant translators. The following words in Romans follow Rheims: 'separated' (1:1), 'impenitent' (2:5), 'approvest' (2:18), 'remission' (3:25), 'glory' (5:3), 'commendeth' (5:8), 'concupiscence' (7:8), 'revealed' (8:18), 'expectation' (8:19), 'conformed' (8:29), 'emulation' (11:14), 'concluded' (11:32), 'conformed' (12:2) and 'contribution' (15:26).[49] Now, the Protestants were well capable of using such vocabulary without prompting from Rheims, as in 'tribulations' (also found in Rheims) and 'maketh intercession' (Rom. 5:3, 11:2), which go back to Tyndale. Nevertheless, such words make Martin a drafter of the KJB. Since most of them are transliterations of Jerome's Latin, they also make Jerome an author of the KJB.

---

[49] Westcott, *History of the English Bible*, p. 253.

CHAPTER 2

Drafting the King James Bible

JOSEPH AND MARY

In this chapter, two short passages, one from each Testament, will be examined to give an impression of how the drafting of the KJB went in practice. Each is given in modern spelling and presentation in order to make the real similarities and differences as clear as possible. This kind of study inevitably presents the work of revision as a matter of either choosing between possibilities offered by preceding drafts or rejecting them all in favour of a new version. Some of the dynamics of translation such as those revealed by Lawrence's notes are omitted as being almost impossible to trace.

Matthew 1:18–21 involves one of the first problems for a translator of the NT, how to deal with the relationship between Mary and Joseph, a matter that is particularly difficult if the translator is unable to give a note explaining the theological and social background. Here is the first draft of the KJB, Tyndale's 1525/6 version:

[18]The birth of Christ was on this wise, when his mother Mary was married unto Joseph, before they came to dwell together, she was found with child by the holy Ghost. [19]Then her husband Joseph, being a perfect man, and loath to defame her, was minded to put her away secretly. [20]While he thus thought, behold, the angel of the Lord appeared unto him in his sleep, saying, 'Joseph the son of David, fear not to take unto thee, Mary thy wife. For that which is conceived in her, is of the holy Ghost. [21]She shall bring forth a son, and thou shalt call his name Jesus. For he shall save his people from their sins.'

Jewish marriage customs lie behind the opening verse. Engagement, though celibate, was as binding a tie as marriage, breakable only by divorce. The wedding and living together followed after a year. The

Greek means engaged, but the risk in translating this literally is that it may seem that Jesus was born out of wedlock. Tyndale avoids this by using 'married' – and leaving the reader to figure out how they could be married but not dwelling together. He gives a sense of the force of the situation, in keeping with 'husband' and 'wife' in vv. 16, 20, but at the expense of literalness. 'Came to dwell together' is also not quite literal: the Greek means came together. Possibly he avoided this as suggesting a sexual relationship.

V. 19 also presents problems of understanding essentially common words. Joseph is, literally, a just man, but what does this mean? Joseph's character depends on our understanding of 'just', and of how, faced with Mary's pregnancy, he acts as a 'just' man. Tyndale of course knew the literal sense of the Greek adjective (if he had not, the Vulgate's 'iustus' would have set him right), but always tried to translate according to context. So elsewhere his renderings include 'just', 'good', 'right' and 'righteous'. Here he takes his cue from Luther's 'fromm', pious, dutiful, religious: Joseph is a man of obedience, 'just' in the sense of following God's law. A 'perfect' man can be one who is completely and absolutely obedient. This fits the context, which shows him accepting without question what God tells him in this – and subsequent – dreams, and acting with perfect propriety. It also fits with other biblical texts, such as 1 John 2:5, which Tyndale translates, 'whosoever keepeth his word, in him is the love of God perfect in deed'. Here the link between obedience and absolute rightness in action is explicit. Tyndale also uses 'perfect' this way in his own writing, describing the effect of God's word on the reader as making 'him every day better and better, till he be grown into a perfect man in the knowledge of Christ and love of the law of God'.[1] Knowledge, love of the law and, implicitly, obedience: this is his idea of what it means for Joseph to be a 'just' man. 'Perfect', then, is not a literal but a carefully considered theological translation.

Two words in this version may have been suggested by Erasmus's *Novum Instrumentum*: 'defame' ('infamare') and 'conceived' ('conceptum est').

---

[1] 'W. T. unto the reader', New Testament, 1534, fol. *iiii*.

Tyndale's 1534 revisions make the translation more literal. 'Married' becomes 'betrothed', opening up the question of whether they were actually husband and wife. 'Loath to defame her' becomes 'loath to make an example of her', which is closer to the literal sense of the Greek, to make a paradigm of her. Now, 1534 has some annotations; one of them explains 'example': 'that is to say, to bring her out to punishment for the example of others'. Evidently he felt that 'defame' was too vague, simply giving a rough sense of the situation, and that, with the help of annotation, he could now give a truer sense of the original. In v. 18, 'Christ' becomes the Greek's 'Jesus Christ': his first translation, whether deliberately or no, corresponded to the Vulgate, Erasmus's Latin and Luther. 'Her husband Joseph' is changed to the Greek word order, 'Joseph her husband'. In the first version of v. 20, 'the Lord appeared unto him in his sleep', 'his' has no equivalent in the Greek (or the Latin), but 'in . . . sleep' follows the Latin. The Greek is literally what Tyndale changed it to, 'in a dream'.

There are limits to how far Tyndale is prepared to move towards literalness: he does not make Greek word order into a fetish, and he frequently avoids participial phrases. Overall, his choices and changes show him as a deeply thoughtful translator whose priority, having once translated, was to bring his work closer to the literal meaning, and even to the word order of the Greek, while always maintaining a strong sense of normal English structures.

Two elements of the model Tyndale gave for English biblical translation are apparent in this passage. One is the judicious fidelity to the syntax and grammar of the original languages, even to the point of including a present participle in the Matthew passage, 'being a perfect man' (v. 19), and so delaying the main verb until the latter part of the sentence: this would not have troubled an educated man, but was not the basic English of the ploughboy. The other key element is the choice of predominantly native English vocabulary. 'Married' (1525), 'perfect', 'defame' (1525), 'example' (1534), 'secretly', 'appeared' and 'conceived' come from Latin by way of Old French and Middle English. All were familiar English. Only 'perfect' is used in a sense that might have eluded an ordinary reader or hearer.

The subsequent drafts made only a few changes. Here is Coverdale's 1535 version (it has no changes after 'son of David'):

[18]The birth of Christ was on this wise: when his mother Mary was married to Joseph before they came together, she was found with child by the holy ghost, [19]but Joseph her husband was a perfect man, and would not bring her to shame, but was minded to put her away secretly. [20]Nevertheless while he thus thought, behold, the angel of the Lord appeared unto him in a dream, saying, 'Joseph thou son of David . . . '

Most of this is a mixture of Tyndale's two versions reflecting Luther's influence. The most obvious sign of Luther is 'thou son of David', which has no warrant in the Greek: Luther was imagining what the angel would have said rather than giving a close translation. Coverdale gives the text more flow by making the first two sentences into a single sentence and by including two 'but's, the second of which has no warrant from the Greek or Latin. 'Nevertheless' (v. 20) strongly brings out the way the angel's appearance changes his mind.

The Matthew Bible follows Tyndale's 1534 text except that, as in Coverdale, it changes 'betrothed' back to Tyndale's original rendering, 'married', presumably for doctrinal reasons. It includes Tyndale's note to 'example' and adds one more note, 'angel, that is, messenger'.

Though Taverner's Bible was almost entirely a discarded draft, his solution to Mary's situation is worth noting: 'when his mother Mary was espoused to Joseph, before they companied together'. 'Espoused' is subtle: it may mean either married or betrothed. 'Before they companied together' is perhaps the clearest indication of the intermediate nature of their relationship. 'Espoused' was to be the KJB's word here.

The Great Bible mixes Tyndale 1534 and Coverdale's first Bible with some original readings; these readings are given in italics here:

[18]The birth of Jesus Christ was on this wise. When his mother Mary was married to Joseph (before they came to dwell together) she was found with child by the holy Ghost. [19]Then Joseph her husband (*because he* was a *righteous* man, and would not *put* her to shame) *he* was minded *privily to depart from her.* [20]*But* while he thus thought, behold, the angel of the Lord appeared unto him in [*omission*] sleep, saying, 'Joseph, thou son of David: fear not to take unto thee Mary thy wife. For that which is conceived in her, *cometh* of the holy Ghost. [21]She shall bring forth a son, and thou shalt call his name Jesus. For he shall save his people from their sins.'

In every other version Joseph, in Tyndale's words, 'was minded to put her away secretly', but here he thinks to leave her secretly. This is a misunderstanding through over-literal reading of Erasmus's 'voluit clanculum ab ea divertere',[2] 'he wished secretly to divorce her' ('divertere', to turn away or depart, can have the sense of divorce and is the origin of that word). Two other readings also come from Erasmus. 'Cometh of the holy Ghost' follows his 'a spiritu sancto profectum est', and 'in sleep' follows 'in somnis' (the Vulgate has 'in somnis ei').[3] Though there are variations from Erasmus such as 'Jesus Christ' instead of 'Christ', and some new choices of words such as 'a righteous man', Coverdale had his eye mainly on Erasmus and tended to follow him literally. One curious insertion is the superfluous 'he' after the parenthesis in v. 19: it is an attempt to keep the grammar of the sentence clearer to the reader or listener.

The Geneva NT of 1557 seems to owe nothing to the Great Bible in this passage; rather it stands as an intermediate draft between Tyndale's later version and the Geneva Bible itself. Its primary source is Beza's Latin. 'Loath to make her a public example of infamy' (v. 19) translates Beza's 'nollet eam ignominie exponere'.[4] Most of the other changes also correspond with Beza ('reasoned with himself' for 'cogitasset' is perhaps an exception). 'Came together' (v. 18), though anticipated by Coverdale in 1535, is exactly Beza's 'convenissent'. This is the first version to describe Joseph as a 'just man', which follows Beza but could as easily have come from the Vulgate or the Greek.

The Geneva Bible builds on 1557 and is also clearly based in Tyndale's later version. Here agreements with what is new in 1557 are in italics (*'for'*, v. 20 is 1560's italics), and 1560's changes are in **bold**:

[18] *Now* the birth of Jesus Christ was **thus**, when **as** his mother Mary was *betrothed to Joseph, before they came [omission] together, she was found with child of the holy Ghost. [19] Then Joseph her husband being a *just* man, and **not willing** to *make *her* a *public* example [omission], was minded to put her away secretly. [20] But while he thought **these things**, behold, the Angel of the Lord appeared unto him in a dream, saying, 'Joseph, the son of David, fear not to take [omission] Mary *for*[5] thy wife: for that which is

---

[2] The Vulgate is unambiguous: 'voluit occulte dimittere eam'.
[3] As given in Coverdale's 1538 diglot NT.
[4] I have used the 1570 edition with annotations by Camerarius; the margin, whether by Joachim Camerarius or Beza, strengthens the sense that this is different from simply making an example of her, since it gives as an alternative translation, 'exemplum in ea fieri'.
[5] So 1560; deleted in Geneva-Tomson NT.

conceived in her, is of the holy Ghost. [21]**And** she shall bring forth a son, and thou shalt *call his [r]name Jesus: for he shall *save his people from their sins.'

* Luke 1:27.

[m] Before he took her home to him.

[n] As the angel afterward declared to Joseph.

[o] Upright and fearing God, and therefore suspecting that she had committed fornication before she was betrothed, would neither retain her, which by the law should be married to another, neither by accusing her put her to shame for her fact.

* Deut. 24:1.

[p] This dream is witnessed by the holy Ghost, and is a kind of revelation. Num. 12:6.

[q] This name putteth him in remembrance of God's promise to David.

* Luke 1:38.

[r] That is, a Saviour.

* Acts 4:12. Phil. 2:10. Isa. 7:14.

Some may be changes for change's sake, some reflect the Greek. 'Thus' for 'on this wise' (v. 18) might be explained either way: a single word may have been used because the Greek has a single word. Yet 'when as' for 'when' is a matter of style (none of the translations here follow the grammar of the Greek). 'Not willing' for 'loath' (v. 19) looks like change for change's sake since there is no difference in meaning, though it does reflect the Greek's use of two words. Adding 'a public' to 'example' adopts half of 1557's 'a public example of infamy', either giving a fuller sense to the Greek to make a paradigm or adding a redundant word, according to one's judgement. 'While he thought these things' for 'while he thus thought' (v. 20) and the addition of 'and' at the beginning of v. 21 are literal changes to match the Greek. Overall, these show the continuing drift towards literal translation mixed with some stylistic revision.

The notes (originally placed in the margin) are reasonably characteristic. Note m paraphrases without going into detail, while note o first paraphrases then gives a detailed explanation: such notes diminish the burden on the text to be completely comprehensible by itself. Note n is like the notes taken over from 1557, a comment filling out the story. The cross-references are study aids, taking the reader to the parallel passage in Luke, and to Deuteronomy on divorce.

The Bishops' Bible gives the Great Bible text with some revisions taken from Geneva: 'came together', 'not willing to make her a public example' and 'these things'. There is one small variation: 'fear not to take [unto thee] Mary' (v. 20). Perhaps responding to Geneva's omission of the Great Bible's 'unto thee', this is the way the first edition marks words with no equivalent in the original language.

Rheims also follows Tyndale's model, but turns it towards the Latin of the Vulgate. The beginning is characteristic: 'and the generation of Christ was in this wise' follows 'Christi autem generatio sic erat', and Mary is 'spoused', 'desponsata' to Joseph.

After all this drafting, the KJB translators made just a few changes to their basic text, Bishops' Bible, 1602 edition, of which only one is original, 'while he thought on these things' (v. 20). This evokes Joseph's ongoing turmoil and overcomes the seeming contradiction between his having thought one thing and Geneva and the Bishops' Bible's literal 'while he thought these things'. They use the one word that did not define Joseph and Mary's situation in familiar English terms of either engagement or marriage, Taverner's 'espoused' (possibly not getting it directly from him but reinventing it, perhaps following Rheims's suggestion). In v. 19 they follow Geneva's word order, 'was minded to put her away privily', but 'privily' comes from the Bishops' Bible. This looks like a revision for style and sound as it moves away from the Greek word order to a slightly more natural English order that has a pleasing alliterative cadence. They also follow Geneva in inserting 'now' and 'and' at the beginnings of verses 18 and 21, and in describing Joseph as 'just' rather than 'righteous'.

The retention of Coverdale's (and Luther's) 'thou son of David' might be carelessness. It is untrue to the Greek; Geneva, following Tyndale, and Rheims had offered more accurate renderings. Overall, this looks like light work, but the revisions come from careful thought about the English, the Greek and the contextual meaning of individual phrases.

It is worthwhile to look at this passage in another way, as the collective result of revisions to Tyndale's second draft, with the KJB's readings given as interlinear changes. This confirms that Tyndale provided the solid base, and also shows a significant quantity of revision (what is hidden is the number of rejected drafts, all of which required thought to create and then to reject):

Now   as
[18] ^ The birth of Jesus Christ was on this wise. When ^ his mother
        espoused   [omission]
Mary was ~~betrothed~~ to Joseph, before they came ~~to dwell~~ together,
             of
she was found with child ~~by~~ the holy Ghost. [19]Then Joseph her
        just   not willing to make her a public example
husband, being a ~~perfect~~ man, and ~~loath to make an example of her~~,
             privily   But thought on these things
was minded to put her away ~~secretly~~. [20] ^ While he ~~thus thought~~,

behold, the Angel of the Lord appeared unto him in a dream,
          thou
saying, 'Joseph, ~~the~~ son of David, fear not to take unto thee

Mary thy wife. For that which is conceived in her, is of the holy
       And
Ghost. [21] ^ She shall bring forth a son, and thou shalt call his

name Jesus. For he shall save his people from their sins.'

In terms of origins, eight changes come from Geneva, two each from Coverdale 1535 and the Great Bible, one perhaps from Taverner or possibly Rheims, and one from the KJB translators. Such observations, however, give only a partial truth: here the KJB may well have reinvented some of the earlier changes, and the role of the Bishops' Bible in transmitting the text vanishes from sight.

In terms of fidelity to the Greek, there are some improvements: the translation is generally more literal in phrases like 'not willing to make her a public example' and 'but while he thought on these things', and in the omission of 'to dwell'; occasionally it is less close to the Greek, as in 'thou son of David'. In more literary terms, the greater use of conjunctive words (something that is also an increase in fidelity to the Greek), 'now', 'but' and 'and' helps the flow, and there is the cadence of 'put her away privily'. There is no change to the level of vocabulary. Overall, Tyndale had worked well, and his version remains very readable, but the revisions enhance the accuracy and do just a little for the literary qualities.

THE FALL

The first passage gave a glimpse of some of the problems with Greek word order and grammar. If Tyndale's sense of the fitness of English as a language for translating Hebrew is right (above, p. 13), we might expect English translation from the Hebrew to be closer to the Hebrew in word order and expression than the NT translation, and at the same time to preserve more of the Hebrew's qualities as writing. Here is Tyndale's version of a passage where the language of the original is fairly simple, the narrative of the Fall, Genesis 3:1–13:

[1]But the serpent was subtler than all the beasts of the field which the Lord God had made, and said unto the woman, 'Ah sir, that God hath said, "ye shall not eat of all manner trees in the garden".' [2]And the woman said unto the serpent, 'Of the fruit of the trees in the garden we may eat, [3]"but of the fruit of the tree that is in the midst of the garden," said God, "see that ye eat not, and see that ye touch it not: lest ye die".'

[4]Then said the serpent unto the woman, 'Tush, ye shall not die: [5]but God doth know that whensoever ye should eat of it, your eyes should be opened and ye should be as God and know both good and evil.' [6]And the woman saw that it was a good tree to eat of, and lusty unto the eyes, and a pleasant tree for to make wise, and took of the fruit of it and ate, and gave unto her husband also with her, and he ate. [7]And the eyes of both them were opened, that they understood how that they were naked. Then they sewed fig leaves together and made them aprons.

[8]And they heard the voice of the Lord God as he walked in the garden in the cool of the day. And Adam hid himself and his wife also from the face of the Lord God, among the trees of the garden. [9]And the Lord God called Adam and said unto him, 'Where art thou?' [10]And he answered, 'Thy voice I heard in the garden, but I was afraid because I was naked, and therefore hid myself.' [11]And he said, 'Who told thee that thou wast naked? hast thou eaten of the tree of which I bade thee that thou shouldst not eat?' [12]And Adam answered, 'The woman which thou gavest to bear me company, she took me of the tree and I ate.' [13]And the Lord God said unto the woman, 'Wherefore didst thou so?' And the woman answered, 'The serpent deceived me and I ate.[6]

For the most part the word order is the same as that of the Hebrew; very little adjustment would be necessary for this to be used as an

---

[6] The passage is unchanged in Tyndale's 1534 'newly corrected and amended' Genesis.

interlinear gloss. The commonest difference is that Hebrew's preference for giving the verb before the subject is changed to the normal English order – 'and the woman said' instead of 'and said the
woman'. Also changed is the order of 'thou wast naked': the Hebrew
gives 'naked thou'. There are a few omissions such as the omission of
the definite article before 'Adam', a Hebrew word for man that came
to be the name of the first man, and so was traditionally taken as a
name in translations (the Hebrew gives the cue for this: once there
are other men, it drops the article, making Adam into a name, Gen.
4:25 onwards). More commonly there are additions. Hebrew often
takes the verb 'to be' as understood, so omits it, as in 'naked thou':
English does not allow this. The last set of changes in response to the
differences between Hebrew and English is to make several singulars
plural: 'all the beast of the field' would have seemed very odd.

Some touches show Tyndale as an imaginative translator. We might
think of 'tush, ye shall not die' as combining an addition and an
omission to register the intensity that Hebrew gives to the verb by
doubling it ('not to die you will die', infinitive followed by the future
tense); 'tush' has no equivalent, but the phrase conveys the mocking
intensity of the Hebrew. 'Ah sir' is similar if perhaps less successful,
a colloquial attempt to pick up the force of the Hebrew conjunction
often translated as 'also' or 'yea'. 'The cool of the day' is a nice
compromise between literal translation and paraphrase. The Hebrew
has 'in the wind of the day'. The Septuagint and the Vulgate gave
Tyndale a simple temporal solution, the afternoon, while Luther
suggested something better with a paraphrase, 'when the day had
become cool'. Picking up 'cool', Tyndale went back to the Hebrew
phrasing, allowing 'cool' to suggest the time of day and perhaps imply
wind.

'The cool of the day' suggests a tendency to change the exact
Hebrew image. 'Whensoever' shows this tendency more clearly. The
Hebrew phrase is, literally, 'in the day'; Tyndale could have used this
but went for the natural expression of the meaning rather than the
foreign way of saying it. He does not go out of his way to follow images
and idioms, and the result, as in most translation, is a compromise
with the exact way the original works.

Hebrew has few conjunctions, relying chiefly on 'vav', 'and'. Whole
strings of sentences begin with it, something that normal English style

is averse to: in this passage every one of the thirteen verses does except v. 5; in the whole passage it is used thirty-four times. The number of 'and's used by a translator – especially to begin sentences – is a useful indicator of the degree to which he is being literal. So the Septuagint, made by writers to whom Hebraic forms came naturally, follows exactly at the start of ten verses, and has twenty-nine overall, whereas the Vulgate begins only three verses with 'et' (eighteen overall). For the most part Tyndale follows the Hebrew nearly as closely as does the Septuagint, beginning nine of the verses and three other sentences within verses with 'and'. In all he uses 'and' twenty-nine times. This shows considerable respect for the original, and becomes one of the basics of English biblical style not only in the OT but also in the parts of the NT that are written in a Hebraic manner. Where Tyndale uses alternatives – of which English has a good number – he shows that he is a servant to, rather than a slave of, the Hebrew. He has a good sense of the connections between sentences, so begins the passage with 'But', alerting the reader to danger, and he uses it in three other places. He also uses 'then', and once adds 'therefore': 'and therefore hid myself'. The prose remains co-ordinated, but an awareness of the progress of the passage shows itself when necessary.

His treatment of the Hebrew verb 'to say' is similar. Three times he uses 'answered' (vv. 10, 12, 13). He does not aim at consistent vocabulary but picks the appropriate English word for the context.

In one place a Hebrew structure – and perhaps Luther – leads Tyndale into trouble. 'And Adam hid himself and his wife also from the face of the Lord God' is the same as Luther except that 'and his wife also' would, following Luther, have been 'with his wife'. This seems to mean that Adam hid Eve as well as himself from God, but the right sense is that both hid themselves. Literally, the Hebrew is, 'and he hid himself, the man and his wife'. Tyndale has kept the singular verb, and added 'also' to suggest that 'also hid herself' should be understood. Not wanting to move far from the Hebrew, he has missed the simple solution later given in the Great Bible, to make the verb plural, and to place both man and wife before it: 'and Adam and his wife hid themselves'.

As in the first passage, there is nothing in this largely monosyllabic and occasionally colloquial language that the ploughboy would have found difficult. Only one word, 'serpent', directly echoes the Latin of the Vulgate. Tyndale had perhaps four other words available, 'snake', 'adder', 'asp' and 'viper'. The last two were probably not serious alternatives, being new to English and used to denote particular kinds of snakes. 'Snake', from Old English, now seems a more obvious choice, but it too was primarily a zoological word, not taking on a figurative or allusive sense until late in the sixteenth century, and then in reference to ingratitude or infidelity. Only 'adder' had been used for centuries in association with the devil, but from about 1300 'serpent' was becoming the usual word for this sense. By 1530 it was the only current English word with the requisite associations. Tyndale had no choice.

While 'serpent' looks like an unavoidable choice, 'aprons' looks decidedly odd. Here Tyndale has followed Luther. Translators continued to struggle to find an appropriate word.

There is little in the language that is difficult to a modern reader even though this is obviously not modern English. There are obsolete senses such as 'lusty' meaning 'pleasing', and strange constructions such as 'for to make wise'. The most pervasive archaic aspect is the verb forms and the accompanying pronouns. Occasionally these may mislead the modern reader, as when the serpent says to the woman, 'ye shall not die': this is not singular but plural, referring to both Adam and Eve. Such forms were of course standard English for the time, and still have limited usage in some English dialects. What was familiar to Tyndale's ploughboy has, through nearly five hundred years, become strange but not impossible to us: that strangeness is part of what is now biblical or religious style. Tyndale's everyday language, coupled with his willingness to follow elements of the style of the original, forms the basis of our high religious English.

COVERDALE'S 1535 TRANSLATION AND THE GREAT BIBLE

For all the diffidence shown in the dedication and prologue, Coverdale did not act as a diffident translator. Again he did not hesitate to revise Tyndale. Here is his 1535 version of the first six verses presented as an interlinear revision of Tyndale:

¹But the serpent was subtler than all the beasts of the field

which the Lord God had made, and said unto the woman,
Yea, hath God said indeed
'~~Ah sir, that God hath said~~, "ye shall not eat of all manner trees in the
      ?   Then said the woman   We eat
garden" ~~:~~ ²~~And the woman said~~ unto the serpent, "` Of the fruit of
                            as for
the trees in the garden ~~we may eat~~, ³"but ~~of~~ the fruit of the tree
                      God hath said, "Eat not ye of it
that is in the midst of the garden," ~~said God, "see that ye eat not~~,

and ~~see that ye~~ touch it not: lest ye die".'

    ⁴Then said the serpent unto the woman, 'Tush, ye shall not
the death. For   in what day soever
die ^: ⁵~~but~~ God doth know that ~~whensoever~~ ye ~~should~~ eat of it,
    shall   shall
your eyes ~~should~~ be opened and ye ~~should~~ be as God and know
                                    the tree was good
both good and evil.' ⁶And the woman saw that ~~it was a good tree~~

to eat of, and lusty unto the eyes, and a pleasant tree ~~for~~ to

make wise, and took of the fruit of it and ate, and gave
                   thereof   Then were the eyes of
unto her husband also ~~with her~~, and he ate. ⁷~~And the eyes of both~~
them both   and they perceived
~~them were~~ opened, ~~that they understood how~~ that they were
 , and
naked. ~~Then they~~ sewed fig leaves together and made them aprons.

This is Tyndale Lutherised. In the first three verses, the following
changes correspond with Luther: 'yea, hath God' ('ja, solt Gott'),
'then said the woman' ('da sprach das weib'), and 'God hath said,
"Eat not ye of it, and touch it not"' ('hat Gott gesagt: Esset nicht
davon, rührets auch nicht an'). 'We eat' ('wir essen') is placed at the
beginning of the speech as in Luther; the form of the verb and the
placing move away from Tyndale's adherence to the Hebrew word
order and his reflection of the Hebrew imperfect. Overall, some of
Tyndale's sensitivity to the Hebrew is lost, together with some of

his imaginative renderings, yet the result is sometimes closer to the Hebrew in relatively simple matters such as word order or phrases such as 'die the death' ('des todes sterben') and 'in what day soever', a mixture of Tyndale with Luther's 'an dem Tage'. Some of the variety also goes: following Luther, 'answered' disappears.

There are fewer interesting changes in the latter part of the passage, but it is worth noting that in the last two verses, where the Tyndale is almost an interlinear gloss to the Hebrew, the Coverdale is just such a gloss to Luther.

The Matthew Bible gives Tyndale's text with two readings from Coverdale, 'yea hath God said indeed' (v. 1) and 'to give understanding' (v. 6). Taverner is also a light revision, making a few changes of words and expressions. Notably he removes Tyndale's colloquialisms, giving, for instance, 'why? hath God commanded you not to eat of all manner trees in the garden?' (v. 1).

By contrast, the Great Bible shows wholesale rewriting of the draft Coverdale was now revising, the Matthew Bible. A few of the changes are for style; most come because the base text is now Münster's Latin. Münster often follows the Hebrew fairly literally, so some of Coverdale's changes seem reasonable as translations of the Hebrew. Inevitably, Münster often gives the same reading as the Vulgate. Here is the last part of the passage with differences from Matthew given in italics:

[8]And they heard the voice of the Lord God *walking* in the garden in the cool of the day. And Adam *and his wife hid themselves* from the *presence* of the Lord God among the trees of the garden. [9]And the Lord God called Adam and said unto him, 'Where art thou?' [10]*which said*, '*I heard thy voice* in the garden, *and* <> was afraid because I was naked, and <> hid myself.' [11]And he said, 'Who told thee that thou wast naked? hast thou *not* eaten of the *same* tree, *concerning the* which I *commanded* thee that thou shouldst not eat *of it?*' [12]And Adam *said*, 'The woman *whom* thou gavest to *be with me*, she *gave* me of the tree, and I *did eat.*'
    [13]And the Lord God said unto the woman: '*Why hast thou done this?*' And the woman *said*, '*Yonder* serpent *beguiled* me, and I *did eat.*'

'Walking' (v. 8, also used in 1535) corresponds to the Hebrew participle and follows both Münster's and the Vulgate's 'deambulantis'; here Tyndale had avoided the idea of a voice walking by giving 'as he walked', but Coverdale has made the translation more literal. Less literal, however, is 'which said, "I heard thy voice"' (v. 10): where the Hebrew began a new sentence, Münster and the Vulgate prefer a relative clause, 'qui ait: uocem tuam audiui'. Two of the readings exactly follow Münster where he is neither quite literal nor the same as the Vulgate: 'concerning the which I commanded thee' ('de qua praecepi tibi', v. 11), and 'yonder serpent beguiled me' ('ipse serpens seduxit me', v. 13); here 'beguiled', which remains in the KJB, neatly responds to Münster's note, referring to Kimchi's interpretation, 'persuasit aut seduxit'.

Coverdale's most significant stylistic change is 'I did eat' for 'I ate' (vv. 12, 13). It gives an appropriately confessional tone as well as creating a poetic rhythm for the KJB, later used by Milton in *Paradise Lost*: 'she gave me of the tree and I did eat', and, with a change of word order, 'the serpent me beguil'd and I did eat' (x: 143, 162).

GENEVA

Translating from Münster rather than the Hebrew was a characteristic Coverdale false step, but he and Münster left their mark as Geneva and the KJB returned to the Hebrew. Geneva revised the Great Bible text in this way:

Now   more subtle   any
¹B̶u̶t̶ the serpent was s̶u̶b̶t̶l̶e̶r̶ than e̶v̶e̶r̶y̶ beast of the field which the
            had   to
Lord God ^ made. And he said u̶n̶t̶o̶ the woman, 'Yea, hath t̶h̶e̶ ̶L̶o̶r̶d̶
      indeed
God ^ said, "ye shall not eat of every tree of the garden"?' ²And

the woman said unto the serpent, 'We eat of the fruit of the
trees   of
t̶r̶e̶e̶ of the garden, ³but a̶s̶ ̶f̶o̶r̶ the fruit of the tree which is in the

midst of the garden, God hath said, "Ye shall not eat of it, neither

shall ye touch it: lest h̶a̶p̶l̶y̶ ye die".'
            Then   to
      ⁴A̶n̶d̶ the serpent said u̶n̶t̶o̶ the woman, "Ye shall not die
at all   when   shall
t̶h̶e̶ ̶d̶e̶a̶t̶h̶: ⁵but God doth know that t̶h̶e̶ ̶s̶a̶m̶e̶ ̶d̶a̶y̶ ̶t̶h̶a̶t̶ ye ^ eat

thereof, your eyes shall be opened, and ye shall be ~~even~~ as gods,

knowing good and evil.' ⁶~~And~~ so the woman (seeing that the ~~same~~
        for meat   that it was pleasant   a
tree was good ~~to eat~~, and ^ ~~lusty~~ to the eyes, and ~~that the same~~
  to be desired   knowledge
tree ~~was pleasant~~ to get ~~wisdom~~) took of the fruit thereof and
      also to   and he
did eat, and gave ^ ~~unto~~ her husband ~~being~~ with her, ~~which~~ did
  Then
eat ~~also~~. ⁷~~And~~ the eyes of them both were opened: and they knew
                figtree
that they were naked, and they sewed ~~fig~~ leaves together and made
  breeches
themselves ~~aprons~~.
  Afterward
⁸~~And~~ they heard the voice of the Lord God walking in the
           the man
garden in the cool of the day, and ~~Adam~~ and his wife hid themselves

from the presence of the Lord God among the trees of the garden.
  But   to the man
⁹~~And~~ the Lord God called ^ ~~Adam~~ and said unto him, 'Where
      Who
art thou?' ¹⁰~~which~~ said, 'I heard thy voice in the garden, and was
          therefore I
afraid because I was naked, ~~and~~ hid myself.' ¹¹And he said,

'Who told thee that thou wast naked? Hast thou ~~not~~ eaten of
         whereof
the ~~same~~ tree ~~concerning the which~~ I commanded thee that thou
        in no case? ¹²Then the man   which
shouldst not eat ~~of it~~?' ¹²~~And Adam~~ said, 'The woman ~~whom~~
  to be
thou gavest ~~to be~~ with me, she gave me of the tree and I did eat.'
          to
¹³And the Lord God said ~~unto~~ the woman: 'Why hast thou done
     The
this?' And the woman said, '~~Yonder~~ serpent beguiled me and I did eat.'

Some of the changes respond to the Hebrew. Instead of the tree being 'good to eat' (Great Bible) or 'good to eat of' (Tyndale, Coverdale 1535, Matthew), it is 'good for meat' because the Hebrew has a noun ('meat' in the English of the time means food in general); and the tree is not 'pleasant' but 'to be desired' because the Hebrew has a passive participle (v. 6). Adam is not 'Adam' but 'the man' because 'Adam' means 'man' and the Hebrew has the definite article.

Enough of Tyndale's original words are restored to show that Geneva kept an eye on his work, so the decision not to use 'ah sir' and 'tush' shows a disapproval of his colloquial touches.

Some of the changes are stylistic. Coverdale's clumsy 'concerning the which' is replaced by his 1535 'whereof' (v. 11). On the other hand, Geneva could be quite as clumsy in the same verse, 'that thou shouldst not eat in no case'; the last three words survived for nearly twenty years, then disappeared.[7] The Hebrew conjunction 'vav' is variously 'now', 'then', 'so', 'afterward' and 'therefore', giving more of a sense of temporal and logical structure, as well as more variety, than its predecessors (there are twenty-three 'and's). There are changes of words: 'subtler' becomes 'more subtle', 'unto' sometimes becomes 'to', 'wisdom' becomes 'knowledge' and 'aprons' becomes 'breeches', whence the nickname, 'Breeches Bible'. Seeming to imply some sort of trousers, and so to be comically inappropriate for Eve, 'breeches' has an older sense, 'a garment covering the loins and thighs: at first perh. only a "breech-cloth"' (*OED*); in other words, a loin-cloth. A century and a half earlier, the Wycliffite translations had used the same word (Geneva here is almost exactly the same as the early Wycliffite version). The Geneva margin perhaps indicates unease at this old sense of the word by giving a good attempt at the literal meaning: 'Hebr. things to gird about them to hide their privities'; this would have been unnecessary if 'loin-cloth' was the unambiguous sense. Here the margin carries out the duty to convey the literal sense. The same thing happens with the change to 'ye shall not die the death'. The Geneva translators relegate 'die the death' to the margin as a Hebraism, and substitute what was to them a more English form, 'ye shall not die at all' (we are now accustomed to Hebraisms such as 'die the death' or 'dream a dream' from their frequent use in the KJB). Such changes are independent – in this last case, deliberately

---

[7] They are present in Barker's 1576 edition and the Edinburgh edition of 1579, but omitted from Barker's 1578 edition.

independent – of the original, and, without being an obvious attempt to raise the style, do a little to improve the flow of the passage.

By now the process of drafting included some good backward steps as well as some bad forward steps. Overall, some aspects of the passage read a little better, and Coverdale 1535 and the Great Bible's movement away from the literal sense of the Hebrew has been substantially corrected.

THE KING JAMES BIBLE

The Bishops' Bible contributes nothing new of significance. It gives the Great Bible text with some touches of Geneva, especially in v. 6; its most blatant change is 'peradventure' for 'haply' (v. 3). Also notable is its near-restoration of Tyndale in v. 6, 'to make one wise': 'one' is an addition to Tyndale's strictly literal translation. In its 1602 form 'the Lord' (v. 9) returns to being 'the Lord God' (possibly the omission of 'God' in the first edition was a printer's error).

There is very little that is new in the KJB. The bedrock of its version is again Tyndale. The Great Bible makes a significant contribution, and there is more from Coverdale 1535 than from Geneva. The Bishops' Bible supplies only one word, and the Matthew Bible none. The KJB translators contributed a mere seven words, and they marked another four as having no equivalent in the Hebrew. One of the seven words is 'surely' in 'ye shall not surely die' (v. 4). This is another attempt to find an English equivalent for the intensive effect of the Hebrew. It has one quality that distinguishes it from 'ye shall not die the death' (Great and Bishops') and 'ye shall not die at all' (Geneva), a mocking tone not too far removed from that of Tyndale's snake. This is more obvious if we change the word order: 'surely ye shall not die': it is as if we were to say 'of course you won't die'. Another of the words is a restoration – or recreation – of Tyndale, 'may' in 'we may eat' (v. 2). There was nothing wrong with 'we eat' as literal translation, but the KJB agrees with Tyndale in taking the verb in the context of God's command, generally expressed by the snake in v. 1 and specified by Eve in v. 3: she and Adam are *allowed* to eat of the other trees. This is sensitive literal translation. The KJB contributes only one sentence, 'what *is* this *that* thou hast done?' (v. 13). It is a literal version of the Hebrew's 'what this you have done', adding only the words essential to make it English, and marking them as additions.

This view of the passage rightly suggests that the KJB translators made a judicious combination of earlier work and that their additions tended to increase the literalness of the text, but it wrongly suggests that they did very little work. First, a decision not to make a change can involve as much work as making a change because it too can come from detailed consideration of the original language and all the possibilities present in the translations. Second, this geological view hides how much they had to change their base text, the Bishops' Bible of 1602.

We can get a visual impression of how much they did from a surviving draft of their work, a 1602 Bishops' Bible with their handwritten annotations. The exact status of this work is uncertain. My tentative suggestion is that it represents the work of a company translator whose brief was to show where Geneva differed from the Bishops' Bible (and who occasionally noted readings from other translators). Almost all these annotations note Geneva readings and are accompanied by 'g' for 'Geneva'. Only half a dozen of these Geneva readings were adopted in the final text, and none of the distinctive KJB readings are present. More remained to be done.

With omissions where there are no changes, the following represents what the translators did to get from the 1602 text to theirs, with the KJB changes in italics:

¹~~And~~ *Now* the serpent was ~~subtler~~ *more subtle* than ~~every~~ *any* beast of the field which the Lord God had made, and he said unto the woman, 'Yea, hath God said, "Ye shall not eat of every tree of the garden"?' ²And the woman said unto the serpent, 'We *may* eat of the fruit of the trees of the garden: ³but ~~as for~~ *of* the fruit of the tree which is in the midst of the garden, God hath said, "Ye shall not eat of it, neither shall ye touch it, lest ~~peradventure~~ ye die".' ⁴And the serpent said unto the woman, *saw* "Ye shall not *surely* die ~~the death~~. ⁵For God doth know that ~~the same day that~~ *in the day* ye eat thereof, *then* your eyes shall be opened and ye shall be as gods, knowing good and evil.' ⁶And *when* the woman, ~~seeing~~ *saw* that the ~~same~~ tree was good ~~to eat of~~ *for food*, and *that it was* pleasant to the eyes, and a tree to be desired to make one wise, *she* took of the fruit thereof, and did eat, and gave also unto her husband ~~being~~ with her, and he did eat. ⁷~~Then~~ *And* the eyes of them both were opened . . . ⁹And the Lord God called *unto* Adam, and

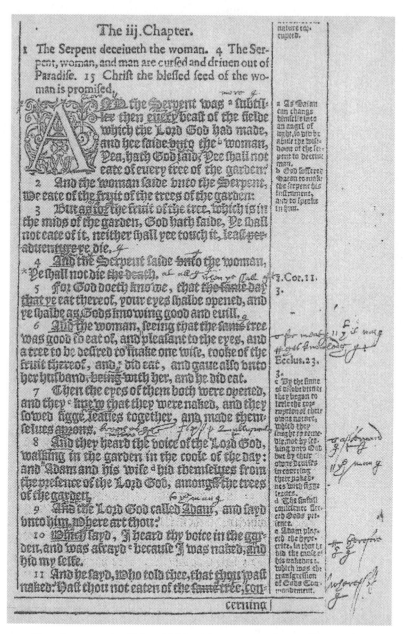

1. Genesis 3:1–11, 1602 Bishops' Bible with annotations by the KJB translators.
Bodleian Library Bib. Eng. 1602 b. 1.

said unto him, 'Where art thou?' ¹⁰~~which~~ *And he* said, 'I heard thy voice in the garden, and *I* was afraid because I was naked, and *I* hid myself.' ¹¹And he said, 'Who told thee that thou wast naked? hast thou ~~not~~ eaten of the ~~same~~ tree ~~concerning the which~~ *whereof* I commanded thee that thou shouldst not eat ~~of it~~?' ¹²And ~~Adam~~ *the man* said, 'The woman whom thou gavest to be with me, she gave me of the tree and I did eat.' ¹³And the Lord God said unto the woman: '~~Why hast thou done this~~? *What is this that thou hast done?*' And the woman said, 'The serpent beguiled me and I did eat.'

A few of the changes such as 'more subtle' for 'subtler', 'any' for 'every' (v. 1), 'food' for 'meat' (v. 6), and some changes to the conjunctive words are independent of the Hebrew and are either stylistic or, perhaps, changes for change's sake. However, most of the changes appear to be prompted by the Hebrew. The overall drift of the translators' work is clear: they gave most attention to the relationship between the English and the Hebrew, either selecting an earlier version that better reflected this relationship, or supplying their own version where none of the alternatives was as close as reasonably possible to the Hebrew. A marker of this increased literalness is that the KJB has more 'and's than any of the others, 31.[8]

---

[8] Total numbers of 'and's in the passage: Hebrew: 34; KJB: 31; Septuagint: 29; Tyndale: 29; Bishops' Bible: 28; Coverdale: 27; Geneva: 23; Great Bible: 22; Luther: 22; Vulgate: 18.

CHAPTER 3

'*I was a translator*'

'CERTAIN LEARNED MEN'

'There were many chosen that were greater in other men's eyes than in their own, and that sought the truth rather than their own praise':[1] this is the KJB translators' modest description of themselves. Though Bishop (soon to be Archbishop) Richard Bancroft circulated a letter from the King, sealed 22 July 1604, that states 'we have appointed certain learned men, to the number of four and fifty',[2] the surviving lists give forty-seven names, divided into six companies, two each at Westminster, Oxford and Cambridge.[3] Whatever the exact number, the translators describe it as 'not too many, lest one should trouble another; and yet many, lest many things haply might escape them'.[4] There are indications in the extant lists of translators that some of the companies divided their work in two; while this is not certain, I show the divisions in the following list.[5] The brief notes give (where

---

[1] 'The translators to the reader'; *NCPB*, p. xxxi.

[2] Pollard, *Records of the English Bible*, p. 331; for the date, see p. 48. Nicolson sees the fifty-four as made up of a proposed eight members of each company, plus six 'directors supervising them', and offers some nice thoughts about the possible numerological significance: six companies is the number of the Trinity multiplied by the number of the Testaments, forty-eight is the number of the Apostles multiplied by the number of Gospels (p. 71).

[3] These seem initially to have been thought of as three companies. Bancroft in July 1604 asked that learned men should send observations on the text to three people, Edward Lively at Cambridge, John Harding at Oxford and Lancelot Andrewes at Westminster, 'to be imparted to the rest of their several companies' (Pollard, *Records of the English Bible*, p. 333). The rules for the translation, especially rules 12 and 13, can as easily be read as referring to three companies as six. But as soon as lists of translators began to be written out with the parts they were to revise listed in biblical order, three companies naturally appeared as six, and in practice they must have worked as six companies.

[4] 'The translators to the reader'; *NCPB*, p. xxxii.

[5] Based on BL MS Harley 750, which may be a copy of John Bois's list, since it is followed by a copy of his notes on the translation work and then by an early, incomplete version of

known) each translator's position at the time the work began, followed by significant positions held at other times, significant works and special skills or claims to fame outside of what is taken for granted with all of them, expertise in the biblical languages.

First Westminster company, Genesis–2 Kings

Pentateuch: Lancelot Andrewes (1555–1626), head of company, Dean of Westminster; fellow of Pembroke College, Cambridge, Bishop of Chichester, Ely and Westminster; *Tortura Torti* (1609) and *Responsio ad Apologiam Cardinalis Bellarmini* (1610), both against Cardinal Bellarmine; posthumous publications include *XCVI Sermons* (1629), *Opuscula quaedam posthuma* (1629), and two volumes of notes from his lectures, *A Pattern of Catechistical Doctrine* (1630) and *The Moral Law* (1642).

John Overall (1561–1619), Dean of St Paul's, Regius Professor of Divinity at Cambridge; Bishop of Norwich.

Adrian Saravia (1532–1613), Prebend of Canterbury, Canon of Westminster; Dutch scholar and educator, Professor of Theology at Leiden; *De diversis ministrorum evangelii gradibus* (1590, English translation 1591), *De imperandi authoritate et christiana obedientia* (1593), *Examen tractatus de episcoporum triplici genere* (1610), the last two attacking Beza's views.

Richard Clerke or Clark (d. 1634), clergyman; fellow of Christ's College, Cambridge; posthumous, *Sermons preached by... Richard Clerke... one of the most learned translators of our English Bible* (1637).

John Layfield (1562/3–1617), clergyman; fellow of Trinity College, Cambridge, traveller to the West Indies, expert on architecture; posthumous, abbreviated 'A large relation of the Puerto Rico voyage' (1625, in Samuel Purchas's *Pilgrimes*).

Joshua–2 Kings: Robert Tighe or Teigh (d. 1620), clergyman; Oxford and Cambridge.

Francis Burleigh, clergyman; Cambridge.

Geoffrey King, fellow of King's College, Cambridge; Regius Professor of Hebrew.

his *Veteris Interpretis*. See Norton, *Textual History*, pp. 6–7. The biographical information that follows draws chiefly on McClure, Nicolson, Opfell, Pollard, Westbrook, Wood and individual articles in *ODNB*.

Richard Thomson (d. 1613), fellow of Clare College, Cambridge; *Elenchus refutationis torturae torti* (1611), supporting Andrewes's views; posthumous, *Diatriba de amissione et intercisione gratiae, et justificationis* (1616).

William Bedwell (?1562–1632),[6] clergyman; Cambridge, Arabist and Mathematician; compiled an unpublished Arabic–Latin dictionary and translated an anti-Islamic dialogue, *Mohammedis imposturae*, with an explanation of Islamic terms (1615), wrote several mathematical works, and edited an unusual work for one of the translators, *The Tournament of Tottenham. Or, The wooing, winning and wedding of Tib the reeve's daughter there* (1631).[7]

First Cambridge company, 1 Chronicles–Song of Solomon
Edward Lively (c. 1545–1605), head of company (successor as head of company unknown, perhaps Spalding, then Bing),[8] Regius Professor of Hebrew; *A true chronologie of the times of the Persian monarchy and after to the destruction of Jerusalem by the Romans* (1597).

John Richardson (d. 1625), fellow of Emmanuel; Regius Professor of Theology, Master of Peterhouse, Master of Trinity College, Vice-Chancellor.

Laurence Chaderton or Chatterton (?1536–1640), Master of Emmanuel College.

Francis Dillingham (d. 1625), clergyman; fellow of Christ's College; *A Dissuasive from Poperie* (1599), *Disputatio de natura poenitentiae adversus Bellarminum* (1606), *Enchiridion Christianae Fidei* (1617).

Thomas Harrison (1555–1630), fellow of Trinity College.

---

[6] His gravestone gives his age at death as seventy; see Daniel Lysons, *The Environs of London* (1795), vol. III, p. 532n.

[7] An engagingly light pastiche medieval poem which he says he copied from a manuscript. A commendatory poem relates to the KJB. It is 'to my learned and reverend friend, Mr Wilhelm Bedwell, one of the translators of the Bible', and begins:

> That learned pen, whose aid did heretofore
> Enrich our tongue with Salem's wealthy store,
> And made our language speak, with faithful skill,
> The oracle of Sion's holy hill,
> Doth now vouchsafe (a lower exercise)
> To grace, poor Totnam, thy antiquities.

[8] The Regius Professor of Hebrew was the designated head of the company.

Roger Andrewes, fellow of Pembroke College; Master of Jesus College; brother of Lancelot.

Robert Spalding, fellow of St John's College; Lively's successor as Regius Professor of Hebrew.

Andrew Byng (1574–1652), fellow of Peterhouse; Regius Professor of Hebrew.

First Oxford company, the Prophets

John Harding, head of company,[9] Regius Professor of Hebrew; President of Magdalen College.

John Rainolds or Reynolds (1549–1607), President of Corpus Christi College; leader of the puritan delegation to the Hampton Court conference; *Sex theses de sacra scriptura et ecclesia* (1580), *The Sum of the Conference betweene John Rainolds and John Hart: touching the head and the faith of the Church* (1584), *De Romanae Ecclesiae idolatria* (1596), *The Overthrow of Stage Plays . . . wherein all the reasons that can be made for them are notably refuted* (1599); posthumous works include *Censura librorum apocryphorum veteris testamenti, adversum Pontificios* (lectures, 1611).

Thomas Holland (d. 1612), Regius Professor of Theology, Rector of Exeter College.

Richard Kilbye (1560/1–1620), Rector of Lincoln College; Regius Professor of Hebrew; his only publication, a funeral sermon for his fellow translator Thomas Holland, does not mention work on the KJB.[10]

Miles Smith (d. 1624), Prebend of Hereford; Bishop of Gloucester; with Thomas Bilson, one of the two final revisers of the KJB, and author of the preface; posthumous, *Sermons* (1632).

Richard Brett (1567/8–1637), fellow of Lincoln College; two translations Greek to Latin, *Iconum sacrarum decas* (1603).

Mr Fairclough. Identification uncertain.[11]

---

[9] Harding's name appears first in the list; as Regius Professor of Hebrew, he was designated head, and Bancroft refers to him in the same sentence as Lively and Andrewes as if each are heads (Pollard, *Records of the English Bible*, p. 333). However, the translators met in Rainolds's rooms until his death – perhaps because of his ill health – and he is sometimes named as head or *de facto* head of the company.

[10] Omitted from MS Add 4254.

[11] McClure, *Translators Revived*, p. 145, proposed Daniel Featley, noting that Featley 'is a corrupt pronunciation of the name Fairclough', who was at most twenty-four when the

Second Cambridge company, the Apocrypha[12]
John Duport (d. 1617/18), head of company,[13] Master of Jesus College; four times Vice-Chancellor.

William Branthwaite (1563–1619), fellow of Emmanuel College; Master of Gonville and Caius College, Vice-Chancellor.

Jeremiah Radcliffe (d. 1612), Vice-Master of Trinity College.

Samuel Ward (1572–1643), fellow of Emmanuel College; Master of Sidney Sussex College, Vice-Chancellor.

John Bois or Boys (1561–1644), clergyman; fellow of St John's College, prebend of Ely; posthumous, *Veteris interpretis cum Beza aliisque recentioribus collatio* (1655).

Andrew Downes (*c.* 1549–1628), Regius Professor of Greek; *Eratosthenes, hoc est brevis et luculenta defensio Lysiae pro caede Eratosthenis* (1593), *Praelectiones in Philippicam de pace Demosthenis* (1621).

Robert Ward, fellow of King's College; prebend of Chichester.

Second Oxford company, Gospels, Acts and Revelation
Thomas Ravis (?1560–1609), head of company,[14] Dean of Christ Church, Canon of Westminster; twice Vice-Chancellor, Bishop of Gloucester, Bishop of London.

George Abbot (1562–1633), Dean of Winchester, Master of University College; three times Vice-Chancellor, Bishop of Coventry and Lichfield, Bishop of London, Archbishop of Canterbury; *Quaestiones*

---

translators were selected. John Featley (his nephew) makes no mention of his having been a translator. Though this identification is sometimes repeated, as in Paine, *Men Behind the King James Version*, p. 76, and Westbrook, *ODNB* makes no mention of his involvement with the translation in its entry for him. Wood describes him as 'sometime of New College' (*History and Antiquities*, vol. II, p. 282); Pollard, *Records of the English Bible*, p. 51, followed by Opfell, *King James Bible Translators*, p. 62, gives Richard Fairclough, fellow of New College and Rector of Bucknell, Oxford. Nicolson, *Power and Glory*, p. 255, gives the same name but with details, other than dates, which fit Daniel Featley.

12 This is described as 'the Prayer of Manasses and the rest of the Apocrypha', an instruction or reminder not to follow the Geneva Bible's practice of placing Manasses after 2 Chronicles.

13 Duport is first named in this company, hence the presumption that he was head. In four of the other companies the first-named member is also the head as specified by rule thirteen for the translation. If that rule was followed in this company, Downes, as Regius Professor of Greek, would have been head, and similarly Harmar (or perhaps Perin) in the second Oxford company.

14 One list of translators gives 'Dr Raynes' instead of Ravis, presumably an error (BL MS EG 2884). As with Duport, the presumption that Ravis was head is because he is named first. *ODNB* article on Savile suggests that he was head of company, noting that the company met in his rooms.

sex totidem praelectionibus (1598), *A Brief Description of the Whole World* (1599), *An exposition upon the Prophet Jonah contained in certain sermons* (1600), *The Reasons which Dr Hill hath brought for the upholding of Papistry . . . unmasked* (1604), *A Treatise of the Perpetual Visibility and Succession of the True Church in all Ages* (1624).

Richard Edes (?1544–1604), Dean of Worcester; died before starting work on the translation.

John Aglionby (1566/7–1610), Principal of St Edmund Hall, Oxford, as replacement for Richard Edes.[15]

Giles Tomson (1553–1612), fellow of All Souls College; Bishop of Gloucester.

Henry Savile (1549–1622), Warden of Merton College, Provost of Eton; only translator not to have taken holy orders, tutor in Greek to Elizabeth, polymath, knighted 1604, founded Savilian Chairs of geometry and astronomy at Oxford; *The End of Nero and Beginning of Galba. Four books of the Histories of Cornelius Tacitus. The Life of Agricola* (first part original work; 1591), edition of the works of Chrysostom (1611–12), *Praelectiones tresdecim in principium Elementorum Euclidis* (1621).

John Perin (d. 1615), Regius Professor of Greek.

Ralph Ravens, fellow of St John's College.[16]

Leonard Hutten (1556/7–1632), canon, later subdean, of Christ Church Cathedral, Oxford, sometimes listed instead of, and probably substitute for, Ralph Ravens.[17]

John Harmar (*c.* 1555–1613), Warden of Winchester College, Prebend of Winchester; fellow of New College, Regius Professor of Greek; translated into English sermons of Calvin (1579), six homilies of Chrysostom (1586), sermons of Beza (1587).

Second Westminster company, the Epistles
The Pauline Epistles: William Barlow (d. 1613), head of company, Dean of Chester; son of the Bishops' Bible translator, William Barlow,

---

[15] Not in MS Harley 750. Named among the translators in the Merton College Register (*Registrum Annalium*), final entry for 1604 old style, i.e., February 1605.

[16] Pollard takes this name as an error, *Records of the English Bible*, p. 53.

[17] Not in MS Harley 750. Named among the translators in the Merton College Register, final entry for 1604 old style. See also Wood, *History and Antiquities*, vol. II, p. 183, and *Athenae Oxonienses*, col. 489.

fellow of Trinity Hall, Cambridge, Bishop of Rochester, Bishop of Lincoln; *A Defence of the Articles of the Protestants' Religion* (1601), *The Sum and Substance of the Conference . . . at Hampton Court* (1604), *Answer to a Catholic Englishman* (1609).

Ralph Hutchinson (?1552–1606), President of St John's College, Oxford.

John Spenser (1558/9–1614), fellow of Corpus Christi College; President of Corpus Christi; editor of Hooker's *Laws of Ecclesiastical Polity* (1604).

Roger Fenton (1565–1616), clergyman; fellow of Pembroke College, Cambridge; *A Perfume against the Noisome Pestilence Prescribed by Moses unto Aaron* (1603), *A Treatise of Usury* (1611); posthumous, *A Treatise against the Necessary Dependence upon that one Head, and the present reconciliation to the Church of Rome* (1617).

The canonical Epistles: Michael Rabbett (1552–1630), clergyman; Cambridge student.

Thomas Sanderson (?1560–1614), fellow of Balliol College, Oxford; Archdeacon of Rochester, canon of St Paul's; *Of Romanising Recusants and Dissembling Catholics* (1611).[18]

William Dakins (1568/9–1607), fellow of Trinity College, Cambridge, Professor of Divinity, Gresham College, London.

Several others took part in the work, either as replacements for those who died or in some other way. Thomas Bilson (1546/7–1616), Oxford scholar, theologian and Bishop of Winchester, is not recorded as belonging to any of the companies but helped to co-ordinate the work and, with Miles Smith, saw the KJB through the press; he is supposed to have written the chapter summaries.[19] William Thorne, Oxford scholar, Dean of Chichester, is described in a 1606 letter as a member of the Oxford OT company.[20] William Eyre, fellow of Emmanuel College, Cambridge, Hebraist and Orientalist, seems to have become a member of the Cambridge OT company: he lent James Ussher a manuscript of the company's work (see below,

---

[18] I assume the Thomas Sanderson who wrote this book and has the dates I have given is the same man.
[19] Opfell, *King James Bible Translators*, p. 105.
[20] Paine, *Men Behind the King James Version*, pp. 75–6.

p. 90), and a name that looks like, but is not certainly his appears added to the names for this company in BL MS Add 4254. George Ryves (1569–?), Warden of New College, Oxford, was an overseer at Oxford.

Others whose names we know who may have been involved are James Montagu (later Bishop of Bath and Wells), whose name appears in one list as replacement for Edes in the second Oxford company (but he was not an Oxford man), Arthur Lake (1559–?), fellow of New College, Oxford, and Thomas Sparke, one of the delegates to the Hampton Court conference. Finally, there is Richard Bancroft (?1544–1610), created Archbishop of Canterbury in 1604: his role was primarily organisational, but he contributed some changes to the text.

All these men had two things in common, scholarship and, except for Savile, positions in the Church, primary qualifications for the work. Beyond these, they were a mixture, from archbishops-to-be to country parsons, and from distinguished writers of sermons, theological and controversial works, and makers of scholarly editions to men who published nothing and would otherwise be absolutely forgotten. Doctrinally, they ranged across the spectrum of the established Church, from high church establishment figures to puritans. One thing very few of them did was to write imaginative literature, and, with a few exceptions such as Lancelot Andrewes viewed through the eyes of T. S. Eliot, none had reputations for their ability to write English.

In the primary respects of scholarship and devotion, therefore, they are an apt group for the work, but in other respects they seem unlikely to produce either the central book of English religion and culture or 'the noblest monument of English prose'.[21] How could individuality emerge from committees? Where is the genius worthy to be compared with – and by some even found superior to – Shakespeare? Such questions have been asked but are in some ways wrong questions. They are asked through a perspective of time that sees the KJB as something it was not seen as in its own time, and they are asked as if these many men were the sole creators of the KJB. What is needed is to see how they worked, not to make the KJB,

---

[21] Lowes, etc. See Norton, *History of the English Bible as Literature*, pp. 401–2.

but to polish the work already so intensely drafted. What qualities did they have that enabled them to do this, and how well did they do it?

In order to give an idea of their qualities, I want here to sketch the mental world of two Cambridge translators, William Branthwaite and John Bois, starting with a glimpse of a third, Samuel Ward. His diary and papers give a vivid sense of a troubled puritan conscience, the political realities of college life and the financial concerns that were also a part of the translators' mental world, but he is useful here as one of the few translators to show open pride in having worked on the KJB. Seeking the Archdeaconry of Bath, he feared losing his prebendaryship of Yatton, and itemised reasons why he should have both:

First, [Yatton] is my stay of maintenance, 2, it cost me £50, 3, that Archdeacon is the least dignity, 4, the King will have all first fruits.

My lord may have good pretence for making me Residentiary: first I was his first Chaplain; 2^d I have small means, 3, I am Doctor and Master of a College, 4, I was a translator. Mr Young may have one of the other Prebends.[22]

Valuable as Ward is for showing some of the realities the translators lived with, Branthwaite gives a strong sense of something more directly important for the KJB, the translators' world of books, and Bois, through his diary, reveals a translator's scholarship, devotion and interests.

A TRANSLATOR'S LIBRARY

The translators' mental lives were above all in their books. This was a time when a scholar could place limited reliance on college or university libraries. When the Bodleian Library at Oxford opened in November 1602 it had about 2,000 books.[23] College libraries at Cambridge and Oxford typically held between 250 and 500 books in the late sixteenth century. Trinity College, Cambridge, had about

---

[22] Thomas Baker, selections from Ward's manuscripts (Cambridge University Library, Baker Mss, Mm 2 25), p. 320. For a picture of Ward as a young man, see Nicolson, *Power and Glory*, pp. 125–30.
[23] *ODNB* Bodley. Thomas James, *Catalogus Librorum Bibliothecae Publicae... Thomas Bodleius* (1605) gives a valuable record of its contents in the time of the translators.

325 in 1600, of which about 75 were recently acquired law books, and about 160 were religious.[24] In these circumstances the translators' own libraries tell a great deal about their reading. Many of them had, by these college standards, huge collections. At his death, George Abbot bequeathed over 2,000 books to Lambeth Palace library; in 1614 he described his collection as 'not much inferior unto that ... of any private man in Europe', though his predecessor as Archbishop, Bancroft, had three times as many, including 102 Bibles.[25] William Branthwaite's library remains as an almost complete collection, said to have been worth about £230, of 1,405 books in Gonville and Caius College library (he also left seventeen volumes, mostly of the Church Fathers, to Emmanuel College; there was a proviso in his will that if books were missing from either college and not restored, the remainder should go to the other college).[26]

Branthwaite had a reputation as a Greek scholar but published nothing. His career was spent entirely at Cambridge. He was appointed Master of Gonville and Caius in contentious circumstances because of irregularities in the way the fellows had gone about the election of their preferred candidate.[27] He was more often involved in factious contention than Ward, though at the last his relationship with the college was harmonious. He died while holding the Vice-Chancellorship.

One of the most striking things about his library is its lack of English literature. There is *Jack Up Land*, 'compiled by the famous Geoffrey Chaucer' (?1536) – but it is neither literature nor by Chaucer: it is a short anti-Catholic tract. And there is *The Spider and the Fly* (1556), a 450-page satirical poem in ninety-eight chapters by John Heywood, better known as a dramatist, epigrammatist and John Donne's father-in-law. This omission of English literature is suggestive. Admirers of the literary qualities of the KJB have argued, in Paine's words, 'that the great poetry of the age was all around the scholars as they worked on the Bible, was in their thought and feeling, and quickened the flow of their language' (p. 17). It was all

---

[24] Gaskell, *Trinity College Library*, pp. 86, ix.   [25] *ODNB*, Abbot, Bancroft.
[26] Venn, *Biographical History*, vol. III, p. 72; Bush and Rasmussen, *Library of Emmanuel College*, p. 24; Stubbings, compiler, *Forty-Nine Lives*, portrait 4.
[27] Venn, *Biographical History*, vol. III, p. 70.

around them, in a manner of speaking, but it is by no means certain that they were aware of it.

There is also a shortage of English Bibles. Even though Branthwaite helped to create it, there is no KJB. Nor is there the Bible the translators were to base their work on, the Bishops' Bible; nor Tyndale, Coverdale nor the Great Bible.[28] There is a 1584 octavo Geneva Bible with two or three underlinings and a number of blots that might suggest that it was sometimes open while he was studying. The only substantial writing is on the inside back cover, some twenty-five capital 'B's, twice followed by 'ranthwaite': this is the young Branthwaite developing an ornate signature. This 'B', or more often a 'WB' monogram, became his characteristic marginal attention mark. And there is Fulke's parallel edition of the Rheims and Bishops' NTs; this probably represents interest in Catholic–Protestant controversy (and controversy in general: he also owned a confuted Koran). Branthwaite, it would seem, was no expert on the English Bible, but it is worth noting that the Bodleian Library in 1605 held only a Matthew Bible besides a copy of Fulke,[29] Lively had only a Coverdale OT, and the library of Emmanuel College had no English Bibles among its less than 500 volumes.[30] It may be that the command to consult the earlier English translations took most of the translators into unfamiliar territory. Indeed, it is possible that some groups of the translators did not have access to the work of all their predecessors.

As with most collections of books, there is no certainty that Branthwaite read them all, and sometimes the annotations in them come from others, either because they were secondhand (he had for instance William Whitaker's copy of Sixtus Senensis's *Bibliotheca Sancta*), or because others used them. Nevertheless, his library gives a very substantial picture of his interests as well as a tantalising glimpse of how he used some of his books. Continental religious works in Latin (including Catholic works) dominate. This is an important reminder not just that scholarship was international and dominated by

[28] Wood says of the Oxford translators that they 'all, for their better information, had the copies of such Bibles that could be found in the public, or those libraries belonging to colleges' (*History and Antiquities*, vol. II, p. 283).

[29] By 1620 these had been joined by 'the Bible of the New translation' (i.e., the KJB), Geneva, the Bishops' Bible, and the first volume of the Douai OT.

[30] Leedham-Green, *Books in Cambridge Inventories*, vol. I, p. 549; Bush and Rasmussen, *Library of Emmanuel College*, pp. 18–19, 21.

western Europe, but also that Latin was its common language. At work, the KJB translators, creators of what has been called the 'greatest of English classics', thought and wrote in Latin, a language they describe themselves as having been exercised in 'almost from our very cradle'.[31] John Overall, for instance, appointed to preach before Elizabeth, said 'that he had spoken Latin so long, it was troublesome to him to speak English in a continued oration'.[32]

Branthwaite had a small collection of non-English Bibles. It included a six-volume Latin Bible with the Glossa Ordinaria (1498–1508), a 1565 edition of the French scholar Johannes Benedictus's emended and annotated Vulgate, Estienne's folio Greek NT of 1550, a 1570 parallel Greek and Latin NT with commentary by Matthias Flacius Illyricus, Philipp Melanchthon's 1545 Greek Bible, giving the Septuagint OT and Apocrypha as well as the NT (here using the text of Erasmus's fifth edition),[33] Plantin's interlinear Bible of 1584, and Antonio Brucioli's Italian OT with commentary (1540). The rather inexact 1778 manuscript catalogue of the collection adds several others that are no longer in the collection. There were at least two more Greek NTs, two copies of a Latin NT with notes by Junius and Tremellius, and a German NT from 1525.[34] Many of Branthwaite's commentaries also gave the text, usually in Latin. Though this is far from a thorough collection, these Bibles gave Branthwaite the Hebrew text in the Plantin, various versions of the Greek for the whole Bible, and a range of Latin versions, including that of Pagninus in the Plantin interlinear.

The Plantin interlinear and the Melanchthon Greek Bible would have been particularly significant for a translator of the Apocrypha. The Plantin gave the Greek text of the Complutensian Polyglot, with some emendations, while the Melanchthon used the reputedly superior Aldine Press text of 1518–19.[35] The Plantin was effectively a translator's crib: the Latin, printed above the line rather than under as in modern interlinear Bibles, was as easy for a translator as English

---

[31] Hoare, *Evolution of the English Bible*, p. 3; 'the translators to the reader', quoting Jerome, *NCPB*, p. xxxi.
[32] Fuller, *Worthies*, vol. III, p. 61.
[33] Greenslade (ed.), *Cambridge History of the Bible*, vol. III, p. 57.
[34] Leedham-Green, *Books in Cambridge Inventories*, vol. I, p. 549.
[35] *Cambridge History of the Bible*, vol. III, p. 57.

would be nowadays. It has occasional markings from a neat hand that is probably not Branthwaite's (but it does appear elsewhere in his books) which show that the OT and the Apocrypha were closely studied, but there are no marks in the NT. A couple of alternative Hebrew readings are noted (Gen. 20:16 and Exod. 10:15), and in parts there are inconspicuous crosses that are most easily understood as marking what has been studied – or, possibly, translated – in a session. If, as seems probable, the KJB translators divided up the work on the Apocrypha, and if this was one of the copies Branthwaite – or they – worked from, the Apocrypha annotations suggest one of the divisions. Throughout Wisdom there are underlinings of individual Greek characters and sometimes of whole words; in places a verse number for a particular bit of the text is written in the margin (neither this Bible nor the Melanchthon has verse numbers). There is nothing in Ecclesiasticus, then attention marks of a different sort run from Baruch 6 to 1 Maccabees 3:27. The same marks in the same hand run from here to the end of 2 Maccabees in the Melanchthon, indicating that this annotator changed the text he was working on. If this reflects work on the KJB, his portion was Wisdom and Baruch 6 (the Epistle of Jeremy, as it is called in the KJB) to the end.

The same hand dominates in the Melanchthon, and can be traced through much of the OT. Branthwaite's much coarser hand annotates part of Melanchthon's preface and occasional parts of the OT. In the Apocrypha he makes frequent marks and some annotations in Judith and Ecclesiasticus. These include underlinings, sometimes of several lines at a time, with his WB monogram in the margin, occasional short English versions of the Greek and even more occasional notations of alternative readings. The English versions differ from the KJB, sometimes in sense as well as wording, as at Ecclesiasticus 44:23, where Branthwaite gives the Geneva rendering. Branthwaite's allotted portion may have been Judith and Ecclesiasticus, but his annotations reveal nothing more than that he looked at these books particularly carefully.

No more than an indication of the range of religious works can be given here. There is an extensive – approaching exhaustive – collection of the Church Fathers, mostly in Latin, sometimes in Greek. Also extensive is the collection of commentaries, medieval, Roman

Catholic and Protestant. Here lists of names may be useful. Besides the treasury given in the Bible with the Glossa Ordinaria, his medieval collection included Hugo Cardinalis, Thomas Aquinas, Theophylact of Bulgaria, Peter Lombard, Ambrosius Anspertus, Ludolph of Saxony, Albertus Magnus, Nicolai Gorrani and Haymo of Halberstadt. Roman Catholic authors included Erasmus, Jerome Oleaster, Thomas Cardinal Cajetan, Luigi Lippomano, Johannes de Turrecremata, Johannes Mercerus, Cornelius Jansen, Lucas Brugensis, Benedictus Arias Montanus (editor of the Antwerp Polyglot), Jacobus Naclantius, and Cornelius Mussus. Protestant authors included Calvin, Beza, Augustin Marlorat, Brucioli, Johannes Oecolampadius, Rodolphe Gualther, Mathias Flacius Illyricus, Martin Bucer, Benedictus Aretius, Nicolaus Hemmingius, Jerome Zanchius, Johannes Drusius, a Scot, Robert Rollock (Rollocus), and three Englishmen, Thomas Cartwright, William Perkins and John Jewel. Perkins on the first five chapters of Galatians and Jewel on the epistles to the Thessalonians were both posthumous works, notable as early works of commentary in English (he also had an English commentary on Obadiah). Each included the text in English, Jewel using Geneva and, interestingly, Perkins giving a lightly revised version of Geneva. In short, Branthwaite possessed the collective wisdom of the centuries about the interpretation of the Bible, something immensely useful for a translator.

Other books were of very particular use for a translator. He owned Robert Estienne's 1555 concordance to the whole Latin Bible and Henri Estienne's of 1594 to the Greek NT (less useful would have been Antonius Broickwy a Konygstein's *Concordantiae Breviores*, which is a brief thematic concordance, but this was a book Branthwaite annotated intensively). For a Greek dictionary he had the greatest not only of the time but for generations to come, Henri Estienne's *Thesaurus Linguae Graecae*, and he also had Johannes Posselius's *Syntaxis Graeca* and John Cheke's work on Greek pronunciation: these are scholars' books, but they are curiously few for a man who had a reputation as a Greek scholar. For Hebrew and Chaldee (as Aramaic was then called), he had a variety of works by Petrus Martinius, Münster, Pagninus, Elias Levita, Johannes Reuchlin, Theodore Bibliander, Antonius Cevallerius, Nicolao Clenardo and Franciscus Stancarus. Unlike the

Greek works, many of these are introductory, and several have annotations that are those of someone (not always Branthwaite) trying to
learn the language. These books suggest he had limited knowledge
of Hebrew and Chaldee.

His collection of theological and controversial works was even more
extensive and adds many names, medieval, Catholic and Protestant,
to those given earlier. Again the abundance of Catholic works is
notable, including works by More, Cardinal Pole and *Disputationes
de controversiis christianae fidei* by Bellarmine, a major work that
dealt systematically with controversies and engendered a great deal
of Protestant refutational effort. For a translator, one of the most
significant works is by Gregory Martin, *A discovery of the manifold
corruptions of the Holy Scriptures by the heretics of our days, specially the
English sectaries, and of their foul dealing herein, by partial and false
translations to the advantage of their heresies, in their English Bibles.*
This, with Fulke's work, made Martin's translation and arguments
about translation a huge presence in the translators' consciousnesses.
Among the Protestants, there are four volumes of Luther, three of
Calvin and two of Beza. There are upwards of thirty volumes in
English, some containing multiple works, but nothing from the early
English Protestants such as Tyndale. Most notable are John Foxe's
Acts and Monuments, and some parts from both sides of the contro-
versy that followed Jewel's championing of the Church of England
against the Church of Rome, *Apologia pro Ecclesia Anglicana* (trans-
lated into English as *Apology or Answer in Defence of the Church of
England*). Cranmer's *Defence of the True and Catholic Doctrine of the
Sacrament of the Body and Blood of our Saviour Christ* is annotated
throughout in the same neat hand seen in Melanchthon's Greek Bible,
usually drawing attention to key words and phrases, and at the end
elaborating a few of the summaries of contents. Future translators
of the KJB are represented by Bilson's *The Perpetual Government of
Christ's Church*, Abbott's *The reasons which Doctor Hill hath brought
for the upholding of papistry, which is falsely termed the Catholic religion:
unmasked and shown to be very weak*, Rainolds's *Sum of the conference
between John Rainolds and John Hart touching the head and the faith
of the Church*, with his *Six conclusions touching the Holy Scripture and
the Church*, and, in Latin, Andrewes's *Tortura Torti*, a response to
Bellarmine.

Branthwaite's mental world was preoccupied with religion but not limited to it. He had a good collection of literature, that is, the Greek and Latin classics. On one shelf, standing side by side, are Apuleius, Aesop (in Greek and Latin), Pindar, selected tragedies of Aeschylus, Sophocles and Euripides, Homer's *Iliad* (also in Greek and Latin),[36] Seneca's tragedies, Plautus and Martial. There are a few books of history, including Josephus, Thucydides, Herodotus and Xenophon, a life of Alfred the Great, and histories of Scotland and England, notably William Camden's *Britannia*. Beyond this there are some travel books and various miscellaneous works such as Machiavelli's *The Prince*.

There is little that is philosophical or scientific, but some of the translators, notably Savile and Samuel Ward, had considerable scientific interests. Nevertheless, Branthwaite's collection gives a very good sense of the predominantly Latin and religious world of books that filled the minds of the translators. Not all the books show obvious signs of use, but if we assume that Branthwaite had read at least a good proportion of them, then he brought substantial knowledge as well as his reputation as a Greek scholar to the work of translation.

Some of the other Cambridge translators and libraries supplement this picture, particularly in relation to Hebrew studies. The inventory of Edward Lively's books includes four Hebrew Bibles, one with the Syriac (or Chaldee) NT, another Syriac NT, the Prophets with Targum, a Latin Targum to the minor prophets and commentaries by David Kimchi and others. He had upwards of thirty-five Hebrew and Chaldee grammars, commentaries and concordances, including Kimchi's *Michlol* (Bois thought Kimchi easily the best of the Jewish grammarians),[37] Pagninus's *Thesaurus Lingue Sanctae* and Hebrew concordance, and Münster's Chaldee and Hebrew dictionaries.[38] A number of the translators came from Emmanuel and would have studied in its library, which at the end of the sixteenth century held

---

[36] Out of place here is a work catalogued as 'Homer and Vergil Centones', an account of biblical history in the form of a catena of verses from Virgil.

[37] 'Grammaticorum apud Hebraeos facile princeps' (diary, fol. 10ʳ).

[38] Leedham-Green, *Books in Cambridge Inventories*, vol. I, pp. 547–8. See also Rosenthal, 'Edward Lively: Cambridge Hebraist', in Winton Thomas (ed.), *Essays and Studies Presented to Stanley Arthur Cook*, pp. 95–112, esp. pp. 99, 104.

eight Hebrew Bibles, including Münster's 1534 Hebrew–Latin OT, and thirteen volumes of lexicography and philology mostly devoted to Hebrew.[39] This collection probably reflects Laurence Chaderton's interests and influence.

Chaderton owned what is perhaps the most interesting Bible connected with the translators, a two-volume third edition of Bomberg's Hebrew Bible (1547–9).[40] The markings and annotations show that he – or one of his contemporaries[41] – read not just the text but also the surrounding material. The annotations and marks cluster in the part that the first Cambridge company worked on, 1 Chronicles to the Song of Solomon, and in some of the prophets (Amos and Habakkuk were worked over intensively, and, more lightly, Isaiah, Hosea, Obadiah, Micah and, though not one of the prophets in the Hebrew Bible, Daniel). In Chronicles, there are underlinings in both Kimchi's and Rashi's commentaries, and occasional corrections in Hebrew. There are also signs of attention to the correctness of the Hebrew text, as at 1 Chronicles 8:8 where the printing of two words as one is underlined. Markings resume in Ecclesiastes, where Ibn Ezra's commentary attracts considerable attention, but not Rashi's. Psalms 22 and 23 have verse numbers inserted in both the text and the Targum, and again Ibn Ezra is closely marked, and then there are a couple of marks in the commentary on Proverbs. As with Branthwaite's work, this gives a tantalising glimpse, possibly of work being done for the KJB. What it does show with certainty is that the translators could and did read this Jewish material.

SCHOLAR AND NOTEMAKER

Had John Bois not been one of the translators he would simply have been one of the many country parsons who were admired by some of their peers but made very small contributions to scholarship. In Bois's case the published contributions were annotations to parts of Savile's

---

[39] Bush and Rasmussen, *Library of Emmanuel College*, p. 18.

[40] Cambridge University Library, S 816 bb 60 5–6.

[41] I am not familiar enough with Chaderton's hand to affirm that he made the notes, but his biographer takes them as his and refers to them as evidence of his Hebrew scholarship (William Dillingham, *Vita Laurentii Chadertoni* [1700], p. 15).

monumental edition of Chrysostom and a posthumous compilation of annotations on the Gospels and Acts, *Veteris interpretis cum Beza aliisque recentioribus collatio* (1655; he had meant to cover the entire NT but left the work incomplete in his papers). Yet he is, in terms of what we know about the making of the KJB, the most important of the translators, for 'he, and he only, took notes of [the translators'] proceedings: which notes he kept till his dying day'.[42] He was a lifelong student, truly a scholar's scholar. By the age of five he had read his Bible through, and his father was teaching him Greek and Hebrew pre-school. He was admitted to St John's College aged fourteen, and given special tuition in the most demanding Greek authors by Downes. Aged twenty, he was elected fellow. He frequently worked from four in the morning till eight at night in the University library. Elected a lecturer (praelector) at the age of twenty-two, he voluntarily supplemented normal teaching with a 4 a.m. Greek lecture 'read in his bed . . . to such young scholars who preferred *antelucana studia* before their own ease and rest'.[43] 'He was a most exact grammarian, having read near sixty grammars, Latin, Greek, Hebrew, Syriac; with some other few', and 'even in his extreme old age, he would study eight hours in the day'.[44] At University he collected so many Greek books that 'he knew of but few Greek authors, great or small, extant, which he had not in his own private library'.[45] He left the University for the parsonage of Boxworth near Cambridge and an arranged marriage. His predecessor had given his daughter the patronage of the living, and requested some friends that, 'if it might be by them procured, Mr Bois of St John's might become his successor by the marriage of his daughter'.[46] The marriage had its rough patches. He left money matters to his wife and unawares found himself in debt. To clear this, he sold at great loss 'his darling', his library. (It is his biographer and step-grandson – or perhaps grandson[47] – Anthony Walker who calls the library 'his darling', perhaps implying that he loved it more than his wife; at least one other translator's wife, Henry Savile's, felt she came second to books, saying to him once, 'I would I were a book too, and then you would a little more respect me'.)[48]

[42] Walker; Allen, *Translating for King James*, p. 141.   [43] Fuller, *Worthies*, vol. III, p. 71.
[44] Walker; Allen, *Translating for King James*, pp. 146, 145.   [45] Ibid., p. 138.
[46] Ibid., p. 137.   [47] *ODNB*, Walker.   [48] Walker; Allen, *Translating for King James*, p. 141.

At this time, Bois was rumoured to have thought of going overseas. Nevertheless, though her temper was not always the best, things mended, and at her death he described her as his 'dearest wife, with whom, in blameless marriage, I have lived five and forty years and more'.[49] In 1615 he became a prebend of Ely and eventually moved there in 1628.

What are of interest here are one of his surviving books and a volume of his diary or notebook which runs from 28 July 1627 to 5 November 1639, giving a picture of his life from the age of sixty-six to seventy-eight. Bois was probably a lifelong diarist. Walker tells of his practice of writing up not only the date and text of a sermon, and the preacher's name, but 'as much of the sermon as he thought fit, or his memory would give him leave'; he refers to a 'pocket-paper-book' which Bois kept in his early years at Boxworth, and he quotes fifteen notebook entries through to 1642.[50] Seven come from the time of the surviving diary but are not found in it, so he must have used more than one notebook at a time. Perhaps this notebook survives because it has a special character. There are places in it where Bois clearly has a reader in mind, and it lacks entries which might have embarrassed his family and friends such as this in the manuscript version of the Life: 'Nov. 5. 1632. Today, I know not what storm stirred up my wife, for she threw the money she had been given on the ground, and so departed in a rage.'[51]

Yet if he did have a feeling that this notebook might have a public character, he could not maintain the distinction between public and private. Three weeks after beginning it with study notes he started putting private notes, which he calls 'Varia', at the back of the notebook. After a while private entries can be found among the study entries at the front, and there are notes on his reading in the back part of the notebook. In practice, he found it difficult to write for anyone but himself, but, with some justification, he maintained a

---

[49] Ibid., p. 144 (translated).
[50] Ibid., pp. 150, 138. Thirteen of the entries are found in the printed version, a further two in an eighteenth-century manuscript copy of the Life, BL MS Harley 7053. Except where noted, all quotations from the diary are translated from Latin.
[51] 'Hodie, nescio quae intemperiae uxorem meam agitarunt, nam pecuniam traditam projecit humi, ac sic irata discesserat'. MS 7053, fol. 42ʳ or p. 104. The right edge is cut off, so 'discesserat' is conjectural; only 'discess' is visible.

belief that these writings would be of interest and value to others. He could never quite be a public writer.

Latin is the diary's principal language, with some Greek and English, and a little Hebrew. The latter, shorter part, the *Varia*, sometimes has a confessional element. Bois's best remedy for lustful thoughts in old age is Luther on Isaiah 36, but he has no qualms about drinking good wine, except that French wine 'rarely does me good, and most often makes me ill'.[52] More commonly, he likes to record anecdotes, and has a special taste for ones that are witty or, by modern standards, sexist. Health, aging and death are frequent subjects, and he frequently brings his learning in, as when he writes, probably while he was reading Martinius's Hebrew Grammar, about his age using the numerical values assigned to Hebrew characters. Throughout his life he made notes on the deaths of prominent men, including Downes (he noted his eminence as a Grecian and composed a Greek epitaph for him), friends, neighbours and family, usually with some recollections of them.[53] He also noted with feeling anniversaries of certain deaths, particularly those of Whitaker and Downes, 'the noblest master of Greek letters at Cambridge'.[54] Once he tells of Downes appearing to him in a dream, saying, incomprehensibly, 'heaten roots'.[55]

The deaths of two of his children a month apart in 1628 particularly affected him and produce some moving entries, including some poems in English. To give more of a sense of the *Varia*, here is one of these poems with the surrounding entries on the page either translated from the Latin or summarised:

1628. Ely. Varia

Sept. 10. The chamber pot which I used last night suffered a strangury, that is, a trickle of urine: for having a small crack in the base, it gave back the urine it had received in drops or a trickle without my knowing it.

Sept. 12. Just as, not without reason, we daily wash our hands: so, not without reason, we daily beseech God to forgive us our sins.

[52] Fols. 138ᵛ, 140ᵛ. For a fuller account of the diary, especially the *Varia*, see Norton, 'John Bois, Bible translator, in old age'.
[53] Walker; Allen, *Translating for King James*, p. 147.
[54] Ibid., p. 141; 2 Feb. 1638. For Whitaker, see diary, fols. 96ᵛ and 109ʳ.
[55] Fol. 162ᵛ; 24 May 1630.

Nov. 11. Mirabel and Robert, recently dead, spoke thus, in English, to their grieving father, John Bois, still living on the earth:

$$\left\{ \begin{array}{l} \text{Give ear to us} \\ \text{O Father dear} \\ \text{out of thy breast} \\ \text{cast needless fear} \end{array} \right\} \left\{ \begin{array}{l} \text{All troublous thoughts} \\ \text{away remove} \\ \text{For we are both} \\ \text{in heaven above,} \end{array} \right\}$$

$$\left\{ \begin{array}{l} \text{And there we both} \\ \text{enjoy a place,} \\ \text{with Abraham} \\ \text{and all his race,} \end{array} \right\} \left\{ \begin{array}{l} \text{Of this be sure,} \\ \text{we can not lie,} \\ \text{and thou thy self} \\ \text{ere long shalt die.} \end{array} \right\}$$

Nov. 19. [Fictional narrative set in Utopia. A widower, urged to remarry, asks for a mirror and says it tells him to think rather of the coffin than of a second wife.][56]

The opening entry gives a sense of his medical knowledge and wit, the second his liking for wisdom and balanced phrases, while the final entry, which appears to be his invention, shows, rather lugubriously, his taste for striking responses. In the middle of these, the poem is a moving song of innocence, mixing his anguish with his faith and his expectation of – sometimes, his longing for – death. Complexity is added by the possibilities of reading across the lines. Though one might not think it from his attempt elsewhere to translate one of Martial's epigrams into English verse,[57] Bois could write effective English verse.

On 29 October 1629, Bois wrote, 'never do I use my genius better than when I devote myself to the study of letters. Indeed, I can do a little in letters: outside letters I am nothing: outside letters what am I but the lowest of all animals? Go where the genius [spirit, talent, intellect] summons you'.[58] The diary is full of evidence of this 'genius' and how he followed it. He had an insatiable curiosity about words, and they might lead him anywhere. In Mercer's Grammar, a rabbinic dialectic term meaning 'on the contrary' catches his eye; he notes it in Hebrew characters but omits the final letter, giving ADRAB, and adds in brackets a note that shows his mind working: 'hence I deduce the English word *drab*, or, *a drab*, i.e., adulteress, harlot, because such

---

[56] Fol. 169[r].   [57] Fol. 143[r].

[58] 'Nunquam magis propitio utor genio meo, quam cum literarum studiis totus incumbo. In literis quidem parum possum: extra literas tamen nihil sum: extra literas quid nisi animal sum omnium vilissimum? vade quo te invitat genius' (fol. 165[r]).

a woman is contrary to her husband, if she has a husband, or if she has not, she is contrary to good laws'.[59] It matters not whether he was serious about the etymology: an obscure word only a scholar would find has led him irresistibly to moral reflection.

On a large scale, the diary shows where his 'genius' for letters and his perpetual quest for religious insight led him. No doubt picking up from a previous diary, it begins with fourteen months reading, in his words, the 'incomparable man', St Augustine.[60] In ten months he read letters 96–239, the *Retractions* took another month, and *On Christian Doctrine* the final three. Representative of the kind of notes he took is this concerning a short letter, now numbered 100; he places a large asterisk at the beginning, suggesting that he thought it of special value:

This letter gives special testimony as much to Augustine's moderation as to his good sense. He wishes heretics to be converted, not killed. 'So check their sins,' says Augustine to Donatus, proconsul of Africa, 'that some may repent of having sinned: to forget that you have the power to kill, but not to forget our wish (that is, that they should not be killed). Do not think it a base thing that we ask you that they should not be killed, for whom we pray God that they should be converted,' etc. And a little before: 'We desire them to be converted not killed; we neither wish their punishment to be neglected, nor the full punishments which they deserve to be applied. (Perhaps, to be inflicted.)'

☞ However great the evil to be abandoned and the good to be held, the effort is more burdensome than effective if men are merely forced rather than persuaded by teaching.[61]

Bois has highlighted what is to be admired in the letter, and backed this up with well-chosen quotations: history – whether of fifth-century Christianity or the Reformation, Bois may have thought (and we might think of the present day) – would have been a different and better thing if Augustine's moderate and sage counsel had been followed. Yet this is a note that highlights Bois's limitations: he gives nothing new. It is essentially the kind of note a student makes for himself: the extended time and daily labour, Christmas

---

[59] Fol. 141ᵛ.
[60] Fol. 5ʳ. Elsewhere he begins an entry, 'Augustine (but what a man! what a Bishop!)' ('at quantus vir! quantus Episcopus!'; fol. 71ʳ).
[61] Fol. 43ʳ.

day included, that he devoted to Augustine do indeed show habitual, tenacious but essentially sterile study.

There was one interruption. On 24 August 1627 began something like a holiday. Heading the page, 'of private things', he begins: 'today I did what perhaps a diligent and provident family man should not have done'. He went to Ely for a few days' relaxation with his close friend Daniel Wigmore, archdeacon of Ely.[62] They made a three-day visit to Snailwell, a village just north of Newmarket where Wigmore was vicar; Bois describes the setting and view, observing how well the place suits fish, ducklings and songbirds. Wigmore preached on Ephesians 4:30; Bois gives the text in Greek. In the afternoon, at Wigmore's suggestion, Bois preached on Proverbs 18:10; this time he gives the text in Hebrew with his own Latin translation. Bois's habitual recourse to and facility with the original languages is clear. There is no note here of what he said, but the first page of the Varia gives an account of Wigmore's sermon. They dined that night with a local knight. Then came a day riding and enjoying the delights around Snailwell. Back in Ely for a week, he turned his mind to study, writing scholarly notes while browsing in Marcus Brixianus's *De arca Noe* and *Praefatio thesauri linguae sanctae*. The day after his return to Boxworth, he noted the anniversary of his father-in-law and predecessor's burial and wondered how long he had been vicar of Boxworth. He returned to Augustine's letters on 5 September.

On 2 October 1628, Bois marked in Greek the end of his reading of *On Christian Doctrine*, then added two passages from William Whitaker's *Disputatio de Sacra Scriptura* (1588), giving his very short summary of *On Christian Doctrine* and arguing for the necessity of prayer if one is to understand the Bible.[63] Such references to other parts of his reading are quite common, and give further evidence of his scholarship and care in making his notes. On the following page there is a surprise. He wrote the date in his usual way at the top. Then, underneath '1628' there is a line and '1634', and an entry that begins, 'here the pen slept a full five years and more than that. August 6, 1634, I have begun to read Samuel Petit's *Miscellanea*, and I thought

---

[62] 'Hodie id feci quod diligens fortassè et providus paterfamiliâs non fecisset. In ipso enim initio triticeæ messis, propriis relictis ædibus, Eliam me contuli, ut dies ibi aliquot cum Domino Archidiacono hilaris consumerem' (fol. 9ʳ).

[63] Fol. 109ʳ. The passages from Whitaker are from pp. 368–9, 349.

it would not be off the point while reading if I put down here for the sake of memory things as they occur'.[64] One can understand the need for a rest, yet it is clear Bois did not intend to rest. There are signs of depression throughout the diary, especially of a feeling of lack of achievement. He may have realised that his notes on Augustine would never be publishable, and so stopped attempting such notes. These new notes are explicitly 'for the sake of memory', that is, his own memory.

Yet the habit of study never died. It is possible to fill in – if not all, then much of – the gap. He still made notes among the Varia on some of his reading, most extensively on the Jesuit José de Acosta's *De natura novi orbis* and *De promulgatione Evangelii apud Barbaros, sive de procuranda Indorum salute*, famous early books about Peru and religion, and the letters of Joseph Scaliger. He spent three years editing for publication a Greek manuscript; this was nearly finished when his collaborator died in his study in 1634.[65] He is said to have worked on the Cambridge Bible of 1638.[66] And, over the better part of a year, he studied perhaps the most extraordinary of the 'near sixty grammars, Latin, Greek, Hebrew, Syriac; with some other few', that he had read,[67] the French scholar Budaeus's (Guillaume Budé) 967-page *Commentarii Linguae Graecae* (1529). At the bottom of the final page on 13 May 1634, he recorded (as usual, in Latin) his exhausted yet admiring judgement, concluding:

When I first began to read these commentaries, and had hardly tasted one or two pages, I was very happy with myself, believing that no more work remained for me but to run my eyes over each page. But when I had gone a little further in, I felt myself as if in an enormous sea, unable to reach land without great, indeed mighty work. So now at last I rejoice at having come to the end of this book, and how I came here and with what difficulty, the

---

[64] 'Hic quievit calamus per integrum quinquennium, aut eo amplius. Augusti 8, 1634, cœpi legere Samuelis Petiti Miscellanea, et inter legendum non abs re fore putavi, si quaedam, ut occurrebant, memoriæ causâ hîc reponerem' (fol. 109ᵛ). Samuel Petit (Petitus) was a French Protestant whose *Miscellaneorum* was published in 1630.

[65] Walker; Allen, *Translating for King James*, pp. 145–6.

[66] Kilburne, *Dangerous Errors*, p. 6. An almost identical manuscript note in the Jesus College copy of this edition (quoted by Scrivener, *Authorized Edition*, p. 22) is either dependent on Kilburne or his source. Corroboratory evidence is lacking for Bois's work on this Bible or for that of the other scholars named. John Worthington's life of Joseph Mede prefaced to the fourth edition of Mede's *Works* (1677) does not mention work on the 1638 Bible.

[67] Walker; Allen, *Translating for King James*, p. 146.

notes added throughout the margin of this book testify. If a new edition of
this book should be prepared, either I am wrong or consulting my notes
will help it along.

Believing in the value of his notes (and the worth of the book), he
left it to St John's College, where it remains yet another labour that
had no hope, unless others took it up, of reaching publication.[68]

The annotations are an immense contrast with those in Branthwaite's books. Only a few pages have even a single line that is
unmarked by his pen. He underlined to such an extent that the
underlining is redundant, for attention is drawn to everything: the
underlining becomes like the tracing of his eye moving along the text.
The annotations include quotation marks in the margins against all
the citations, a variety of attention marks, names of authors quoted
written in the margin against the quotations, corrections of errors,
including in the index and errata, headings added, cross-references,
additional material (usually references to other writers with page
references included), discussion of readings and of points raised,
and translations and similar idioms in Latin, English, and occasionally other languages. Because they show his sensitivity to English,
some of the most interesting are those which deal with vocabulary and idioms. Under a discussion of sweating and sweatbaths,
Bois summarises Budaeus's move from Greek to Latin, and adds
English:

Θόλος ξηρὸς, i.e. Laconicum, sudatorium, vaporarium, hypocaustum, *a
stove, a sweatbath or sweating bath, or dry bath to sweat in*. (p. 353)

Where Budaeus notes the vernacular phrase, 'they could have it in
their mind or heart, and, as the Italians say, it was enough for the
mind', Bois writes, 'in English, *could find in their heart*' (p. 758).
Budaeus translates ἀνθρακίας into Latin as 'black as a charcoal-
burner, having a face like a firelighter', and Bois glosses, 'as black as a
collier', probably using 'collier' to mean charcoal-burner. Elsewhere
Bois notes an idiom comparable to one used by Demosthenes, '*give
a thing and take a thing. He is the Devil's darling*' (p. 800). Such notes
show a sensitivity to – and interest in – English idiom that is also
occasionally visible in the diary.

[68] St John's College Library, Cambridge, G.7.7.

One annotation is of special interest in relation to the notes he made about the making of the KJB. At the top of p. 872, Bois writes large and clear, Συμβιβάζω, one of several verbs discussed on the page. In all likelihood, this is because the translators discussed its meaning as it is used in Colossians 2:2, which reads in the KJB: 'that their hearts might be comforted, being knit together in love, and unto all riches of the full assurance of understanding'. This is Bois's record of the discussion; the translators are considering whether to add to the Bishops' Bible text the words, 'and instructed' (the italicised words are in English, the rest in Latin):

being knit together in love] [and instructed] in all riches &c. The word συμβιβάζω signifies both at once, join together, and instruct, or teach: it is not inconsistent with the truth therefore, that the Apostle took account of both meanings.[69]

The key question was whether there was a deliberate play on the meaning of συμβιβάζω. Bois remembered this discussion when, in 1634, nearly a quarter of a century later, he saw in Budaeus a similar discussion of its meaning:

The word συμβιβάζειν signifies to reconcile, and to draw together in friendship and agreement . . . It also signifies to accommodate, and to bring together in harmony . . . From a collation of the sacred prophets, it seems to mean to teach and to prove.

Now in his seventies, his interest in languages and his memory for details were as sharp as ever.

The Life, the diary and the annotations together give a sharp picture of Bois's character and scholarship. An obscure, diligent, immensely knowledgeable scholar of languages and lover of theology, he was an ideal man to help examine the extant English Bibles against the original Greek and Hebrew, though his occasionally evident interest in English idioms and his few pieces of English poetry are not enough to make him seem a good person to give style to the English Bible, if that is what one thinks was the task and achievement of the KJB translators. Was he also an ideal man to make notes on the work of the translators? The question is necessary because, the more one reads his diary, the more it seems that his notes, discussed

---

[69] Allen, *Translating for King James*, p. 63.

in the next chapter, are exactly in character with it. The only picture we have of the discussions that helped create the KJB is seen through his eyes and reflects his interests. Linguistic matters, especially in relation to the Greek, were his prime study, religious insight his prime concern, and it is important to keep in mind the mixture of public and private observed in the diary: the notes may be more private than at first appears. This must make us wary. Much that went on in making an English translation was grist to these mills – much, but not all: he was not interested in making a record of decisions about particular words in the KJB. It must also make us still more confident that the notes are absolutely authentic Bois. His diary notes on his reading show him far more concerned to report what he has read than to develop his own thoughts about it. If anyone was going to report impartially – though probably not fully – what the translators discussed, it was Bois.

CHAPTER 4

Working on the King James Bible

SETTING UP

By 1604, the idea that a new translation was needed had been around for some time, though perhaps only held strongly by Hugh Broughton. The Bishops' Bible had not succeeded in ousting Geneva as the popular favourite, so England was in the uncomfortable position of using two different Bibles, one the official Bible of the Church, the other generally used by the people and many of the clergy, including the man principally reponsible for the demise of Geneva, the future Archbishop William Laud. Variety of translation had been defended and even extolled by the English translators from Coverdale onwards, but it was a touchy point, especially in controversy with Roman Catholics. It seemed that England did not have the pure truth of the Bible, and there was an uncomfortable awareness of errors in both versions, especially in the Bishops' Bible.

Broughton agitated long and hard for a new version. To him any Bible that had inconsistencies in chronology 'will as it were rend the Bible in pieces, whereby it should become of no estimation'. By contrast, 'a Bible fair printed, standing in the original, or translated with pure dexterity, is the glory of all books': it would settle 'all the stories in order, that no one jar, and all appear chained [linked] with manifold golden chains of times'.[1] He had some success in winning support from Archbishop John Whitgift, and this may be behind a draft Act of Parliament, probably from late in Elizabeth's reign, 'for reducing of diversities of Bibles now extant in the English tongue to one settled vulgar translated from the original'. It echoes Broughton's

---

[1] Broughton, To the Queen, c. 1591, *Works*, ed. John Lightfoot (1662), p. 163.

address to the Queen in being 'for avoiding of the multiplicity of errors that are rashly conceived by the inferior and vulgar sort by the variety of the translations of Bible [*sic*] to the most dangerous increase of papistry and atheism'. It refers to a long-standing desire 'from the high to the low of all sorts' for a translation 'in such sort that such as study it should in no place be snared', and, anticipating the way the KJB was made, it envisages compulsory assistance from scholars of the two Universities. It includes an argument that may have been in King James's mind when he set work afoot on the KJB: it 'will tend to her Majesty's immortal fame'.[2]

James I was still in his first year as king of England when he called the Hampton Court conference of January 1604 to deal with religious friction in his new kingdom. As James VI of Scotland, he had already had dealings with the Bible. Ironically, given his later opinion of Geneva, his approval was invoked on the title page of the first Geneva Bible printed in Scotland, Bassandyne and Arbuthnot's folio of 1579 – but James was only thirteen when this appeared and presumably had no real say in this. His arms are on the title page and, as the dedication reminds him, he had in the past 'ordained that this holy book of God should be set forth and imprinted of new within your own realm'. It goes on to seek his authorisation, assuring him that that this,

no doubt, shall be an exceeding great honour and perpetual renown that shall follow your highness. All other glory shall at last decay, and all commendation that results of other princely acts either is not of long endurance or has commonly mixed therewith such things as be always worthy of blame, but the honour of this act shall endure for ever.[3]

More significantly, James had favoured a new translation in a 1602 meeting of the general assembly of the Scottish Church:

a proposition was made for a new translation of the Bible, and the correcting of the Psalms in metre: his Majesty did urge it earnestly, and with many reasons did persuade the undertaking of the work, showing the necessity and the profit of it, and what a glory the performing thereof should bring to

---

[2] Pollard, *Records of the English Bible*, p. 329.
[3] Original in Scottish spelling. Both this and the next Bible printed in Scotland, Hart's Geneva of 1610, claim royal privilege on the title page, but in Arbuthnot's case this clearly refers to his position as King's Printer.

this Church: speaking of the necessity, he did mention sundry escapes in the common translation, and made it seen that he was no less conversant in the Scriptures than they whose profession it was; and when he came to speak of the Psalms, did recite whole verses of the same, showing both the faults of the metre and the discrepancy from the text. It was the joy of all that were present to hear it, and bred not little admiration in the whole Assembly, who approving the motion did recommend the translation to such of the brethren as were most skilled in the languages, and revising of the Psalms particularly to Mr Robert Pont; but nothing was done in the one or the other.

Yet one thing was done: 'the revising of the Psalms [James] made his own labour, and at such hours as he might spare from the public cares, went through a number of them, commending the rest to a faithful and learned servant'.[4] These were published in 1631, with an authorisation to be printed by Charles I, the only use of 'authorise' on the title page of a biblical version in this century.

On the second day of the Hampton Court conference, Monday 16 January, the leading spokesman for the puritans, John Rainolds (hitherto an antagonist of Broughton's, soon to be a translator), apparently without warning, 'moved his Majesty that there might be a new translation of the Bible, because those which were allowed in the reigns of Henry the eighth and Edward the sixth were corrupt and not answerable to the truth of the original'.[5] He gave three examples. In Galations 4:25, συστοιχεῖ 'is not well translated, as now it is, *bordreth*, neither expressing the force of the word, nor the Apostle's sense, nor the situation of the place'. Psalm 105:28 should read 'they were not disobedient', rather than 'they were not obedient', and Psalm 106:30 is wrong to read 'then stood up Phinees and prayed' because the Hebrew is 'executed judgement'. As reported, this is a very odd request.[6] This was not one of the topics that Rainolds had said he would raise, and, on the surface, the argument is bad because

---

[4] Spottiswoode (Spotswood), *History of the Church of Scotland*, p. 465.

[5] Barlow, *Sum and Substance*, p. 45.

[6] Barlow's report was written at Bancroft's request, read by the King before publication and scorned by those who were not of the Church party (Babbage, *Puritanism and Richard Bancroft*, p. 70). Chaderton, who was present at the conference, noted some vehement disagreements with Barlow's designation of himself, Rainolds and two other puritans as 'agents for the millenary plaintiffs' (p. 2) in his copy of *The Sum and Substance* (Wren Library, Trinity College, Cambridge), but his silence on the discussion of a new translation suggests that there is nothing significantly wrong with it.

he has cited nothing later than the Great Bible (where these readings are found), and there were of course two more recent versions.[7] Looked at more closely, the argument is subtle: he has not attacked the Bishops' Bible, nor therefore the Church establishment, but these three readings remain in the 1602 Bishops' Bible and are corrected in the Geneva Bible. Any investigation would show the inadequacy of the former and the correctness of the latter. Rainolds probably hoped that his suggestion for a new translation would be dismissed and the much simpler solution be followed, adoption of Geneva as the official Bible of the Church.

If this was his subtle intention, he was quickly disappointed. Though Barlow notes that there was 'no gainsaying' or denying this motion, Bancroft, by now the leading establishment figure, was at best lukewarm: 'if every man's humour should be followed, there would be no end of translating'. But James was on familiar territory, and knew his own mind:

Whereupon his Highness wished that some especial pains should be taken in that behalf for one uniform translation (professing that he could never yet see a Bible well translated in English, but the worst of all his Majesty thought the Geneva to be), and this to be done by the best learned in both the Universities, after them to be reviewed by the Bishops and the chief learned of the Church, from them to be presented to the Privy Council, and lastly to be ratified by his royal authority; and so this whole Church to be bound unto it, and none other. Marry, withal, he gave this caveat (upon a word cast out by my Lord of London [Bancroft]), that no marginal notes should be added, having found in them which are annexed to the Geneva translation (which he saw in a Bible given him by an English Lady) some notes very partial, untrue, seditious and savouring too much of dangerous and traitorous conceits: as, for example, Exod. 1:19, where the marginal note alloweth disobedience to Kings. And 2 Chron. 15:16, the note taxeth Asa for deposing his mother only, and not killing her.[8]

---

[7] These texts may have been standard examples. Though the KJB had also corrected them, the two verses from Psalms were mentioned again in 1640 as examples of perversions 'of the meaning of the Holy Ghost . . . by putting in and leaving out of words' (Hughes, *Certain Grievances*, p. 18).

[8] Pp. 46–7. The two notes read, 'their disobedience herein was lawful, but their dissembling evil'; 'herein he showed that he lacked zeal: for she ought to have died both by the covenant and by the law of God; but he gave place to foolish pity, and would also seem after a sort to satisfy the law'. Rainolds might have cited other, stronger examples such as the outline of Saul's career in the argument to 1 Samuel or the note to 1 Kings 20:8 where the elders think

He may have detected the desire to promote Geneva (a natural presumption about a puritan), and his opposition to its annotations was probably wise in that they did not represent the views of the whole Church. His particular objection to notes allowing disobedience to kings we may set down as not just politic but prescient in view of his son's fate. And he may further have thought that agreeing to the proposal would show him sympathetic to the puritans while allowing him to strike a blow at the mainstay of their beliefs. He may also have thought that it would keep the leaders of all parts of the Church busy and working together. Or did he think it would be a monument to his reign? We simply do not know. All we do know is that, in the words of the dedication to Bassandyne and Arbuthnot's Bible, 'an exceeding great honour and perpetual renown' did follow his actions here, and that 'the honour of this act' has endured for 400 years.

The work was not quite set up as James had envisaged it, but the general idea of involving the foremost scholars from the Universities and having a series of review stages was followed. The first steps were to choose the translators and to draw up rules for the work – and to try to find money for the work since James did not provide any. Bancroft, on James's behalf, did most of this, but with little or no success on the financial side. Fifty-four translators had been appointed and approved by James by the end of June 1604,[9] but changes were still happening

---

it their duty to risk their lives rather than allow an unlawful act 'only to satisfy the lust of a tyrant'. This aspect of Geneva leads directly to Benjamin Franklin and Thomas Jefferson's proposed motto for the seal of the United States, 'Rebellion to Tyrants is Obedience to God'.

Anthony Johnson gives two more objections to Genevan notes which appear to be his own but may have been James's; I quote in full since they are rarely reproduced:

To these exceptions may be added two more: the first is their comment on the twelfth verse of the second of St Matthew; here they tell us that 'promise ought not to be kept where God's honour and the preaching of his truth is hindered; or else it ought not to be broken'. What loose casuistry is this? What a desperate expedient is this to justify the breach of promises and oaths; of contracts between man and man? What insurrections and confusions have been raised upon this pretence? The other extraordinary comment is on Rev. 9:3, where the locusts that come out of the smoke are said to be 'false teachers, heretics, and worldly subtle prelates, with monks, friars, cardinals, patriarchs, archbishops, bishops, doctors, bachelors and masters'; a strong composition of ignorance and ill will. What broad innuendos are here upon the English clergy, and all those distinguished with degrees in the universities? These, it seems, according to the skill and charity of the Genevan annotators, are part of the locusts that came smoking out of the bottomless pit.

This produced a resolution in his majesty for a new translation... (*Historical Account*, pp. 86–7)

[9] Bancroft, 30 June, 31 July 1604; Pollard, *Records of the English Bible*, pp. 48, 331.

later in the year that probably account for fewer than fifty-four being named. Thomas James, Bodley's librarian, for instance, was one of the chosen, but Bodley, against James's wishes, interfered in late October: he lobbied Rainolds and was prepared to go to Bancroft if need be. Ultimately he kept James's services for himself. We may guess that the choosing was done by Bancroft through consultation with Lively for Cambridge, Harding for Oxford and Andrewes for Westminster, and that other senior figures such as Rainolds were influential.

Fourteen rules were given to the translators, with a fifteenth added later, and a number of supplementary rules were reported to the Synod of Dort in 1618, presumably by Samuel Ward. Two relate to the English text to be followed and the limitation within which the translators were to work:

1. The ordinary Bible read in the Church, commonly called the Bishops' Bible, to be followed, and as little altered as the truth of the original will permit.

14. These translations to be used where they agree better with the text than the Bishops' Bible, *viz.*: Tyndale's, Matthew's, Coverdale's, Whitchurch's, Geneva.[10]

It was to be a revision of its official predecessor, and the work was to be minimalist, the only criterion for change being 'the truth of the original'. In the words of the Synod of Dort, it was to be 'accuratissime versionis', a most accurate translation.[11] There is no suggestion that the translators should revise for style. Two significant features of rule 14 are the idea that the translators should pick and choose between readings in their predecessors from Tyndale through Coverdale, the Great Bible (Edward Whitchurch, with Richard Grafton, was the printer of the first Great Bible) to Geneva, and the omission of Rheims: implicitly it is forbidden, but not actually. There is one major omission from the rules here: no mention is made of texts to translate from. The issue of textual scholarship is absent. The preface's reply to the question of texts is simplistic: 'if you ask what

---

[10] Three manuscripts in the British Library give the instructions. They vary in details of phrasing and spelling. I have modernised MS Add. 28721, fol. 24ʳ. This and MS Harley 750 omit rule 15 (this suggests they are the older manuscripts, for rule 15 was a late addition); for this rule I follow MS Egerton 2884, fol. 6ʳ. The version of the instructions given in Pollard is commonly followed, but does not correspond exactly with these manuscripts.

[11] Pollard, *Records of the English Bible*, p. 336.

they had before them, truly it was the Hebrew text of the Old Testament, the Greek of the New. These are the two golden pipes, or rather conduits, wherethrough the olive branches empty themselves into the gold'.[12] The report to the Synod of Dort notes that the translators followed the Greek text of Tobit and Judith where there was 'any great discrepancy' between it and the Vulgate. The preface adds a note on secondary sources: 'neither did we think much to consult the translators or commentators, Chaldee, Hebrew, Syrian, Greek, or Latin, no, nor the Spanish, French, Italian, or Dutch'.[13]

Three rules deal with matters of translation practice:

2. The names of the prophets, and the holy writers, with the other names in the text, to be retained, as near as may be, accordingly as they are vulgarly used.

3. The old ecclesiastical words to be kept, *viz.*: as the word 'Church' not to be translated 'Congregation' etc.

4. When a word hath diverse significations, that to be kept which hath been most commonly used by the most of the Ancient Fathers, being agreeable to the propriety of the place, and the Analogy of Faith.

The first of these, to use the commonly known form of names and, implicitly, to use them consistently, was poorly adhered to. The translators paid more attention to the forms used in the originals and did not establish uniformity either of sound or spelling. Isaiah, for instance, is also Esai (2 Kings 19:2), Esaias (NT) and Esay (Apocrypha); Holofernes is Olofernes in Judith 2, and Apollo in the NT is sometimes, following the Greek spelling, Apollos (Acts 18:24, 1 Cor. 16:12 and Titus 3:13). Only some of this variety comes from differences between Hebrew and Greek spelling. The concern to keep 'old ecclesiastical words' is anti-puritan. It harks back to More's attacks on the tendentiousness of some of Tyndale's vocabulary. Here 'congregation' instead of 'church', or, say, 'elder' instead of 'priest', would have had strong anti-establishment implications. Rule 4 underlines the desire to preserve traditional understanding. These things are in keeping with James's respect for the established: 'rather a Church with some faults than an innovation', he had declared at Hampton Court.[14]

---

[12] *NCPB*, p. xxxii.   [13] *NCPB*, p. xxxii.   [14] Barlow, *Sum and Substance*, p. 47.

Next come some more general matters, of which the restriction on marginal notes is by far the most important, for it places attention almost exclusively on the text itself:

5. The division of the chapters to be altered either not at all, or as little as may be, if necessity so require.

6. No marginal notes at all to be affixed, but only for the explanation of the Hebrew or Greek words, which cannot without some circumlocution so briefly and fitly be expressed in the text.

7. Such quotations of places to be marginally set down as shall serve for fit reference of one Scripture to another.

The report to the Synod of Dort summarises rules 6 and 7, then elaborates on the use of the margin:

Secondly, no notes were to be placed in the margin, but only parallel passages to be noted.

Thirdly, where a Hebrew or Greek word admits two meanings of a suitable kind, the one was to be expressed in the text, the other in the margin. The same to be done where a different reading was found in good copies.

Fourthly, the more difficult Hebraisms and Graecisms were consigned to the margin.[15]

The remainder of the original rules deal mostly with organisation. An elaborate system for avoiding individualism, errors or partisan translation is set out. All in a company were to draft a translation, then debate it among themselves; then there was to be what would now be called peer review, circulating the draft to all the other companies before final review at a general meeting. Extending the desire to get collective wisdom, there is a particular care to draw on the wisdom of the whole country (though there is no record of scholars outside the committees contributing 'particular observations'):

8. Every particular man of each company to take the same chapter or chapters, and having translated or amended them severally by himself where he think good, all to meet together, confer what they have done, and agree for their part what shall stand.

---

[15] Pollard, *Records of the English Bible*, p. 339.

9. As one company hath dispatched any one book in this manner, they shall send it to the rest to be considered of seriously and judiciously, for His Majesty is very careful for this point.

10. If any company, upon the review of the book so sent, shall doubt or differ upon any place, to send them word thereof, note the place and withal send their reasons, to which if they consent not, the difference to be compounded at the general meeting, which is to be of the chief persons of each company, at the end of the work.

11. When any place of especial obscurity is doubted of, letters to be directed by authority to send to any learned man in the land for his judgement of such a place.

12. Letters to be sent from every Bishop to the rest of his clergy, admonishing them of this translation in hand, and to move and charge as many as being skilful in the tongues have taken pains in that kind, to send his particular observations to the company, either at Westminster, Cambridge or Oxford.

13. The directors in each company to be the Deans of Westminster and Chester for that place, and the King's Professors in the Hebrew and Greek in each University.

15. Besides the said directors before mentioned, three or four of the most ancient and grave divines, in either of the universities not employed in the translating, to be assigned by the Vice-Chancellors, upon conference with the rest of the heads, to be overseers of the translations as well Hebrew as Greek, for the better observation of the 4th rule above specified.

This final rule was added following uncertainty about rules 3 and 4. Bancroft wrote to the Vice-Chancellor of Cambridge to explain:

To be sure, if he had not signified unto them already, it was his Majesty's pleasure that, besides the learned persons employed with them for the Hebrew and Greek, there should be three or four of the most eminent and grave divines of their university, assigned by the Vice-Chancellor upon conference with the rest of the heads, to be overseers of the translations, as well Hebrew as Greek, for the better observation of the rules appointed by his Highness, and especially concerning the third and fourth rule: and that when they had agreed upon the persons for that purpose, he prayed them send him word thereof.[16]

---

[16] As given in Mombert, *English Versions of the Bible*, p. 348.

The only evidence that this rule was followed is Thomas Bilson's reference to Ryves as 'one of the overseers of that part of the New Testament that is being translated out of Greek'.[17]

The report to the Synod of Dort adds three other rules, that words with no exact equivalent in the original were to be marked by the use of small roman type, that new arguments or summaries to each book and chapter summaries were to be supplied, and that a genealogy and a map of the Holy Land were to be included.

CHRONOLOGY

The first stage, the work of the individual companies, took between three and four, perhaps even five years. By the end of June 1604, James, 'very anxious that the same so religious a work should admit of no delay', commanded that the translators 'should with all possible speed meet together... and begin the same'.[18] By August the translators were 'at it hard in Cambridge',[19] so hard that 'too earnest study and pains about the translation'[20] were reckoned to have hastened Lively's death in May 1605. Work at Westminster also started early, though perhaps less diligently. In November 1604 Andrewes noted a particular afternoon as 'our translation time', but added that 'most of our company are negligent' (a statement that shows this company worked collectively rather than individually as the Apocrypha company did).[21] Work at Oxford seems to have started more slowly: the NT group may have begun as late as February 1605.[22] The companies completed their work in 1607 or 1608. The Oxford OT company, Wood implies, were done by the time Rainolds died, 21 May 1607.[23] Be this as it may, by late 1608 the King had grown impatient, and William Eyre, apparently by now one of the Cambridge translators,

---

[17] Bilson to Thomas Lake, 19 April 1605; as given in Paine, *Men Behind the King James Version*, p. 72.
[18] Pollard, *Records of the English Bible*, p. 48.
[19] Bodley to James, 4 Sept. 1604; Wheeler (ed.), *Letters of Thomas Bodley to Thomas James*, p. 108.
[20] Paine, *Men Behind the King James Version*, p. 74.
[21] Andrewes, *Two Answers to Cardinal Perron, and Other Miscellaneous Works* (Oxford, 1854), vol. XI, xlii; as given in Allen, *Epistles*, p. xii.
[22] Nicolson, *Power and Glory*, p. 154, following Merton College Register for 13 Feb. 1604 (i.e. 1605).
[23] Wood, *History and Antiquities*, vol. II, p. 283.

wrote with some urgency on 5 December to James Ussher, future Archbishop of Armagh, to retrieve a manuscript of their work:

In my absence from Cambridge there was order taken from the King's Majesty by the Archbishop of Canterbury [Bancroft] that the translation of the Bible shall be finished and printed so soon as may be. Two of every company are chosen to revise and confer the whole at London. Hereupon I am earnestly requested to get again that copy of our part which I lent you for Dr Daniel's use; for albeit there be two fair written copies out of it, yet there will be use of it because I noted in the margin . . . the places which were doubted of.[24]

This suggests that the work had been finished for a while but that the King's order caught the translators by surprise.[25]

Now, there should have been two successive outcomes from the companies' work, one interim, one final. First there should have been, if rule 9 was followed punctiliously, drafts of individual books circulated as they were completed to other companies for comment. It is clear there was an intention to follow rule 9 – in spirit if not to the letter: MS 98, discussed below, appears to be a manuscript of this sort, but is not a manuscript of individual books. Then there should have been a completed draft for the general meeting accompanied by (or containing) notes on contentious points as specified in rule 10. All this should have been part of the companies' work, completed in 1607 or 1608.[26] Eyre's letter describes a draft of the latter sort and refers to two fair copies of it which do not identify the doubtful places. These copies must, one assumes, have been manuscript versions of the revision, either made as insurance against loss of the original or so that the general meeting could have several copies to look at, or

[24] Bodleian MS Rawlinson, C. 849, fols. 262ᵛ 3ʳ (as given in Allen, *Epistles*, p. xvi). William Daniel had earlier translated the NT into Irish, and he completed his translation of the Prayer Book at this time; it seems likely that he had been lent the manuscript as an aid to his work (see my *Textual History*, p. 14).

[25] The KJB's Epistle Dedicatory implies more extensive and exhortatory involvement from James: he 'did never desist to urge and to excite those to whom it was commended, that the work might be hastened, and that the business might be expedited in so decent a manner, as a matter of such importance might justly require'.

[26] The uncertainty here is twofold. First, it is uncertain that the consultation process on the interim drafts was completed – possibly it was cut short by James's intervention in late 1608. Second, Allen, presuming that the consultation did take place, suggests that the committees 'revised their texts in light of comments from those who had read the manuscripts and prepared a final text during the year 1609' (*Epistles*, p. xxvii; see also Allen and Jacobs, *Coming of the King James Gospels*, pp. 4–5).

because there were some difficulties in using the primary manuscript. I raise this last possibility because neither of the surviving pieces of work from the translation committees is easy to use: one is in the form of a printed text of the Bishops' Bible with changes written in, the other is MS 98, which gives roughly half of the text, but leaves room for the missing verses to be written in.

The next stage was the general meeting. Delegates had been appointed, as Eyre's letter shows, by the end of 1608, but when it began remains a matter of doubt. Walker's life of Bois gives this account:

> Four years were spent in this first service [the company work]; at the end whereof the whole work being finished, and three copies of the whole Bible sent from Cambridge, Oxford and Westminster to London; a new choice was to be made of six in all, two out of every company, to review the whole work; and extract one [copy] out of all three, to be committed to the press.
> For the despatch of which business Mr Downes and Mr Bois were sent for up to London. Where meeting (though Mr Downes would not go till he was either fetched or threatened with a pursuivant) their four fellow-labourers, they went daily to Stationers Hall, and in three quarters of a year finished their task.[27]

Walker is probably wrong to specify six delegates, but there is nothing to contradict his other details. His account and Eyre's letter both lead one to expect that the general meeting began work some time in 1609, possibly finishing by the end of the year, possibly going into 1610. Allen, however, observes that Bois's notes from the general meeting contain page and line references to the first volume of Savile's Chrysostom, which was published in 1610, and concludes that the notes were made in 1610.[28] Importantly, he draws this inference:

> the falling out of these nine months between 1610 and 1611 makes likely that the company of revisers must, to all intents and purposes, have been solely responsible for the composition of the final version of the Authorized Version, for this computation leaves almost no time for Bishop Bilson and Dr Smith's finishing touch. It is possible that the finishing touch may have been no more than the assembling of the prefaces. (p. 10)

---

[27] Walker; Allen, *Translating for King James*, pp. 139–40. The colourful detail about the pursuivant or officer with a warrant is not in the eighteenth-century manuscript copy of the Life; the manuscript adds that Downes and Bois were sent for 'out of Cambridge company' (p. 106, also numbered 43).

[28] Allen, *Translating for King James*, pp. 9–10.

Now, as has been observed before, nine months is an extremely short time for the review and the printing.[29] The biographical preface to Miles Smith's sermons suggests that more time was spent on the final review by Smith and Bilson than Allen allows, and that the writing of the preface was done after the rest of their work was finished:

after the task of translation was finished by the whole number . . . it was revised by a dozen selected ones of them, and at length referred to the final examination of the learned Bishop of Winchester that then was Dr Bilson, and of this reverend Bishop, Dr Smith . . . who happily concluded that worthy labour. Which being so ended, for perfecting of the whole work as it now it is, he was commanded to write a preface, and so he did in the name of all the translators, being the same that now is extant in our Church Bible, the original whereof I have seen under his own hand.[30]

It is possible to extend our notion of how much time was available to Smith and Bilson and the printer. Since both Bois and Downes worked on Savile's Chrysostom, they may have seen the first volume before its publication. Even if this did not happen, Bois's notes, dealing with the last part of the NT, probably come from the last days of the general meeting. Either of these possibilities would fit with the implication that the general meeting began in 1609 and therefore finished around the middle of 1610. This could leave as much as a year and a half for the finishing touches and the printing. There is no record of the publication date of the KJB beyond the year of the title page, 1611. Though it is inconvenient for centenaries, the latest possible date for the publication of the KJB is not December 1611 but February 1612, because old-style dates were in use.[31] In short, Allen's conclusion gives the minimum possible time for the final stages of

---

[29] Scrivener, who assumes on the basis of Walker's account that the general meeting oversaw the printing as part of their nine months' work, comments that this period 'seems wholly inadequate for the accomplishment of all they had in hand' (*Authorized Edition*, p. 13).

[30] J.S., preface, in Smith, *Sermons of . . . Miles Smith*, fols. ¶¶ᵛ–¶¶2ʳ.

[31] Herbert notes a purchase in 1611, but the same problem applies to this. The earliest known precise date for a purchase is 6 February 1612 (Herbert, *Historical Catalogue*, p. 133). The first edition had to be published in time for Hugh Broughton to write his 'Censure of the late translation'. Its publication date is unknown. Broughton, though terminally ill with consumption, was able to visit England in November 1611, and died in London on 4 August 1612. The 'Censure' probably did not take much writing: it is very brief and most or all of its points relate to readings he had previously argued for. Thus it does not rule out an early-1612 publication of the KJB.

the work, but the maximum possible time is larger and more realistic for what remained to be done.

The finishing touches included the writing of the dedication and the preface, writing the chapter summaries (supposed to have been done by Bilson) and inserting the paragraphing.[32] One task could only have been done while the Bible was being printed, the insertion of the headers summarising the content of the page. One further finishing touch was not part of the translators' work: the historian and cartographer John Speed obtained in 1610 a ten-year (later twice renewed) royal privilege to insert into the new Bible what turned out to be a highly ornate, 34-page genealogy from God through Adam to Jesus. Speed was also responsible for the map and gazetteer that follow. There is an irony here. He had been closely associated with that adversary of the translators, Broughton: the genealogies go back to work they did together, notably *Genealogies Recorded in the Sacred Scriptures* (1592).[33] Besides James, Robert Barker, the printer, and Cornelis Boel, engraver of the title page, Speed is the only one of the creators of the KJB to have his name in it, in an oval frame within the map which states, 'begun by Mr John More and finished by John Speed'.[34]

MANUSCRIPT WORK AND NOTES

Robert Barker, the King's Printer, supplied forty unbound copies of the 1602 Bishops' Bible for the translators' use, not only ensuring they worked from the right text but enabling them, if they wished, to work by annotating it.[35] The only description of how the companies worked comes from John Selden, who knew Andrewes and Bedwell (and no doubt others of the translators) and so may be repeating what he knew from them of the first Westminster company's practice. He says that

---

[32] The Bishops' Bible was unparagraphed, so this was a substantial task. That it is left incomplete in the KJB suggests that it was among the last things done.
[33] *ODNB*, Speed.
[34] John More is presumably 'the Apostle of Norwich', who had a reputation as a map-maker; the name of the engraver appears indistinctly beside the oval frame.
[35] Barker's bill for '40. large churchbibles for the translators', dated 10 May 1605, is given in Morgan, 'A King's Printer at work', p. 370.

that part of the Bible was given to him who was most excellent in such a tongue (as the Apocrypha to Andrew Downes), and then they met together, and one read the translation, the rest holding in their hands some Bible, either of the learned tongues or French, Spanish, Italian, etc.; if they found any fault they spoke, if not he read on.[36]

This does not square easily with each man making his own translation and comparing the results (rule 8), but it probably has a degree of truth. The translation referred to was the Bishops' Bible, and the practice of commenting on it as occasion arose seems sensible; presumably the comments were made in the light of each individual translator's preparation for the meeting and a particular version (or perhaps, versions) he had been designated to keep an eye on.

Two pieces of work survive from the companies, annotations to parts of the Bishops' Bible Gospels and a partial manuscript of the Epistles. The annotated Gospels may well represent the earliest surviving stage of the work. The translators worked on unbound sheets of the 1602 Bible, as is shown by the way many of the annotations disappear into the binding. Sheets from at least two parts of the work (plus unannotated sheets needed to make a complete Bible) were gathered together and bound some time after the work on the KJB was completed as a complete 1602 Bishops' Bible, Bodleian Library Bib. Eng. 1602b (here abbreviated to Bod 1602). The OT is later work which I will discuss separately. The Gospel annotations record work done by the second Oxford company, omitting John 1–16, Acts and Revelation (presumably these were annotated on one or more separate sets of sheets not used in assembling Bod 1602). The work is in three hands. One scribe annotated Matthew and John 17, a second Mark and Luke 1–18, and a third Luke 19–24 and John 18–21. Moreover, there are corrections by one scribe in another scribe's annotations.[37] Allen and Jacobs take the initial annotations as a record – a kind of fair copy – of the first stage of the company's work, and the corrections as the results of the review of the work carried out in accordance with rule 10. Alternatively, the annotations may be viewed as a working copy, perhaps created as the company made their initial decisions, that was then reviewed by the company itself.

[36] *Table Talk*, p. 3.
[37] Allen and Jacobs, *Coming of the King James Gospels*, p. 5.

The scribe who annotated Mark and most of Luke worked in a way that fits with this suggestion. There is a clear process to most of his annotations. First the words to be revised are identified by underlining, then a Greek letter is written by the words and, against the same Greek letter in the margin, the revision is recorded. Finally, if the revision is accepted, the words in the Bishops' Bible are struck through. For deletions, words are underlined twice, with delete signs placed against them and in the margin; if the deletion is accepted, a line is drawn through the deleted words.[38] This meticulous process appears to show the translators recording their decisions as they made them.

The annotations sometimes show alternative readings being created for the KJB margin. These are typically marked with a flower symbol and begin with 'Or'. Sometimes particular words are marked as English additions to the Greek text: the use of what later became italics in the text is being revised.

The result of these annotations is an intermediate draft of the revision. In terms of the number of revisions needed to make the Bishops' Bible into the KJB, the work of the three scribes represents between two-thirds and five-sixths of the total.[39]

The manuscript Lambeth Palace MS 98 comes from the Westminster NT company.[40] It looks like a fair copy made from annotations such as those in the Gospels to enable review and further revision. Formally presented in two columns, it uses only the left column to give a partial revision of the Bishops' Bible Epistles – partial in that this column gives 1,769 verses, and leaves numbered spaces for the remaining 1,013. The natural inference is that the company had made no changes to these 1,013 verses, and that it expected the manuscript to be used in relation to the Bishops' Bible, where the missing text could be found.[41] The space for the unaltered verses allows for a complete version to be written in this column, but I guess that its real purpose is to ensure that there is space for comments on unchanged

---

[38] Ibid., pp. 7–15.   [39] Ibid., pp. 6, 29.
[40] See Allen, *Translating the New Testament Epistles*.
[41] Here also is the evidence that the manuscript was made from an annotated Bishops' Bible, for 21 of the verses show the copyist mechanically copying as he fails to notice that these verses contain no revisions of the Bishops' Bible, and there are a few other places where he began to copy unrevised verses and then, seeing that they had no revisions, left them incomplete (Allen, *Epistles*, pp. lxxi–lxxii).

verses and for revision of these verses. The right column is empty. It must have been either for comments and queries, presumably from another company, or for revisions, either from the company or from the general meeting. This format allows for both possibilities, consultation following rule 9, or the creation of a further revision. It could in due course turn into a printer's manuscript, the printer being required to work from the right column where it had a version, otherwise to use the left column; where both were blank, he would reprint the Bishops' Bible text. Whatever the purpose was, the emptiness of the right column shows that it went unfulfilled, which fits with the suggestion already made that the consultation with other companies was not completed.

Nevertheless, the manuscript does have revisions that show that it was examined by several people. Within the text, different hands have made corrections of omissions, spelling and punctuation, and corrections of corrections. More interestingly, there are annotations in the left margin. Two groups show critical attention, but there is no knowing whether this attention came from within the Westminster company or from review by another company.[42] Thirty-five verses, all but two either omitted or only partially present in the transcript, have q for quaerere (query) against them, thirty-three in one hand, the remaining two in two different hands; all but three of these have a revised reading in the KJB. Thirty-three verses, twenty-eight of them fully present in the transcript, have Greek words written against them, sometimes with an equivalent English word, indicating concern about the accuracy of the English rendering. There are also marginal readings written in an italic hand, perhaps from a reader, but possibly from the copyist since it was common for one person to use more than one hand (Bois used one hand for English, another for Latin). These give alternative renderings, but whether they are work towards the KJB's marginal readings or part of the process of deciding on the English of the text is not clear. By contrast with the empty right column's testimony to incomplete use of this manuscript, these annotations show the care with which the translators examined a draft.

---

[42] Here I summarise parts of Allen's discussion, *Translating the New Testament Epistles*, pp. lxix–lxxx.

MS 98 leaves uncreated a similar proportion of the final readings to that found in the early part of the Gospel annotations, about two-thirds. There are 4,131 revisions of the Bishops' Bible, of which 3,287 make their way into the KJB. Besides these a further 1,765 revisions appear in the KJB. If the rejection of 844 MS 98 readings is added to the later work, the general meeting (or more extensive later work) made a further 3,818 changes, almost as many changes as are found in MS 98. Overall, of the 6,261 revisions that the KJB made to the Bishops' Bible text of the Epistles, just over half come from MS 98, 3,287 as against 2,974.[43]

John Bois's notes made on the general meeting's discussion of the Epistles and Revelation are evidence of a different sort. They are typical Bois: written in Latin except where the original Greek or a possible English translation is given, and still more typical in that they are a scholar's notes, not a historian's. They tell us much more about how the translators thought, how they discussed issues, what knowledge they brought to bear, than they do about what they did and how much they did. He made notes on some 498 items of discussion – sometimes nothing more than an English phrase without a comment – but he shows no special interest in the reading finally adopted. Only fifty-six readings or decisions that are found in the KJB are given, and none are highlighted as a decision taken for inclusion in the text. He is far more interested in the suggestions that were not used than the ones used: of the 367 notes that have English in them, 332 have unused readings, often several to a note. How they travelled, not where they got to, is his interest, as he tells us about translating but not about the translation.

The contrast with Lawrence's notes is stark. Lawrence gave scholarly arguments for particular readings. The same kind of notes could have been made about the KJB, explaining exactly why it reads as it does.[44] They would perhaps reveal the logic behind every contentious reading and the literary awareness behind every perceived

---

[43] Allen, *Epistles*, p. xxi.
[44] A recollection of Richard Kilbye of the first Oxford company shows that translators carried in their heads detailed memories of such discussions. Kilbye heard a sermon in which

the young preacher [had] no more discretion than to waste a great part of the hour allotted for his sermon in exceptions against the late translation of several words (not expecting such a hearer as Dr Kilbye), and showed three reasons why a particular word should have been otherwise translated. When Evening Prayer was ended, the preacher was invited to the

felicity. They might also reveal the state of the text received by the general meeting and indicate where (if anywhere) there were later changes made to the text. Bois's notes afford only glimpses of these sorts but nothing more. It is like watching Shakespeare's brain at work while writing *Hamlet* without getting *Hamlet* itself.

From a historical perspective, Bois's notes present problems. The first is their extent. There is good reason to think that they constitute a complete manuscript,[45] but the general meeting was to review the whole translation. Why then do the notes only cover the Epistles and Revelation?

Here I want to put up two possibilities.[46] The first, following the discussion of Bois's diary (above, p. 79), questions the seemingly obvious notion that Bois took notes on the translation work because of his interest in the translation. It may be that, while Romans was being discussed, he began to make notes for theological reasons. The beginning of the notes is peculiar, notes on Romans 3:25–6 and 4:17, then a numerical sequence of notes beginning from 1:9 and including an extended note on the verses that were the subject of the first note, 3:25–6. Except for the addenda, nowhere else is the numerical sequence broken.[47] Once he had started making notes he recorded them sequentially. This suggests that he began making notes at 3:25–6 because something there was of particular interest,

---

Doctor's friend's house, where after some other conference the Doctor told him, he 'might have preached more useful doctrine, and not have filled his auditors' ears with needless exceptions against the late translation; and for that word for which he offered to that poor congregation three reasons why it ought to have been translated as he said, he and others had considered all them, and found thirteen more considerable reasons why it was translated as now printed.' (Walton, *The Life of Dr Sanderson*, fol. a7^{r-v})

45 William Fulman, who made the published copy, writes at the end that he has 'transcribed [them] out of a copy taken by some unskillful hand, very confused and faulty, especially in the Greek' (Allen, *Translating for King James*, p. 113). There is another copy, again faulty, but evidently made from Bois's own copy by one of his colleagues at Ely, the future Bishop of Dunblane, James Wedderburn, BL MS Harl. 750, fols. 3^r–16^r. There are variant readings but the general contents are identical (see my 'John Bois's notes on the revision of the King James Bible New Testament'). Bois's diary confirms that he knew Wedderburn: he quotes 'ex ore D. Doctoris Wedderburnii', fol. 144^r.

46 I leave on one side the possibility that Bois did make notes on the rest of the work but that these are lost. This is at best unlikely in view of Walker's statement that he kept the notes till his dying day (Allen, *Translating for King James*, p. 141) and the fact that Wedderburn, who copied the notes, predeceased Bois; Wedderburn would surely have copied more if there was more to copy.

47 Some comments on Phil. 3:13 make up the last part of the note on 3:14, but this seems to be part of a single discussion.

then went back and filled in what had happened previously. Allen, whose suggestion this is, develops the point this way:

A guess: Bois had not kept notes concerning the discussions of revisions for the Old Testament, Apocrypha, and Gospels. A discussion of vv. 25–6 caught his attention. Then a discussion of 4:17 caught his attention. He took a notion then to keep notes on the discussion of the Epistles, these being central books for the establishment of doctrines held by the Church. For example, the conflicting views of original sin, held by the East and West, have grounds in a single verse, Rom. 5:12. Bois's brief note, 16 words, rejects the view held by St Augustine, Beza, and generally the West.[48] The difficulty must have called for a great deal of discussion. It ended in a compromise, the East in the text and the West in the margin.

Having taken this notion, Bois then went back and reviewed the discussions from 1:9 though 4:11. Now he adds a full account of his views on 3:25–6, [giving] a full explanation of his argument, of which the first note was a sketch to remind himself of what he had said . . . In the extended note Bois notes why this verse caught his eye: 'scarcely another place is to be found more apt to this point'.[49]

This is an attractive argument because it fits with Bois's character to explain the extent and nature of the notes. Once he had applied his habitual note-taking to the translation, the notes turned into a record of philological discussion, though the theological, reflective character never entirely disappears, as in his Latin note to James 1:15, 'Suggestion, Delight, Agreement, Act, the four steps of sin' (p. 87).

The second – less attractive – possibility is that Bois was not present at all the discussions, perhaps because review work was divided among the delegates. This possibility becomes a little stronger if we consider another problem: who was present at the discussions of the Epistles and Revelation? Downes, Bois's fellow Grecian and delegate from the Cambridge Apocrypha company, is frequently mentioned and appears to have dominated the discussions. John Harmar from the Oxford NT company is mentioned either twice or, if 'D. H.' (i.e. Dr H.) also refers to him, four times, and 'D. Hutch.' (Dr Hutch.) or 'Hutch' three times (or five if 'D. H.' refers to him). Three other

---

[48] KJB: 'wherefore, as by one man sin entered into the world, and death by sin: and so death passed upon all men, ∥for that all have sinned'; margin, '∥ or, in whom'. Bois's note: 'In quo, i.e. according to Beza, in Adam. Which is difficult, nor is it necessary' (Allen, *Translating for King James*, p. 39).

[49] Personal letter, 2009. Reproduced with permission.

single letters appear which may refer to translators but all have a degree of doubt to them.[50] At most, eight translators including Bois are indicated but there may only have been four, Bois, Downes, Harmar and 'Hutch.' (Hutchins or Hutchinson and variants, otherwise unknown among the translators, Ralph Hutchinson having died in 1606). Now, the infrequency of recorded comments from others does suggest a historical limitation in Bois's notes, but the implication is strong that only some of the delegates were present for discussion of the Epistles and Revelation. If some were absent from this part of the discussions, Bois may equally have been absent from other parts. While there is no more evidence than this to suggest it, the general meeting may have divided up its work. The most sensible division would have been for the Hebraists to work on the OT (by far the larger task), and the Grecians to take the Apocrypha and the NT.

The other problem is inherent in the kind of notes Bois made. In particular, they do not show how the text moved from the state represented by MS 98 to the printed text. All we can say is that, if 498 represents the total number of items the general meeting discussed, a great deal of revision went on elsewhere. They do not even suggest that the readings in MS 98 were a real factor in the discussions, since only twenty readings from it appear in the notes.

Even if skewed by Bois's particular interests, what the notes do show us is how the translators thought. They thought primarily in Latin, sometimes in Greek and English, and they thought about two languages, Greek and English. A quarter of the notes involve discussion of the Greek without any mention of a possible English translation, many more mix discussion of the Greek with English possibilities. Refined understanding of the Greek was the translators' starting point even at this late stage of the work. The argument that they worked primarily or even solely to polish the English of the Bible *as English* is absolutely untenable set against these notes.

Here is the complete set of notes on 1 Corinthians 7, a chapter in which MS 98 makes some forty-seven changes to the 1602 text:

---

[50] In MS 750, 'C' at at Rom. 4:11 appears to have been added later. 'H' at 1 Cor. 9:5 looks more like a deletion in Fulman's manuscript; MS 750 gives 'al.' 'B' at Heb. 12:23 is lower case in MS 750, and Fulman's 'B. A. D.' is equally curious since there is usually 'et' when two names or initials are given.

Cap. 7.2. ἐχέτω] habeat, i.e. inquit A.D. rem habeat cum etc.

Ibid. v. 22. ἀπελεύθερος sit ἐλεύθερος nascitur.

Ibid. v. 26. ἀνάγκην] i.e. θλίψιν, διωγμόν, Photius, διὰ τὴν ἐνεστῶσαν τῶν πειρασμῶν φοράν.

Ibid. v. 29. ὅτι ὁ καιρὸς] h.e. jam instant et impendent calamitates. A.D. ὅτι ὁ καιρὸς ἐστι δύσκολος καὶ κινδύνων ἀνάμεστος]. cui non assentior. Lege Gr. Scholia.

Ibid. v. 35. but that you may decently and without distraction wait upon the Lord.

Cap. 7. 36. ἐπὶ τὴν παρθένον. toward his virgin. i.e. περὶ τὴν παρθένον, concerning his virgin. ἐπὶ ἀντί τῶ περί.[51]

In verse 2, Downes gives the Latin equivalent of the Greek in order to bring out the full sense, 'let him have, i.e. he may have relations with'.[52] There is no change here to the 1602 reading (MS 98 records the insertion of italics earlier in the verse).

In v. 22 the precise significance of the Greek word is noted by observing the difference in sense if the prefix was removed, from 'a freedman is made' to 'free is born'. MS 98 does not give this verse; the KJB's text is unchanged from 1602, 'is the Lord's free man', but the observation leads to the KJB's margin, 'Gr. made free'. This allows the scholarly reader to get closer to the precise sense of the text.

V. 26 shows the weighing of a single word which might mean distress or necessity. Greek synonyms are given, followed by a paraphrase from Photius of Constantinople that supports 'distress' rather than the word previously used in English translations, 'necessity'. Knowledge of Greek and the Greek patriarchs leads to a judgement that the best English word is 'distress', but 'necessity' remains possible, so appears in the KJB margin.

At v. 29 the KJB retains a few words that go back through the 1568 Bishops' Bible to Tyndale, 'the time is short. It remaineth'. 1602 gave a slightly revised version, 'because the time is short: it remaineth', but MS 98 has a significant change, changing the structure to connect 'remaineth' with 'time': 'because the time is short that remaineth'.[53] Bois's note can be read as a discussion of the issue that relates to this

[51] Allen, *Translating for King James*, pp. 44–7, 104–5; the final note is in the addenda.
[52] The translations are from Allen, *Translating for King James*.   [53] Allen, *Epistles*, p. 62.

change, whether 'the time is short' concerns the brevity of human
life or, in the words of the Geneva-Tomson margin here, 'the latter
end of the world'. But what he deals with is 'that the time' (his Greek
here follows Beza; usually the first word is omitted). The Latin draws
out the meaning, 'now calamities draw nigh and threaten', though
it is unclear whether Bois gives this end-time paraphrase as his own
understanding or as a rough equivalent of Downes's Greek, 'that
the time is troublesome and filled full of dangers'. Perhaps adding
something he did not say at the time, he observes 'to which I do not
assent. Read the Greek Scholia', that is, the Greek glosses. Again there
is uncertainty: is he dissenting from Downes's particular elaboration
or from the apocalyptic reading? What is clear is that significant
discussion has taken place, probably followed by research on Bois's
part, and that the translators decided on the traditional reading. So
much work could go on to produce a decision to keep a reading.
Further, if this sense of the discussion is right, the obliqueness of
Bois's notes is demonstrated. Settling a reading involved close examination of a word, 'time', that was apparently not at issue.

The English for the latter part of v. 35 is a rejected but nevertheless
pleasing alternative to what was obscure in 1602 and only slightly
improved in MS 98. 1602 presents three obscurities: what do 'comeliness', 'sitting fast unto' and 'separation' mean in its rendering of the
whole verse: 'this speak I for your profit: not that I may cast a snare
upon you, but for comeliness sake, and sitting fast unto the Lord
without separation'. MS 98 gives an alternative for 'separation': 'distraction'. 1611 followed this, tinkered with 'comeliness' and clarified
'sitting fast': 'but for that which is comely, and that you may attend
upon the Lord without distraction'. The rejected revision given by
Bois also deals with 'comeliness' and gets a more natural English word
order: 'but that you may decently and without distraction wait upon
the Lord'. It may have been rejected because it reduced three Greek
words to one English word, 'decently', and did not follow the Greek
word order as closely as the other versions. That it might have been
better English did not count against this. And again, Bois, by giving
what was eventually rejected rather than what was accepted and why,
allows us to see the kind of possibilities the translators tested.

The final note, v. 36, is deceptively simple: one Greek preposition
is used with the meaning of another, and the result is a change from

the reading in all the other Protestant English versions, 'for his virgin', to 'toward his virgin'.[54] Up to this point Tyndale's meaning had been kept with slight changes of language. This is how 1602 gives the verse: 'but if any man think that it is uncomely for his virgin, if she pass the time of marriage, and need so require, let him do what he will, he sinneth not: let them be married'. MS 98 picked up one change of wording from Geneva, a somewhat more literal phrase, 'if she pass the flower of her age' for the explanatory 'if she pass the time of marriage'; this remains in 1611. But in 1611 the change to 'toward his virgin' either goes along with or necessitates a change of meaning. The Tyndalian rendering, 'if any man think that it is uncomely for his virgin' leaves it uncertain whether the uncomely behaviour is by the virgin or the man – it seems more likely to be by the virgin. 'Toward' makes it certain that the behaviour is by the man, and so the translation becomes unambiguous (even if arguably less literal), 'if any man think that he behaveth himself uncomely toward his virgin'. Attention to a Greek preposition has made quite a change.

One further example widens the picture of how the translators worked with the Greek and thought about the English, 2 Peter 2:2, where a variant reading in the Greek texts is noted:

ἀπωλείαις, al. ἀσελγείαις. ἀπωλείαις, pernicious ways; ἀσελγείαις, lascivious ways, impure ways, flagitious facts. flagitium, peccatum flagris dignum.[55]

'Al.', others, is frequently used, always with reference to the Greek or other non-English versions. ἀπωλείαις is the reading in the received text, and had been translated from Tyndale through to 1602 as 'damnable ways' (MS 98 omits this verse); ἀσελγείαις has become the preferred reading. From these observations comes the KJB's new reading, 'pernicious ways', and its margin, 'or, lascivious ways, as some copies read'. 'Flagitious facts' is a delicious phrase, clearly prompted by alliteration. The translators are playing with words ('facts' hardly fits the context: 'many shall follow their flagitious facts' would make little sense here though it would fit detective fiction). Yet it is serious play, as the Latin explains: 'an outrage, a sin worthy of lashes'. Textual scholarship, playful inventiveness and sober judgement combine to produce the KJB's text and margin.

---

[54] Rheims has 'upon his virgin'.   [55] Allen, *Translating for King James*, pp. 94–5.

Bois's notes give little evidence of adherence to rule 14, to use the earlier Protestant English translations 'where they agree better with the text than the Bishops' Bible'. They are never named (Rheims is mentioned once, in relation to Col. 2:18), and nowhere do we see Downes and company collating English readings. They thought for themselves, though often their sober decision, as the KJB text shows, was to obey rule 1, leaving the Bishops' Bible 'as little altered as the truth of the original will permit'.

Nor do the notes show much evidence of revising for style. The translators do bring literary issues into their discussions, but they concern the rhetoric of the Greek. One note only shows a concern for English effect. At Hebrews 13:8 MS 98 gives a version not found in the earlier English translations, 'Jesus Christ the same yesterday, and today and for ever', and this became the KJB reading. Downes had an alternative suggestion, clearly based on this: 'yesterday, and today the same, and for ever'. He commented, 'if the words be arranged in this manner, the statement will be more majestic'.[56] He is surely right: the words have a felicitous cadence, with 'the same' at its emphatic peak. Moreover, though this is not noted, this is the order of the Greek. There is no knowing why this one piece of apparently literary revision – but also successful as literal revision – was not used.[57]

While Bois was recording what interested him in the discussions, someone else must have been recording the changes decided on by the general meeting. In all likelihood, most of the OT annotations in Bod 1602 are part of this record.[58] Their extent makes this probable. They run from the beginning of Genesis to the end of the Song of Solomon, then, perplexingly, cover the first four chapters of Isaiah, Jeremiah, Ezekiel and Daniel, and finish with all of the minor prophets. Thus they traverse work initially done by the first Westminster, Cambridge and Oxford companies. Both places where one company's work ends and another's begins come in the middle of a page, and there is no change of hand, so these annotations must come after the company

---

56 Allen, *Epistles*, p. 244. Downes's comment is given in a mixture of Latin and Greek.
57 I previously suggested seven of the notes might be read in terms of care for English style, but the others no longer appear to sustain this reading (Norton, *History of the English Bible as Literature*, pp. 71–2).
58 The Genesis annotations appear to be earlier (above, p. 51). Other possibilities have been suggested and are discussed in Norton, *Textual History*, pp. 22–3.

work. On the other hand, they do not represent the finished text of the KJB, so cannot be a post-1611 collation of the 1602 and 1611 texts. They must, therefore, come from the time in which the general meeting took place, but with some possibility that they antedate its finished work.

An important aspect of the annotations is that they appear to represent the text at a single stage, for there is little sign of subsequent correction. If they are indeed a record of the general meeting's work, they show that it considered every word rather than adding final decisions on doubtful places to an already annotated Bishops' Bible.

The real importance of the OT annotations is the evidence they give for the translators' decisions about the OT text, for Bod 1602, despite not having all the KJB's new readings and its incompleteness in the major prophets, is very close to being the final manuscript for the OT. That the KJB was printed from an annotated Bishops' Bible – possibly from Bod 1602 – is almost certain from the presence of peculiarities and errors that come directly from the printed 1602 text. Among the errors are 1602's 'the Lord your God' for 'the Lord our God' at 1 Kings 8:61, and 'Amorites' for 'Ammonites' at 1 Kings 11:5. In each case earlier editions of the Bishops' Bible and the other versions had the correct reading.[59]

Just how important Bod 1602 was to the final text of the KJB and how it can clarify whether a 1611 reading is a deliberate decision or an error by the translators is readily shown. The 1602 text spells Noah's first son 'Sem' throughout, and this is followed by 1611 until Genesis 9, where he becomes, more correctly, 'Shem'. The change in spelling exactly follows Bod 1602: the translators began inserting an 'h' from chapter 9 on. This reflects something that happens a number of times in translation and editorial work: a change is decided on after several examples of the need for it have occurred, but there is no looking back to the earlier examples. Moreover, it shows work being done in a linear fashion, apparently once only.

Another such variation derives from the particular nature of the annotations in Bod 1602. 'Ishmael' occurs forty-seven times in the OT, but at 1 Chronicles 9:44, 1611 gives the form consistently used in the Bishops' Bible, 'Ismael'. What looks like carelessness on the printer's part is probably due to difficulties in following Bod 1602:

'h' is inserted but only visible if one looks very closely because the insertion is obscured by other work. This makes it highly probable that the relationship of Bod 1602 to 1611 is paternal or grandpaternal, for the reading descends directly from a scribal peculiarity of Bod 1602.

The most striking example of Bod 1602 as evidence for the text comes at Hosea 6:5. Here what appears to be a misprint that was immediately corrected in subsequent editions is shown to be a deliberate creation of the translators. The standard text of the KJB reads 'therefore have I hewed them by the prophets; I have slain them by the words of my mouth'. 'Have I hewed them' corresponds to the earlier versions' 'have I cut down'; it is a good literal rendering of the Hebrew and goes appropriately with 'I have slain them'. Now, the first printing has 'shewed' (1611 spelling) for 'hewed'. This is not the literal sense of the Hebrew, and later editors apparently had every justification in rejecting it as a misprint. But it is not a misprint: in Bod 1602 'cut down' is struck through and 'shewed' substituted. 'Shewed' responds to an exegetical difficulty, the violent presentation of God (the speaker here). A Geneva annotation explains the sense this way: 'I have still laboured by my prophets, and as it were, framed you to bring you to amendment, but all was in vain: for my word was not meat to feed them, but a sword to slay them'. God's word, which should have led to reform of life, has been ignored, so, rather than saving, it condemns. Figuratively, what should have been food has become a sword. 'Shewed' follows this note, removing the figurative sense and rephrasing the note's 'laboured by my prophets' with 'shewed them by the prophets'. Here we have a glimpse of what may have been in translators' minds, but it does not seem enough to explain what now appears as a paraphrastic removal of an image through theological embarrassment. The KJB is too steadfastly literal for this. Yet the Geneva note points in the right direction. The Aramaic translation-paraphrase of the prophets, Targum Jonathan, could well have been taken by the translators as having a certain authority and was available to the translators not only in the Bomberg Bibles but also in manuscript in Oxford.[60] It reads 'I warned them', giving the sense found in the Geneva note.[61] So what seemed like a printer's mistake,

[60] Daiches, *King James Version of the English Bible*, p. 166.
[61] Sperber (ed.), *Bible in Aramaic*, vol. III: *The Latter Prophets According to Targum Jonathan*, p. 395.

easily correctly by the removal of 'h', is a deliberate and reasoned translation. Only Bod 1602 gives this kind of insight into details of the KJB.

Another such change comes in 2 Chronicles 32:5. Here is the verse as it was in 1602 and as it appears in standard KJBs:

1602	Standard KJBs
And Hezekia went to lustily, and built up the wall where it was broken, and made the towers, and another wall without, and repaired Millo in the city of David . . .	Also he strengthened himself, and built up all the wall that was broken, and raised it up to the towers, and another wall without, and repaired Millo in the city of David . . .

Only the last two phrases appear untouched, yet the translators did revise 'repaired Millo' in Bod 1602: they inserted 'p' at the beginning and deleted the 'i', creating 'prepared Millo'. In 1616, whether as a correction or by accident, 'repaired' found its way back in, with the consequence that standard KJBs keep a reading the translators deliberately rejected. Again we can guess at the translators' reasoning. The Hebrew is now usually translated 'and strengthened Millo' (Revised Version, etc.). The difference in sense from 'repaired' is that 'strengthened' does not imply previous damage. 'Prepared' similarly omits the suggestion of damage, and this sense of the meaning presumably prompted the translators. But this change seemed wrong or inexplicable to somebody involved with the printing of the 1616 edition, somebody perhaps familiar with 'repaired' as the standard reading (first found in the Matthew Bible): he treated it as a printing error and restored the old reading.

Bod 1602's OT annotations are almost as close as we will ever get to the final manuscript of the KJB (the only thing closer is the first edition itself, but we want the manuscript to tell us about the first edition rather than the other way round). It may be that Bod 1602 is part of the final manuscript, but that leaves the problem of understanding how, where and by whom the remaining changes were made.

If Bod 1602 fathered a further manuscript, it is lost. There are various reports of it. A pamphlet of 1651 declares 'that the sole right of printing of the Bible was Matthew Barker's, in regard that his father paid for the amended or corrected translation £3,500, "by reason whereof the translated copy did of right belong to him"'.[62] An entry in the Stationers' Register by Oliver Cromwell allocating Bible printing to the printers Henry Hills and John Field was objected to in 1656 on the grounds 'that the Bible copy was not Barker's, but Bill's, and that it was only held in trust for Bill'.[63] Barker, however, as reported in a 1659 pamphlet, 'by the mediation of Mr Marchamont Needham [Nedham], sold the several tomes of K. James's translation to Henry Hills and John Field'.[64] This purchase of 'the Bible copy' was probably in 1656, and cost Field and Hills £1,200.[65] Later in 1656 a new edition of the Bible by Field and Hills was advertised in Nedham's *Mercurius Politicus* as 'being examined, corrected, and amended according to the original manuscript copy of the translators'.[66] This was advertising as we are used to it: the value to Field and Hills of the 'Bible copy' was the legitimacy it gave them as monopolists of the Bible copyright. Though we cannot tell which edition is being referred to, none of their editions from this time show any signs of examination, correction and amendment: rather, they were notoriously poor, and the 1659 pamphlet defending them admits the faultiness.

The later references to the original are all secondhand and of questionable value. William Kilburne refers to Hills and Field 'purchasing the translated copy, made in . . . 1611', and he also alludes to 'the original' in his 'Humble proposals'.[67] A pamphlet printed about June 1660 repeats Hills and Field's claim in an attack on them: they have 'obtained, (and now keep in their actual possession) the manuscript copy of the last translation of the Holy Bible in English (attested with the hands of the venerable and learned translators in

[62] Plomer, 'King's Printing House', p. 370; the date is given by Herbert, *Historical Catalogue*, p. 132.

[63] McKitterick, *A History*, vol. I, p. 462, n. 89, with reference to *Calendar of State Papers Domestic*, ed. R. Lemon *et al.* (1856–), 1655–6, p. 289.

[64] Anon., perhaps William Bentley, 'The case of the printery at Finsbury'.

[65] Anon., 'A true state of the case of John Field and Henry Hills', pp. 1, 2.

[66] No. 334, 29 Oct.–6 Nov. 1656, p. 7366. Nedham had substantial dealings with the Stationers' Company in the mid-1650s (*ODNB*, Nedham), and was alleged to have been bribed more than £100 a year by Field (Kilburne, *Dangerous Errors*, p. 14).

[67] Kilburne, *Dangerous Errors*, p. 14; 'Humble proposals', as given in McKitterick, *A History*, vol. I, p. 388. Kilburne is discussed in Chapter 6.

King James's time) ever since 6 March 1655'.[68] Finally, in a lawsuit against Christopher Barker, Roger Norton refers to 'the moiety of a manuscript of a Bible in English called the Bible of King James's translation'.[69] Perhaps the partial or half manuscript ('the moiety of a manuscript') is not the same manuscript as that referred to in the other references, or perhaps it is a variation on the report of 'several tomes'; not impossibly, it could refer to Bod 1602 or another volume of a similar sort. Speculation that the manuscript was lost in the Great Fire of London, 1666, may be right,[70] but there may be new discoveries waiting to be made.

Whatever the final manuscript was, there is no clear evidence it was ever used for printing from after the first edition had been printed: it may have been referred to but subsequent editions were made, with an increasing degree of randomness, from earlier editions, not from the manuscript.

Looking back over the evidence for the making of the KJB, I think the good luck of having as much as we do outweighs the regret that we do not have more. We know much more about the KJB than about any previous version, and it is worthwhile reflecting that Shakespeare scholars would be delighted to have even a single autograph manuscript of one of his plays, or a printed text that he himself had supervised. That so much survives is partly testimony to the grandeur of the scheme initiated by King James. Involving so many people, some of them of considerable fame outside their participation in the translation, it was always likely to leave more historical traces than any other version. Moreover, in spite of the modesty exhibited by many of the men who were, after all, merely revising many good previous versions, the occasional sense of pride epitomised in Samuel Ward's declaration, 'I was a translator', shows that there was some sense that this was a special work. This sense contributed to the survival of treasures such as Bois's notes.

---

[68] *The London Printer's Lamentation, or, the press oppressed, and overpressed*; as given in Arber, *A Transcript*, vol. III, p. 28.

[69] Plomer, 'King's Printing House', p. 373; the lawsuit is no earlier than 1664.

[70] Arber, *A Transcript*, vol. III, 28; Herbert follows this suggestion, p. 131.

CHAPTER 5

1611: the first edition

THE HOLY SCRIPTURES AND 'THE TRANSLATORS TO THE READER'

Coming now to the result of all this labour by generations of men, it is good to begin with the translators' praise of the Holy Scriptures in the preface, 'the translators to the reader'. It is a reminder – if reminding is needed – of what the Scriptures were and are to so many:

But now what piety without truth? what truth, what saving truth, without the word of God? what word of God, whereof we may be sure, without the Scripture? The Scriptures we are commanded to search (John 5:39, Isa. 8:20). They are commended that searched and studied them (Acts 17:11 and 8:28–9). They are reproved that were unskilful in them, or slow to believe them (Matt. 22:29, Luke 24:25). They can make us wise unto salvation (2 Tim. 3:15). If we be ignorant, they will instruct us; if out of the way, they will bring us home; if out of order, they will reform us; if in heaviness, comfort us; if dull, quicken us; if cold, inflame us. 'Tolle, lege; tolle, lege', take up and read, take up and read the Scriptures (for unto them was the direction), it was said unto St Augustine by a supernatural voice. 'Whatsoever is in the Scriptures, believe me,' saith the same St Augustine, 'is high and divine; there is verily truth, and a doctrine most fit for the refreshing and renewing of men's minds, and truly so tempered that every one may draw from thence that which is sufficient for him, if he come to draw with a devout and pious mind, as true religion requireth.' Thus St Augustine. And St Jerome: 'ama Scripturas, et amabit te sapientia', etc. Love the Scriptures, and wisdom will love thee. And St Cyril against Julian: 'even boys that are bred up in the Scriptures become most religious', etc. But what mention we three or four uses of the Scripture, whereas whatsoever is to be believed, or practised, or hoped for, is contained in them? or three or four sentences of the Fathers, since whosoever is worthy the name of a Father, from Christ's

time downward, hath likewise written not only of the riches, but also of
the perfection of the Scripture? 'I adore the fulness of the Scripture,' saith
Tertullian against Hermogenes. And again, to Apelles a heretic of the like
stamp he saith, 'I do not admit that which thou bringest in' (or concludest)
'of thy own' (head or store, 'de tuo') without Scripture. So St Justin Martyr
before him: 'we must know by all means', saith he, 'that it is not lawful' (or
possible) 'to learn' (anything) 'of God or of right piety, save only out of the
Prophets, who teach us by divine inspiration'. So St Basil after Tertullian:
'it is a manifest falling away from the faith, and a fault of presumption,
either to reject any of those things that are written, or to bring in' (upon the
head of them, ἐπεισάγειν) 'any of those things that' are not written . . . The
Scriptures then being acknowledged to be so full and so perfect, how can
we excuse ourselves of negligence if we do not study them? of curiosity, if we
be not content with them? Men talk much of εἰρεσιώνη,[1] how many sweet
and goodly things it had hanging on it; of the philosopher's stone, that it
turneth copper into gold; of cornucopia, that it had all things necessary for
food in it; of panaces the herb, that it was good for all diseases; of catholicon
the drug, that it is in stead of all purges; of Vulcan's armour, that it was
an armour of proof against all thrusts and all blows, etc. Well, that which
they falsely or vainly attributed to these for bodily good, we may justly and
with full measure ascribe unto the Scripture for spiritual. It is not only an
armour, but also a whole armoury of weapons, both offensive and defensive,
whereby we may save ourselves and put the enemy to flight. It is not a herb,
but a tree, or rather a whole paradise of trees of life, which bring forth fruit
every month, and the fruit thereof is for meat, and the leaves for medicine. It
is not a pot of manna or a cruse of oil, which were for memory only, or for a
meal's meat or two, but as it were a shower of heavenly bread sufficient for a
whole host, be it never so great; and as it were a whole cellar full of oil vessels,
whereby all our necessities may be provided for, and our debts discharged.
In a word, it is a panary of wholesome food against fenowed traditions;
a physician's shop (St Basil calleth it) of preservatives against poisoned
heresies; a pandect of profitable laws against rebellious spirits; a treasury of
most costly jewels against beggarly rudiments; finally, a fountain of most
pure water springing up unto everlasting life. And what marvel? the original
thereof being from heaven, not from earth; the author being God, not man;
the inditer, the Holy Spirit, not the wit of the Apostles or Prophets; the
penmen such as were sanctified from the womb, and endued with a principal
portion of God's spirit; the matter, verity, piety, purity, uprightness; the form,
God's word, God's testimony, God's oracles, the word of truth, the word of
salvation, etc.; the effects, light of understanding, stableness of persuasion,

---

[1] An olive bough wrapped about with wool, whereupon did hang figs, and bread, and honey
in a pot, and oil [KJB margin].

repentance from dead works, newness of life, holiness, peace, joy in the Holy Ghost; lastly, the end and reward of the study thereof, fellowship with the saints, participation of the heavenly nature, fruition of an inheritance immortal, undefiled, and that never shall fade away: happy is the man that delighteth in the Scripture, and thrice happy that meditateth in it day and night.[2]

It is the book of truth, the foundation of religion, knowledge and law, divinely inspired and dictated by the Holy Spirit. To the KJB went the honour of becoming the standard English form of this 'whole paradise of trees of life'. In a sense it is much more than the book made by men that we must treat it as here.

'Happy is the man that delighteth in the Scripture', and many have taken aesthetic delight in the KJB. This is not what Miles Smith and the translators had in mind, which was delight in God's truth. If we think in terms of form and content being inseparable, then the list of 'the effects' of the Bible, 'light of understanding' and so on, have an aesthetic dimension, but the translators did not think in those terms.[3] They present the Bible and their work as purely religious. Moreover, taking this paragraph as a sample of their writing, it is clear that the translators' idea of good writing was different from the English they used for the Bible. The length of the paragraph and the length and complexity of the sentence structures are alien to most of the Bible except some parts of the Apocrypha and the Epistles. Some of the vocabulary has a similar simplicity to that commonly found in the translation, as in 'repentance from dead works, newness of life, holiness, peace, joy in the Holy Ghost', but there are places where the scholarly background shows off in neologisms to rival any inkhorn writer of the period. The resoundingly alliterative description of the Bible as 'a panary of wholesome food against fenowed traditions . . . a pandect of profitable laws against rebellious spirits' was probably as difficult to understand in 1611 as it is now. 'Panary' is a storehouse for bread, and this is the *OED*'s only citation. 'Fenowed' (or 'finewed'), mouldy, is a rare word set against 'wholesome'. 'Pandect', a complete legal system, was probably the easiest word for those with a Greco-Latin education. In passing, the way Smith quotes from Tertullian and Basil, inserting alternatives and bits of the Latin and Greek,

---

[2] *NCPB*, pp. xix–xxi.   [3] See Norton, *History of the English Bible as Literature*, pp. 66–7.

suggests that he would probably have preferred a still more scholarly way of translating than that used in the KJB.

The latter part of the preface gives an account of the work, some of which has already been quoted. After confirming in general terms both the range of sources the translators drew on, and that they went over the translation several times, he discusses two of the translators' practices, their use of the margin to give 'diversity of senses', and their avoidance of uniform translation for particular words or phrases. Both practices had (and have) their opponents. The danger of marginal alternatives is that they might be seen as undermining 'the authority of the Scriptures for deciding of controversies' by making the text seem uncertain. Without denying the divine origin of the Scriptures, Smith notes that

> it hath pleased God in his divine providence here and there to scatter words and sentences of that difficulty and doubtfulness, not in doctrinal points that concern salvation (for in such it hath been vouched that the Scriptures are plain), but in matters of less moment, that fearfulness would better beseem us than confidence, and if we will resolve, to resolve upon modesty with St Augustine (though not in this same case altogether, yet upon the same ground), 'Melius est dubitare de occultis, quam litigare de incertis': it is better to make doubt of those things which are secret than to strive about those things that are uncertain. (p. xxxiii)

Moreover, the Bible has many unique words whose meaning is uncertain, especially for birds, beasts and precious stones; therefore, he argues, 'diversity of signification and sense in the margin, where the text is not so clear, must needs do good, yea, is necessary'. In essence, he argues that man should not presume to be wiser than God: 'as it is a fault of incredulity to doubt of those things that are evident: so to determine of such things as the Spirit of God hath left (even in the judgement of the judicious) questionable, can be no less than presumption' (p. xxxiii).

Identity of phrasing is a particularly difficult issue in translating the Bible. Unvaried translation would have the advantage of allowing the reader to perceive identities in the original languages, but, even setting aside the huge problem of different meanings in different contexts, there was also the very practical problem of achieving consistency across different groups of translators. Even where it would seem to be a straightforward matter, as when two Gospels have the identical

Greek phrase, the KJB often varies its translation. The same Greek that is translated in Matthew as 'they toil not, neither do they spin' (6:28) is 'they toil not, they spin not' in Luke (12:27). Both are good, the Matthew producing a pleasing cadence, while the Luke follows the Greek literally. Sometimes the translators go the other way, and use a single English word for different Greek words (in English the statements just quoted from both begin 'consider', but the Greek has different verbs). Smith's somewhat disingenuous defence is very important because it involves the relationship between the truth and the words that the generations of translations had laboured over. He begins by writing that the translators did try for consistency where it was possible:

> Truly, that we might not vary from the sense of that which we had translated before, if the word signified the same thing in both places (for there be some words that be not of the same sense everywhere), we were especially careful, and made a conscience, according to our duty. (p. xxxiv)

The example just given shows that this care was not always successful. Here, with examples from Patristic times omitted, is Smith's defence of linguistic variety:

> But that we should express the same notion in the same particular word, as for example, if we translate the Hebrew or Greek word once by 'purpose', never to call it 'intent'; if one where 'journeying', never 'travelling'; if one where 'think', never 'suppose'; if one where 'pain', never 'ache'; if one where 'joy', never 'gladness', etc.; thus to mince the matter, we thought to savour more of curiosity than wisdom, and that rather it would breed scorn in the atheist than bring profit to the godly reader. For is the kingdom of God become words or syllables? why should we be in bondage to them if we may be free? use one precisely when we may use another no less fit as commodiously? . . . We might also be charged (by scoffers) with some unequal dealing towards a great number of good English words. For as it is written of a certain great philosopher, that he should say that those logs were happy that were made images to be worshipped; for their fellows, as good as they, lay for blocks behind the fire: so if we should say, as it were, unto certain words, 'Stand up higher, have a place in the Bible always', and to others of like quality, 'Get ye hence, be banished for ever', we might be taxed peradventure with St James's words, namely, 'to be partial in ourselves and judges of evil thoughts' [James 2:4]. Add hereunto that niceness in words was always counted the next step to trifling, and so was to be curious about names too: also that we cannot follow a better pattern for elocution

than God himself; therefore he using divers words in his holy writ, and indifferently for one thing in nature, we, if we will not be superstitious, may use the same liberty in our English versions out of Hebrew and Greek, for that copy or store that he hath given us. (p. xxxiv)

This is at once serious and witty, playing with the idea that the words of the English language are an abundance ('copy' means copiousness) given by God in the same way that he created the original words of Scripture. As God's creations, all have equal title to be in the Bible. As well as seriously invoking the precedent of varied vocabulary and phrasing in the Bible, this ingeniously justifies variety in the English. But, if one fit word is as good as another, there is a strong sense that truth is not tied to the particular words. Earlier, Smith argued that 'the King's speech which he uttered in Parliament, being translated into French, Dutch, Italian and Latin, is still the King's speech, though it be not interpreted by every translator with the like grace, nor peradventure so fitly for phrase, nor so expressly for sense, everywhere' (p. xxviii): essence is separate from verbal form. Now the drift of his argument is to downplay the particular words the translators have chosen: they are not the truth but ways to the truth. There is a paradox here. The translators examined the words of the originals with immense subtlety, they chose their words with fidelity, precision and sensitivity, but they caution against taking them too absolutely. 'Niceness in words', too pedantic an attention to the letter, Smith warns, 'was always accounted the next step to trifling'. In effect he is saying, we have done our best, but do not make too much of it.

In keeping with this argument, the preface's quotations from the Bible are a mixture of Genevan and original versions, presumably made up by Smith as he wrote. This was no idiosyncrasy on his part: Gregory Martin had been similarly loose in the preface to the Rheims NT, and loose rather than verbally precise quotation was to be the general practice for some time to come.[4]

The discussion of language finishes with another important point. The translators have avoided the jargon of both the puritans and the Roman Catholics. Their aim is like Tyndale's, to be faithful to the language of the originals and comprehensible to everybody:

---

[4] See Norton, *History of the English Bible as Literature*, pp. 103–7.

'we desire that the Scripture may speak like itself, as in the language of Canaan, that it may be understood even of the very vulgar' (p. xxxv).

'The translators to the reader' is both heavy and admirable, and much the most important part of the preliminary material that appeared in the original edition of 1611. It has been a casualty of its length, and is rarely reprinted. I have taken it first because of the importance of what it has to say about the nature of the Bible in general and of the translation in particular.

NEW AND FAMILIAR

In appearance, the first edition has a grand formality. Cornelis Boel's copperplate engraving of the title page announces the finely revised newness of the text. It has traditional elements in a new design. The reader seems to be looking at an ornate wall. Inset like a window is the title itself, flanked by the statue-like figures of Moses and Aaron. The latter is a rarity on Bible title pages and may be taken as a statement of the importance of the Anglican priesthood, and so a rejection of Presbyterianism.[5] Seated in the corners below and in front are Luke and John, with their symbols, a bull and an eagle. Between them is the pelican, emblem of piety and the Passion, nurturing her young. Two-thirds up the page is a frieze capping the wall, with emblems or arms of the twelve tribes of Israel.[6] The New Testament rests on the Old, so the top third has posed, but not statuesque, figures of the Apostles, perhaps suggesting new life. Matthew with his angel and Mark with his lion sit forward on the sides, each watching the Lamb of God and writing. The Lamb matches the pelican below; it is in an oval frame held by Peter, who has keys in his other hand, and Paul who has a sword. Grouped behind are the other Apostles, most identifiable by their symbols, several of which refer to the manner of their death.[7] On the left are Jude (Thaddeus) with a sword, Thomas

---

[5] Corbett and Lightbown, *The Comely Frontispiece*, p. 111.

[6] For a clearer presentation of these, see Speed's genealogies, p. 10, 1611 KJB.

[7] Some of the symbols such as the halberd and the carpenter's square are associated with more than one of the Apostles, but comparison with the NT title page, where the Apostles are named, clarifies most of these. With some hesitation, I follow the identifications given by Corbett and Lightbown, *The Comely Frontispiece*, p. 109.

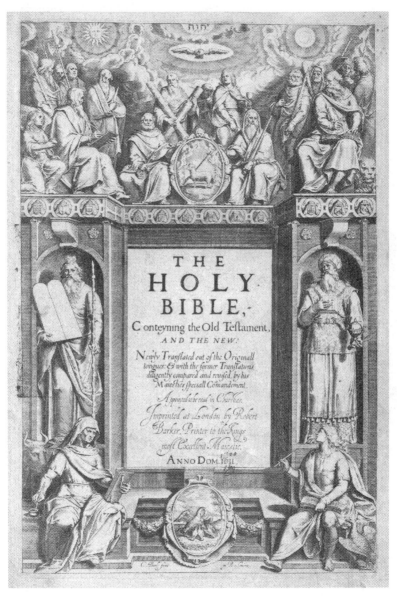

2. 1611 title page by Cornelis Boel. Bible Society: BSS.201.C11 (multiple copies).

with a staff or spear, Matthias with a halberd, and Bartholomew with a flaying knife. Behind Peter stands Andrew with his saltire or diagonal cross, a strong image pointing to the crucifixion. Behind Paul there is the similarly strong figure of John holding a cup or chalice suggestive of Communion.[8] Between these two is Matthew with his carpenter's square. On the right are Simon with a saw, James the Less with a club, and James the Greater with a pilgrim's hat and staff talking to Philip, who holds a spear. Above the Apostles and the Lamb is the dove of the Holy Spirit, above that the holy name of God, the Tetragrammaton. The sun on the left and the moon on the right illuminate the scene, assisting the holy name in dispelling the darkness of the surrounding clouds of ignorance.[9] Nothing in this shows the mortal makers of the translation or their monarch as the Great Bible and the Bishops' Bible title pages had done: it is a grand theological image of Anglican Christianity and the Bible.

But James is very present in the title itself:

The Holy Bible, containing the Old Testament and the New: newly translated out of the original tongues, and with the former translations diligently compared and revised by his Majesty's special commandment. Appointed to be read in churches. Imprinted at London by Robert Barker, Printer to the King's most excellent majesty. Anno Dom. 1611.

Royal authority for the translation and flattery of the King combine. Though 'commandment' did not necessarily evoke divine power, it was surely intended in that sense, for James, in the words of the dedication to him, was 'that sanctified person, who, under God, is the immediate author of all their [his subjects'] true happiness'. He would not have been pleased that 'commandment' became the mundane 'command' in the first Cambridge edition (1629).

The NT has its own title page, a woodcut design cluttered with ornamentation surrounding the title itself. This baroque ornamentation, like that of an elaborately carved wooden chest, is much more Barker's normal style. On the left are the emblems of the twelve tribes, on the right the twelve apostles. The evangelists and their symbols sit at the four corners of the title, looking into it. The Lamb and the Tetragrammaton are at the top. Rather than 'C Boel fecit', there

---

[8] John's chalice usually holds a serpent, in reference to an attempt to poison him.
[9] Corbett and Lightbown, *The Comely Frontispiece*, p. 110.

are two monograms at the bottom of the title panel, apparently 'RL' and, with an accompanying shield, 'OS'. The title text is adapted to use for the NT, and there is one change of substance: 'appointed to be read in churches' is omitted. This title page was first used for some copies of the 1602 Bishops' Bible, and became the standard Barker title page for the whole Bible as well as the NT, probably because Boel's engraving was damaged or lost, possibly because it was free of Anglican, or even Anglo-Catholic particularity. Some first edition KJBs have it rather than Boel's title page.[10]

The only curious thing about the Epistle Dedicatory to King James is that this piece of dignified flattery is included in most KJBs. A most particular part of the praise of James is for his care 'for the Church as a most tender and loving nursing father' (alluding to Isa. 49:23), especially for his 'vehement and perpetuated desire of the accomplishing and publishing of this work'. So the Epistle offers this Bible to him as 'the principal mover and author of the work', begging for his 'approbation and patronage'. His authorisation is sought rather than assumed. Fear of attack by 'Popish persons' and 'self-conceited Brethren, who run their own ways, and give liking unto nothing but what is framed by themselves, and hammered on their anvil' (no doubt Broughton was in mind) will count for little if James gives his approval. The last word is a blessing on James, wishing that he 'may be the wonder of the world in this later age'. That wish was unfulfilled, but, as the preface to Bassandyne and Arbuthnot's Bible anticipated, his fame has been kept alive by his involvement with this Bible (above, p. 82).

'The translators to the reader' follows the dedication. Then comes material from the Prayer Book given only in the folio Bibles in the same format as the first edition. A calendar gives the Psalm of the day and the readings for morning and evening prayer, together with various kinds of miscellaneous information, such as feasts, anniversaries, signs of the zodiac and times of sunrise and sunset (these last are not totally trustworthy: the hours for July are reversed, 7.34 instead of 4.34, and 4.26 instead of 7.26, a mistake peculiar to the black-letter folios and not corrected until 1634). This is followed by a 39-year

---

[10] Some copies of the 1613 folio (H322) have Boel's title page. A smaller copy of it was made by Jasper Isaac and used for some of the 1612 quartos but then it too disappeared.

almanac (the 1602 Bishops' Bible had essentially the same calendar and a similar almanac), a perpetual table for Easter, a table of lessons for Sundays, Psalms for Christmas, Easter, Ascension and Whitsun, a table for the Psalms, and a list of holy days. Next is a generic table of contents that follows almost exactly that given in Barker's 1610 Geneva folio. The Prayer of Manasses is moved to the Apocrypha and 1610's 'Manasse' is changed to the still inappropriate spelling of the 1610 text, 'Manasseh'; the contents follow 1610 in giving 'Ester' for 'Esther', 'the idole Bel and the Dragon' and 'Timotheus' for 'Timothie'.

Speed's genealogies, much more commonly printed in accordance with his patent, take up thirty-four pages, numbered and foliated independently from the surrounding material. With the title pages, they are the most ornate part of the KJB. Because work on them goes back to 1592, it is unsurprising that their Bible quotations are either exactly or adapted from Geneva (with one piece of independent translation). Last comes the double-spread map of Canaan with an inset map of Jerusalem and a two-page gazetteer.

Like the translation itself, visually this first edition is both new and familiar. A long history of Bible presentation lies behind it. What had become the standard Protestant order of the books, with the Apocrypha given separately from the Testaments, is based on Jerome's views of the canon.[11] The columns of text go back to early Greek manuscripts, marginal annotations to the Hebrew texts with the Masora, chapter numbers to Stephen Langton, Archbishop of Canterbury early in the thirteenth century, and headers and verse divisions to Robert Estienne in 1540 and 1551. Along with these general features went the particular practices of the King's Printer, now Robert Barker. Every feature of the KJB as a piece of printing was present in the 1602 Bishops' Bible. A churchman opening a new church Bible for the first time would have seen novelty in the title page and the comparative clarity of Speed's genealogies (to say nothing of the superior engraving), but all the other preliminary

---

[11] Tyndale, followed by Coverdale and the Matthew Bible, placed Hebrews after 3 John. Coverdale placed Baruch (with the Epistle of Jeremy, though it is not separately identified) after Lamentations, and noted that it was not in the Hebrew canon; the Matthew Bible moved them to the Apocrypha. The Geneva Bible placed the Prayer of Manasses after 2 Chronicles.

matter exuded the appeal of the familiar. As for the pages of the text, they would have appeared almost exactly what he had seen in the 1602 Bishops' Bible, even down to the use of printed lines to frame the columns of text and the margin. The only differences he might have noticed were the lack of illustrations, and that not only was the margin emptier but what was there was in roman type.[12] Visually, the first edition presented the KJB as a lightly polished revision of the latest version of the Bishops' Bible.

Though the first edition was a folio and so has some features that disappear in the smaller formats, it is useful to look closely at how it presents the text. There is no ornamentation except for a variety of friezes above the titles of books and the ornamental capitals, large ones for the first letter of books, smaller ones for individual chapters. Genesis 16–17 is a convenient specimen page.

The typeface is black letter, originally created in imitation of gothic script but now carrying with it a sense of biblical tradition by contrast with the modern clarity introduced by the Geneva Bible's use of roman type. It now appears difficult to read and perhaps occasionally caused problems in its own time. Because it is so strongly based on thick vertical lines with diagonal connecting lines and serifs, some letters can be confused if the type is at all misformed, worn or broken, notably 'n', 'u' and 'm'. The 'n's of 'Egyptian' (16:3) and of 'in' (16:6, second line) show how the connecting stroke can disappear, making the distinction from 'u' unclear. The 'm's show a tendency for the right side of the letter to separate, making the letter appear 'ni' (compare 'Abrams' in 16:3 with the other 'm's in the verse), or even, under the pressure of printing, to move, apparently giving 'Abrant' in 17:1. Long 's' within a word (as in 'mistresse was despised', 16:4) and 'f', such a problem to modern readers, may also have been a problem even to those thoroughly used to the typeface. This is the likeliest explanation for the variation between 'flay' (first edition) and 'slay' (second edition) at Leviticus 1:6 and 2 Chronicles 29:34.

The text is presented within ruled borders with space delineated for headers and for annotations. Here the printer is following the

---

[12] Most of the marginal material in the 1602 Bishops' Bible is doctrinal and in black-letter type. The relatively few cross-references and alternative readings are in roman. The same is true of Barker's black-letter Geneva Bibles from this time. 1611's use of roman type effectively follows this practice and highlights the omission of doctrinal notes.

Hagar fleeth.   Chap.xvij.   Abraham.

Marginal notes	
‖ Heb.bee builded by her.	obtaine children by her : and Abram hearkened to the voice of Sarai.

3 And Sarai Abrams wife, tooke Hagar her maid,the Egyptian, after A- bram had dwelt ten yeeres in the land of Canaan, and gaue her to her hus- band Abram,to be his wife.

4 ¶And he went in vnto Hagar, and she conceiued : And when shee saw that shee had conceiued, her mistresse was despised in her eyes.

5 And Sarai said vnto Abram, My wrong be vpon thee : I haue giuen my maid into thy bosome, and when shee saw that she had conceiued, I was de- spised in her eyes : the LORD iudge betweene me and thee.

6 But Abram said vnto Sarai,Be- hold,thy maid is in thy hand: doe to her ‖ as it pleaseth thee. And when Sarai † dealt hardly with her, shee fled from her face.

‖ *Heb.that which is good in thy eyes.* † *Heb. affli- cted her.*

7 ¶And the Angel of the LORD found her by a fountaine of water, in the wildernesse,by the fountaine, in the way to Shur:

8 And he said,Hagar Sarais maid, whence camest thou? and whither wilt thou goe? And she said, I flee from the face of my mistresse Sarai.

9 And the Angel of the LORD said vnto her, Returne to thy mistresse, and submit thy selfe vnder her hands.

10 And the Angel of the LORD said vnto her, I will multiply thy seede exceedingly,that it shall not be numbred for multitude.

11 And the Angel of the LORD said vnto her, Behold, thou art with child,and shalt beare a sonne, and shalt call his name ‖ Ishmael ; because the LORD hath heard thy affliction.

‖ *That is, God shall heare.*

12 And he will be a wilde man : his hand will be against euery man, and e- uery mans hand against him : *he shal dwell in the presence of all his brethren.

*Chap. 25, 18.

13 And shee called the name of the LORD that spake vnto her, Thou God seest me : for she said, Haue I also here looked after him that seeth me?

14 Wherefore the well was called, *‖ Beer-lahai-roi: Behold, It is be- tweene Cadesh and Bered.

*Chap. 24. 62. ‖ *That is, the well of him that li- ueth and see- eth me.*

15 ¶And Hagar bare Abram a sonne: and Abram called his sonnes name, which Hagar bare, Ishmael.

16 And Abram was fourescore and sixe yeeres old, when Hagar bare Ish- mael to Abram.

CHAP. XVII.

God reneweth the Couenant. 5 Abram his name is changed, in token of a greater bles- sing. 10 Circumcision is instituted. 15 Sa- rai her name is changed, and she blessed. 17 Izsaac is promised. 23 Abram and Ishmael are circumcised.

AND when Abram was ninetie yeres old and nine, the LORD appeared to Abram, and said vnto him, I am the almightie God, *walke before me, and be thou perfect.

*Chap. 5. 22. ‖ *Or, vpright or sincere.*

2 And I wil make my couenant be- tweene me and thee, and will multiply thee exceedingly.

3 And Abram fell on his face, and God talked with him,saying,

4 As for me, behold, my couenant is with thee, and thou shalt be a *father of ‖ many nations.

‖ *Heb.mul- titude of na- tions.* *Rom.4.17

5 Neither shall thy name any more be called Abram, but thy name shall bee Abraham : *for a father of many nati- ons haue I made thee.

6 And I will make thee exceeding fruitfull, and I will make nations of thee,and Kings shall come out of thee.

7 And I will establish my couenant betweene me and thee, and thy seede af- ter thee, in their generations for an e- uerlasting couenant, to bee a God vnto thee, and to thy seed after thee.

8 And I will giue vnto thee, and to thy seed after thee,the land †wherein thou art a stranger, all the land of Ca- naan, for an euerlasting possession, and I will be their God.

‖ *Heb.of thy soiournings.*

9 ¶And God said vnto Abraham, Thou shalt keepe my couenant there- fore, thou, and thy seede after thee, in their generations.

10 This is my couenant, which yee shall keepe betweene me and you, and thy seed after thee : *euery man child a- mong you shall be circumcised.

*Acts 7.8.

11 And ye shall circumcise the flesh of your foreskinne; and it shal be a *token of the couenant betwixt me and you.

*Acts 7.8. rom.4.11.

12 And he that is †eight dayes olde, *shalbe circumcised among you, euery man childin your generations, he that is borne in the house, or bought with money of any stranger, which is not of thy seed.

‖ *Hebr. a sonne of eight dayes.* *Leuit. 12. 3. luke 2.21 iohn 7.22.

13 He that is borne in thy house, and he that is bought with thy money, must

B 2   needs

3. 1611: Genesis 16–17.

practice of hand-ruling red lines round the text, something that had previously been offered to customers as an extra.

Recto pages like this have the chapter number in the middle of the header (except in the Psalms), while the verso pages have the name of the book. Usually but not always the chapter number is the number of the chapter beginning on the page. On either side of the header there are very brief summaries of the content of each column; occasionally a longer summary deals with the whole page. Such summaries are missing from the Apocrypha, which simply has 'Apocrypha' on either side. The margin is used for three kinds of annotation. There are literal translations designated with an obelisk (†), alternative English renderings with double vertical lines, and cross-references with an asterisk. The cross-references are more extensive than in the Bishops' Bible and similar but not identical to those in the Geneva Bible; more than half of them come from copies of the Vulgate, one consequence of which is that references to the Psalms are wrong.[13] At the beginning of each chapter there is a summary of its contents. The catchword at the bottom of the right-hand column is the word that will begin the next page; it has a line to itself (something the printer could vary according to the demands of space). The first letter or initial of the chapter is typical of the designs used by Barker within – rather than at the beginning of – books; all are given without borders and most occupy five lines (where necessary for reasons of space, he used smaller ones). The second letter of the first word is always printed as a capital.

The most obvious feature of the text is the antiquated spelling, most of which has disappeared from modern versions. Some is simply a consequence of old typographical conventions. 'U' and 'v' are interchangeable: 'v' is used for both 'v' and 'u' at the beginning of a word, 'u' is used within a word. What look like 'J's are black-letter 'I's, as the roman type setting of 'Izsaac' and 'Ishmael' in the chapter summary shows. 'I' or 'i' are used for 'J' or 'j' except in the chapter number in the header, so 'judge' is given as 'iudge' (16:5). Many of the words have a terminal 'e' ('obtaine' and 'bee' in the first line and its margin, etc.), but this is not consistently used, as 16:5 shows: 'when *shee* saw that *she* had conceiued'. A more substantial variation is visible in 16:8 and the chapter summary: the possessive is first modern (save

[13] The only discussion of these is Scrivener's, *Authorized Edition*, pp. 116–27.

that apostrophes were yet to be used), then antiquated, 'Sarais maid', and 'Sarai her name'. Spelling was much more fluid in 1611 than we allow: in general, the fashion was for long forms with what appear to us as superfluous letters (this decorative fashion had a financial basis: lawyer's clerks were paid by the inch, so found ways of lengthening their work).[14] Nevertheless, it was quite acceptable for a word to be given in several different forms, including forms that appear to us to demand different pronunciations. The printer often used shorter forms if that allowed him to save a line, as in 16:12 where '& he shal' stops the verse running to an extra line; sometimes he even omits the space after a punctuation mark, as in 'maid,the' (16:3).

Words that now appear in italics such as 'is' (16:6) are given in small roman type: visually they appear de-emphasised – exactly the opposite to the effect of italics used for such words in roman type and modern editions.[15] And the diminished emphasis is the point: these are words that have no equivalent in the original text. Now, 'is' at 16:6 is the only example of small roman type here, but the page has other such added words: modern editions recognise this by adding a further seven uses of italics, all involving the verb 'to be'. The identification of added words is inconsistent and incomplete in 1611. So is the presentation: the Apocrypha, which rarely notes such words, uses square brackets without variation of type (though the first such word, 'watch' at 1 Esdras 4:11, is given in round brackets).

There are no speech marks. Instead speech begins with a capital letter, and nothing shows where speech ends. Since every verse begins with a capital letter, whether or not it is a new sentence, there can occasionally be uncertainty whether a new verse is speech. Sometimes there are capital letters within sentences, as in 16:4 and 14, which look like errors but were repeated in some later editions.

---

[14] Scragg, *A History of English Spelling*, p. 52.

[15] As roman type is the font used for distinguishing text from the surrounding black-letter type, so italic is used in relation to roman. The practice of setting translators' additions in a different type was introduced into English Bibles in the 1557 Geneva NT, which was set in roman with italic for the additions. Paul Gutjahr suggests that Barker 'used gothic type to delineate what was sacred writ, as opposed to what was human invention . . . manipulating his typographical choices to make clear to his readers what was written by the hand of God and what was not' ('Four centuries of typography in the King James Bible', in Gutjahr and Benton [eds.], *Illuminating Letters: Typography and Literary Interpretation*, pp. 19–21).

Paragraphs are denoted with paraphs following verse numbers (16:4 etc.). One of the curiosities of the KJB is that there are no paragraph marks after Acts 20, only one in Psalms, and six in the whole of the Apocrypha.[16] Like the identification of added words, this bespeaks incomplete work.

'LORD' (16:5 etc.) is a reversion, not an innovation. Tyndale's Genesis had used 'LORde', and Coverdale's 1535 Bible had 'LORDE', but the practice of capitalisation was dropped thereafter. In the KJB 'LORD', and elsewhere 'GOD' and 'Jehovah', represent the specialness of the four Hebrew letters or Tetragrammaton that denote the unpronounceable sacred name. After Genesis this took on the form found thereafter in KJBs, 'Lord'.[17] Besides the Tetragrammaton, the Hebrew scriptures had two other words for God, 'adonai' ('Lord') and 'elohim' ('God'); when 'elohim' follows the Tetragrammaton, the KJB gives 'Lord God', when 'adonai' precedes, it gives 'Lord God'. This is typographical reverence, corresponding to the Jewish refusal to pronounce the sacred name, either substituting 'adonai' or 'the name'. These capitalised forms are not found in the Apocrypha or the NT because their original language is not Hebrew and so does not have the Tetragrammaton.

There is an uncharacteristically high number of what appear to be printer's errors (though it may not always be that the printer was at fault). In 17:4 there is an asterisk before 'father' but no cross-reference in the margin; in the next line of the verse there is a double vertical line where there should be an obelisk, as in the margin. In the chapter summary, 'Izsaac' appears to be an error, as does 'soieurnings' in the margin to 17:8. There is also an error that may go back to Bilson's preparation of the chapter summaries: 'Abram' in the summary for verse 23 should be 'Abraham' because his name changed at v. 5 (the second edition corrected this). 'And' in the middle of 16:4 following a colon looks like an error but was retained for some time, and 'see-eth' (16:14m) is an error by modern standards.

One last thing about this page: at 16:6 it has a different reading from the second edition, 'but Abram' where the second edition reads 'and Abram'. 'But' was the 1602 reading and remains the modern

---

[16] Ps. 92:8 (superscriptions to the Psalms have paragraph marks; the sections of Psalm 119 begin with a three-line drop capital), 1 Esdras 2:8, 3:13, 4:13, 8:25, 2 Esdras 6:11 and 1 Macc. 6:48.

[17] 'LORD' and 'GOD' are only found in the first edition.

reading; however, Bod 1602 shows that the translators struck through 'but' and substituted 'and'.

TYPOGRAPHICAL ERRORS

The specimen page shows mistakes, and the first edition has both obvious and hidden errors. Some come from the copy the printer used, some from the printer. So far it has been a convenient shorthand to write of 'the printer', but there were a variety of functions in the printing house, probably undertaken by several people at once. Different parts of the Bible may have been set simultaneously and several presses employed. The most significant functions were those of the compositor, the proof-reader and the distributor of the type, presumably an apprentice. Compositors take type, a character at a time, from a case, a two-part box (upper and lower case) with compartments for each character. Printers did not have enough type to set the whole of the Bible at once, so parts had to be set and printed, then the type distributed or returned to the case so that fresh text could be set. The apprentice distributing the type might mis-identify a character and so place it in the wrong compartment, or he might simply misplace a character. Consequently a compositor could reach into the correct compartment and pull out an incorrect character. It is as if there were a glitch in the programming of one's keyboard so that once in a while when, say, the 'u' key is struck, an 'n' results.

Not all typographical errors, therefore, represent errors by the man with the first responsibility for rendering the text into print, the compositor. After the compositor, the proof-reader has prime responsibility for seeing that the text is as it should be (I use 'proof-reader' loosely: insofar as there was proof-reading, it was checking of freshly printed sheets, more often for things like broken types than literal fidelity to a copy-text).[18]

Because of the divided responsibility for errors, because they tell only part of the story of the accuracy of the work, and because there is also fallibility in the present identification of them, one should not depend too much on generalisations from errors. But, with this

---

[18] Greetham, *Textual Scholarship*, p. 118; see also Simpson, *Proof-reading in the Sixteenth, Seventeenth and Eighteenth Centuries*, ch. 1.

caveat, some observations may be made. I count 387 clear errors (281 in the text, 106 in the margins etc.) in the first edition, that is, not much more than one in every three and a half chapters.[19] This, surely, is a remarkably low number. The commonest error is 'u' for 'n' (61), followed by 'n' for 'u' (20), 'c' for 't' (9) and 'e' for 't' (4). The commonest incorrect word is 'aud' (28), an error also commonly found in other black-letter Bibles. The confusion of 'u' and 'n' is an error of distribution, not of setting, that comes from the great similarity of the characters in black-letter type.[20] Over eighty of the typographical errors are therefore attributable not to the compositors but to the apprentices who did the distributing of the type.

Some of the 387 errors are blatant: for instance, three lines are repeated at Exodus 14:10, 'plaine' is given for 'plague' (Lev. 13:56), 'Anocrynha' for 'Apocrypha' (1 Esdras 4 header), 'Ecclesiasticus' for 'Baruch' (Baruch 6 header), 'great great multitudes' for 'great multitudes' (Matt. 4:25), 'himt hat' for 'him that' (Luke 10:36), and 'sririt' for 'spirit' (Eph. 4:30). They suggest that proof-reading was not as thorough as it should have been. If this was skimped, it is unlikely that a special effort was made to read the compositor's work against the translators' copy.

Occasionally we can catch glimpses of the proof-reader at work. There are at least eight variations to be found between copies. All but one reflect work done after printing had begun rather than as part of the regular process of composition, proof-reading and correction.[21] Three of the variations show typographical errors being corrected (a misplaced annotation at Joel 3:14, 'seters' at 1 Esdras 5:58, and 'Tyranuus' at 2 Macc. 4:40m),[22] and are useful in indicating that the printer was willing to correct such errors when they were noticed. More interesting are the three or four changes of reading, 'them' to

---

[19] Most are listed in Norton, *Textual History*, appendix 1.

[20] The confusion is unlikely to be caused by inverting the character because each character had a nick showing the compositor which way it was to be held. There are only two instances of inverted characters, at Num. 29:1m, and Ezek. 40:6m.

[21] The exception is '40' for '46' (1 Macc. 13 summary), where the up-stroke of '6' has broken off; what is left of the character happens to be identical in size to a zero. Some copies show the break between the circle and the up-stroke.

[22] Wright, who notes all but the variation at Joel 3:14, suggests that 'probably many other changes might be discovered' (*The Authorised Version of the English Bible 1611*, vol. 1, p. v.). Only a full collation of extant copies would tell, but I suspect he overstates.

'him' (Exod. 21:26), 'she' to 'he' (Song 2:7),[23] and 'by their knowledge of' inserted (Ecclus. 44:4). The possible fourth is 'Abigal'/'Abigail' (2 Sam. 17:25). These changes appear to come from scholarly observation of the text as it is being printed. There is no telling whether such observation was thorough or random, but the survival of blatant errors suggests it was the latter.

All one can reasonably conclude is that the common-sense view is right: the first edition is to be treated with critical respect – respect, because it is made directly from the translators' own work and, probably, with their collaboration, and because it is well done; critical, because it is not perfectly done and may not have been checked against the manuscript.

In addition to the clear ones, there are hidden errors, that is, errors which might well have been invisible to a proof-reader because the printed text appears to make sense, as in 'the hoops of the pillars' for 'the hooks of the pillars' (Exod. 38:11).[24] These errors have various sources. The copy-text may be uncertain or corrupted in some way, earlier translations may have made a mistake that is accidentally retained, the translators themselves may have erred, they may not have written down what they meant to write, their draft may have been incorrectly copied in making the master copy, and the printer may have gone wrong in ways that are hidden.

The bulk of the hidden errors appear to be the fault of the printer. 1 Corinthians 15:6 should begin 'after that', which is the reading of the Bishops' Bible, MS 98 and most editions from 1616 on. Instead, it reads 'and that', which is how the previous verse began. That the printer's eye had wandered back to that verse is confirmed by a manifest printer's error: the verse is misnumbered 5. Sometimes the printer simply misunderstood what he was setting. At Ezekiel 5:1 he put the apparently sensible 'take the balances' where it should have been 'take thee balances' as in the similar phrases earlier in the verse. This error was sufficiently natural and inconspicuous that it survived until 1638.

On occasions the printer misread his copy (the marvel is that this happened so rarely if his copy was Bod 1602 or anything like it). This

---

[23] It is possible that the change was 'he' to 'she' since the Hebrew is feminine.
[24] See Norton, *Textual History*, pp. 59–60 for a list of such errors.

is the likeliest explanation for the strange reading at Ecclesiasticus 44:5, 'such as found out musical tunes, and reiected verses in writing' (original spelling). 'Reiected' surely comes from mistaking 'recited', which is what the subsequent editions have. And carelessness presumably caused 'threescore and seventh' instead of 'threescore and seventeenth', the Bishops' Bible reading, at 1 Maccabees 16:14.

Several times a Bishops' Bible mistake creeps apparently unnoticed into the KJB text. 'If thou knowest any man of activity amongst them, then make them rulers over my cattle' (Gen. 47:6) is, but for the addition of 'then', exactly a Bishops' Bible reading. 'Man' appears to be inconsistent with the second 'them'. Moreover, the Hebrew is plural and always translated as plural elsewhere in both the Bishops' Bible and the KJB, and all the other translations from Tyndale to Geneva have 'men' here. The Bishops' Bible made a mistake, and the KJB failed to correct it until 1762. Small mistakes can go unnoticed for nearly a couple of centuries in spite of the best efforts of translators and editors. Another reading that appears to be a printer's error in the 1602 Bishops' Bible is 'upon earth' instead of 'upon the earth' in the phrase 'since the day that God created man upon earth' (Deut. 4:32). The Hebrew has the definite article and other editions of the Bishops' Bible (as also the Geneva Bible) have 'upon the earth'. No correction was noted in Bod 1602, but the article reappears in the KJB in the 1612 quartos. A more blatant error from the 1602 text is 'the LORD your God' (1 Kings 8:61). The Hebrew, correctly followed by the original Bishops' Bible and brought back into the KJB in 1629, means 'the LORD our God'. Again the translators failed to correct Bod 1602.

Such errors may come from moments of inattention by the translators or from failure to mark intended corrections, in which case they relate to the next group, errors that come from the Bod 1602 scribes. At Exodus 35:11 the translators revised 'and his rings, his boards, his bars' towards Geneva's 'and his taches and his boards, his bars', but the scribe omitted 'and his boards'. The omission was rectified in 1638. At Ecclesiastes 8:17 there is a reading that seems to make sense: 'because though a man labour to seek it out, yea further though a wise man think to know it, yet shall he not be able to find it'. However, a phrase from the Hebrew is missing after 'to seek it out': 'yet he shall not find it'. The omission goes directly back to the Bod 1602 scribe.

Just possibly he struck through more of the text than he meant to, but the likelihood is that he failed to write in a revision, for the Bishops' Bible phrase – 'yet he cannot reach unto them' – does need revision. A similar incomplete correction also produces sense at Daniel 1:12. 'Us have' is struck through in Bod 1602's 'let us have pulse', and 'them give' is inserted. The 1629 Cambridge edition noticed that something from the Hebrew was omitted, and corrected the reading to 'let them give us pulse'.

Most difficult of all are readings which may be hidden or may look odd, and which may or may not be errors. Three similar problems of gender illustrate these. The first edition is nicknamed the 'He' Bible from its reading at Ruth 3:15, 'he went into the city'. This follows the received Hebrew text, but the problem is that the context seems to demand that it is Ruth, not Boaz, who went. Many manuscripts and various translations including the Geneva and the Bishops' Bibles make the verb feminine. Bod 1602 shows that the translators originally left 'she' unchanged, and the second edition has 'she went', hence its nickname, the 'She' Bible.[25] If the translators had followed the practice recorded in the report to the Synod of Dort of noting alternative readings in the margin, it would have been certain that 'he went' was deliberate. There is, then, a good case that 'he went' is an error. Two points go against this. First, the reading is true to the Hebrew; second, 'he went' is a hard reading and therefore difficult to take as a copying or printing error. In short, if 'he went' is an error, the fault lies with the translators not the printer. Changing it to 'she went' represents a disagreement with the translators' original decision.

In Song 2:7 the context seems to demand a masculine verb: although one might take the verse as an interpolation by the man, the woman appears to be speaking, as in the surrounding verses, giving a command about her lover: 'I charge you, O ye daughters of

[25] Pollard writes vehemently of the designations 'He' and 'She': 'all such nicknames for editions of the Bible are objectionable, and this, which suggests that the two editions form a pair, is mischievous. Their relation is not that of equality as between man and woman, but the second is derived from the first, as a child from its parents, an entirely new and distinct edition, reprinted from the original, and not a contemporaneous issue' (*Records of the English Bible*, pp. 72–3). The nicknames are pernicious in a second way: they wrongly suggest that the lineage of later editions can be determined by which of the readings they have at Ruth 3:15.

Jerusalem . . . that ye stir not up, nor awake my love, till he please'. The Hebrew has a feminine verb, 'till she please', and various translations, including the Vulgate, Geneva and the Bishops' Bible have followed this. The KJB translators decided to treat the Hebrew as an error, for they created the first edition's reading in Bod 1602. However, some copies of the first edition read 'till she please'. Because we do not know whether 'he' was corrected to 'she' or the other way round, we do not know whether the translators changed their minds and decided to be literal in spite of the context, or whether the printer, misled by the Bishops' Bible feminine reading because he was working from an annotated text like Bod 1602, incorrectly printed 'she'. 'Until she please' could have been the translators' final decision, but the presence of 'till he please' in the majority of copies and in the second and subsequent editions means that one must take this as the intended reading. In this case the translators decided the Hebrew text was wrong, and the source of the variation in some copies may go back to the nature of the copy the printer worked from.

The eagle in Job 39 is masculine in the Hebrew, but the KJB makes it feminine except in v. 30: 'her young ones also suck up blood: and where the slain are, there is he'. This apparent muddle is a vestige of the Bishops' Bible, which makes the eagle masculine throughout. The translators forgot to mark the necessary alteration to 'there is he' in Bod 1602.

Good as it is, the first edition presents several hundred problems, ranging from the simple to delicate matters of judgement. Subsequent editions dealt with them in a variety of ways that sometimes included changing the text to give what someone judged as a better translation. The first edition represents the prime moment in the making of the KJB, but it does not mark the end of the process that has been traced from Tyndale through to 1611. The text continued to grow in many small ways, and, in due course, to produce children that became new versions in their own right.

CHAPTER 6

Printing, editing and the development of a standard text

If the appearance of the KJB sometime between March 1611 and February 1612 was marked in any special way, all record is lost. We do not even know if the King was pleased. It is as if it crept into the world with no more fanfare than a reprint of the Bishops' Bible. There is no Stationers' Company record of the publication because, presumably, that was what in effect it was: a revision of the Church's official Bible. Had not Broughton carried out his determination to censure it, it might seem that the KJB fell into a vacuum.

WHAT TO CALL THE NEW BIBLE

Coverdale's Bible gave its title first in Latin, then in English, 'Biblia. The Bible', adding, 'that is, the Holy Scripture of the Old and New Testament'. The Matthew Bible omitted the Latin: it was 'The Bible, which is all the Holy Scripture'. Taverner's was 'The Most Sacred Bible, which is the Holy Scripture'. The Great Bible was, to begin with, 'The Bible in English, that is to say the content of all the Holy Scripture', then, even more prosaically, 'The Bible in English of the largest and greatest volume'. Geneva was 'The Bible and Holy Scriptures contained in the Old and New Testament' (shortened to 'The Bible' in some editions from 1578 onwards). It was the Bishops' Bible that first used the words found in the KJB, 'The Holy Bible, containing the Old Testament and the New'. Rheims-Douai also used 'The Holy Bible' in 1610. Given this similarity and, from 1568, identity of short titles, how could people refer specifically to the KJB? All the others were easy, generally referred to by author, size, or place of origin, but the KJB was difficult. Even today it has two names, the King James Bible and the Authorised Version.

For some time the commonest descriptions were variations on 'new' or 'latest'. The earliest description, February 1612, is 'a great Bible of the new translation', which neatly suggests its connection with both its official predecessors. The translator, George Abbot, now Archbishop of Canterbury, in 1619 called it 'the Bible of the new translation', and the 1620 catalogue of the Bodleian Library used the same phrase.[1] In the early days after its publication, clergy asked for 'a Bible of the latest edition' or 'of the last translation' or 'of the largest volume'.[2] From 1630 on, title pages to the concordances by John Downame, Clement Cotton and Samuel Newman referred to the KJB as 'the last translation'. In the 1640s, the KJB and Geneva were distinguished by referring to them as Bibles with or without notes.[3] Robert Gell's huge attack on the KJB, 1659, calls it 'the last English translation' (title page), and thereafter usually refers to it as 'this translation'. In 1620 it was referred to as 'the authorised Bible' in a rival translator's manuscript, and in the 1640s it was described as 'allowed as authentic by special order of King James',[4] but the *OED*'s first citation for 'Authorised Version' is from 1824. Designations connected with James can be traced back to 1627 when Cotton's concordance to the OT used 'the translation allowed by his late Majesty of Great Britain' (title page). In 1645, the first – brief and inaccurate – account of English translations to include the KJB referred to it as 'the last translation procured by King James' – and also as 'the last translation of the Bible', 'the new translation', and, uniquely, 'the reformed and revised edition of the Bible'.[5] In the 1660s, Roger Norton referred to 'the Bible of King James's translation' (above, p. 110). Such designations became common in the next century. A historian of the Bible noted in 1723 that it 'is commonly called King James's Bible'.[6] John Lewis titled the last chapter of his *History of the Several Translations of the Holy Bible* (1731), 'of the translation of the Bible into English in King James the First's reign, and since', and indexed the KJB

[1] Pollard, *Records of the English Bible*, p. 66; James, *Catalogus universalis*, p. 70.
[2] Pollard, *Records of the English Bible*, p. 66.
[3] Sparke, *Scintilla*, pp. 1, 3; Prynne, *Canterbury's Doom*, p. 515.
[4] Ambrose Ussher, epistle dedicatory to his unfinished translation, *Fourth Report of the Royal Commission on Historical Manuscripts* (1874), p. 589; E.W. [Edward Whiston], *The Life and Death of Mr Henry Jessey* (1671), p. 48.
[5] Preface, possibly by Downame, to *Annotations upon all the Books of the Old and New Testament*, fols. B3ʳ–B4ʳ.
[6] Anon., *Bibliotheca Literaria*, p. 22.

as 'Translat. of the Bible into English by . . . K. James'; elsewhere he calls it variously the 'New Translation of the Bible', 'this Royal Translation', 'our present English version' and 'our Translation'; he quotes a Roman Catholic who calls the KJB 'King James's Bible' and 'the King's Bible'.[7] A Protestant writer calls it the 'Royal Version'. 'The King James Bible' became the usual American designation, 'the Authorised Version' the usual English one.

There was another development in naming the KJB that is of real historical significance. About the time of the Restoration it became unnecessary to refer specifically to the KJB because 'the Holy Bible' had come to mean only one Bible. Newman's concordance shows the change. In 1658 it was still a 'concordance to the Bible in English according to the last translation', in 1662 it became, and remained, a 'concordance to the Holy Scriptures'. The KJB had become the only Bible in England.

THE ONLY BIBLE IN ENGLAND

In 1611 the KJB's real rival was Geneva. It had a strong base in popular preference and half a century of market dominance. Above all the people liked it for its annotations. As the KJB began to dominate the market, 'the people complained that they could not see into the sense of the Scripture so well as they formerly did by the Geneva Bibles because their spectacles of annotations were not fitted to the understanding of the new text, nor any others supplied in their stead'.[8] The desire to have the Bible explained was strong, and the KJB did not satisfy it. Yet the demand was not for continued publication of the Geneva translation itself, but for the Geneva notes or something of the sort specifically adapted to the KJB. The 1645 *Annotations* was the first of many attempts to meet this demand, another was the publication abroad not of further Geneva Bibles but of editions of the KJB with the Geneva annotations (1642 etc.).[9]

---

[7] Second edition (1739), pp. 339, 340, 347 and 336. Anthony Johnson, who beat Lewis to the honour of publishing the first book on the history of the English Bible by a year, refers to the KJB as 'this our new translation' (*An Historical Account*, p. 97).

[8] Downame (?), *Annotations*, fol. B4ʳ. Fuller later made the identical point, *Church History*, book x, p. 58.

[9] The first of these, printed in Amsterdam, added these words following the usual title: 'with most profitable annotations upon all the hard places, and other things of great importance. Which notes have never before been set forth with this new translation; but are now placed

4. 1642 KJB with Geneva annotations, printed in Amsterdam. Bible Society (Fry Collection). BSS.201.C42. Genesis 16–17.

All Bibles have a political aspect, and the Geneva notes made Geneva especially political. James had made this clear at the Hampton Court conference, and, as civil war loomed and then materialised, this aspect would have become more obvious to the Bishops and the court. There was reason for the Bishops to promote the KJB and attempt to suppress Geneva. The man chiefly reponsible for this was Archbishop William Laud, even though he had used it himself until the late 1620s.[10] In his trial (1644), he was clear about the political motive. He cited James I's objections and observed 'that now of late these notes were more commonly used to ill purposes than formerly, and that that was the cause why the High Commission was more careful and strict against them than before'.[11]

The other reason for the slow demise of Geneva was commercial. Printing the Church's Bible was part of the King's Printer's monopoly. Real competition came from imported Geneva Bibles. At Laud's trial there was a report that because the KJB was 'most vendible', the King's Printer forbore to print Geneva Bibles for 'private lucre, not by virtue of any public restraint, [and so] they were usually imported from beyond the seas'.[12] 'Most vendible' probably means most profitable to Robert Barker, who had a very substantial investment in the KJB to recoup. Laud's view was that

by the numerous coming over of [Geneva] Bibles . . . from Amsterdam, there was a great and a just fear conceived that by little and little printing would quite be carried out of the kingdom. For the books which came thence were better print, better bound, better paper, and for all the charges of bringing, sold better cheap. And would any man buy a worse Bible dearer, that might have a better more cheap? And to preserve printing here at home . . . was the cause of stricter looking to those Bibles.[13]

in due order with great care and industry'. It gave the KJB translators' preface and chapter summaries, and the Geneva Bible's tables of proper names and of 'the principal things that are contained in the Bible', its poem 'of the incomparable treasure of the Holy Scriptures', arguments and notes, but omitted the diagrams (and the Apocrypha).

[10] Norton, *History of the English Bible as Literature*, pp. 104–5.
[11] Laud, *Works*, vol. IV, p. 262.   [12] Prynne, *Canterbury's Doom*, p. 515.
[13] Laud, *Works*, vol. IV, p. 263. An opposite, somewhat obscure account of imported Bibles is given by Fuller. He describes Bibles imported from Amsterdam and Edinburgh about 1640 'as being of bad paper, worse print, little margin', and having 'many most abominable errata'. These, he says, were complained about 'as giving great advantage to the papists' (*Church History*, book XI, section III, p. 29). The reader may choose betwen his account and

The puritan Michael Sparke, a London bookseller and importer of Bibles in defiance of the monopoly, publisher too of Laud's opponent William Prynne, gave an identical picture in his attack on printing monopolies, *Scintilla*. He documented price rises, noted how much cheaper the imported Bibles were, and charged the King's Printer with commercial exploitation of his monopoly. Like Laud, he writes in several places of the 'better paper and print' of the imports. It is ironic, then, that the KJB's triumph over its rival came about in part because it was an inferior production: in fair competition it would probably have lost, but its supporters had foul means at their disposal.

What is most significant in these arguments is that there is nothing in them to suggest that the triumph of the KJB owed anything to its relative merits as a translation. The question seems not to have occurred to Laud or his opponents. It was not the KJB's merit as a translation or its attractiveness as a book that led to it becoming the only Bible in England. Quite simply, after 1644, to buy a new English Bible meant buying a KJB. There was, fleetingly, only one alternative, Theodore Haak's 1657 translation of *The Dutch Annotations upon the Whole Bible*. Since this buried its text within the very extensive notes, it was unreadable as a translation, and belongs more to the history of commentaries in English. It was never reprinted. There were no other new translations until Daniel Mace's diglot NT of 1729 heralded the arrival of alternative versions, mostly of the NT. By this time the KJB was absolutely established as *the* Bible.

PRINTING THROUGH TO 1800

Until 1629 printing of the KJB was entirely carried out by the King's Printer. He had the monopoly for printing official Bibles, the Bishops' Bible and the KJB, Prayer Books, and some official documents.[14] Robert Barker, King's Printer in the early years of the KJB, also held the monopoly for printing the Geneva Bible in England.[15] His

that of two adversaries immediately concerned with the issue. Judgement of the Bibles of this time, in terms of their printing qualities, would be a complex matter, and Laud, Sparke and Fuller's arguments are all shaped by other interests.

14 Handover gives a history of the office of King's Printer and the travails and rewards of printing the Bible in chapter 3, 'The Bible Patent', *Printing in London*.

15 Barnard, 'Financing of the Authorized Version', p. 29.

position should have been lucrative, though the Bible could be more of a burden than a bounty, and he was, perhaps unavoidably, a poor businessman. The KJB involved him in costs of at least £3,500,[16] and folio Bibles were (and remained) especially expensive to produce and slow to give a return on the investment. Barker raised this money by selling stock at wholesale rates to, and perhaps also borrowing from, two men who became his partners and also his legal adversaries, possibly even his saboteurs,[17] Bonham Norton and John Bill. Litigation, substantial fines, costs and imprisonment dogged them all for the rest of their lives, and titular and effective tenure of the office of King's Printer passed between them as their fortunes varied.[18]

Given such indebtedness and strife, it is no wonder that the early printing history of the KJB is complex and obscure. Barker worked his men hard, apparently trying to flood the market. Between 1611 and 1613 they set the whole KJB text thirteen times, the KJB NT twice, four Geneva Bibles, two or three Geneva NTs and a Bishops' Bible NT. This is an extraordinary amount of work, especially as each edition or reprint involved a complete resetting of the text. The immediate demand from churches for folio Bibles was probably fulfilled, and something had been offered to most other parts of the market, quartos in both black-letter and roman type, including one NT, octavos in roman type and a duodecimo roman type NT.

Two omissions from the octavos are worth noting. 'Appointed to be read in churches' is missing from the title pages, presumably because such small formats were for private reading only. The translators' preface is omitted as an economy measure; as the century went on it became rarer and rarer, even beginning to disappear from folios (it is not found in Oxford folios).

With so much Bible-printing on hand, the highest standards of textual accuracy were hardly likely to be maintained. Barker used the common practice of page-for-page resetting: in each of his formats, every verso page ended at the same point. This allowed for simultaneous working on different parts of the text, either within one printing

---

[16] Ball, *A Brief Treatise*, p. 27.
[17] The omission of 'not' from the seventh commandment (Exod. 20:14) in the 'wicked' Bible of 1631 was probably sabotage on Norton's behalf.
[18] For this complex story, see Plomer, 'The King's Printing House', and Handover, *Printing in London*, pp. 81–5. Barnard corrects Plomer's views and adds to the earlier part of the story.

house or spread round several, greatly speeding production.[19] The various compositors worked from several copies of an edition in the same format, and it is likely that there was little checking of the work against a single master copy. Page-for-page printing also allowed sheets from one printing to be mixed with sheets from another, so making most economical use of any over-supply of particular sheets, and creating variation within the editions. This over-supply was caused by another of Barker's economies, his practice of selling books for quick cash before they were fully printed (and so missing out on the better prices he might have achieved by waiting until a printing was completed).[20]

This is not to say that the printing was wildly inaccurate, especially by comparison with some of the printing from later in the century, but there were mistakes, and a variety of readings developed along with the variety created by deliberate changes. One of the mistakes was probably deliberate, and it suggests workplace tension inevitable under a driving master: instead of 'princes have persecuted me without a cause' (Ps. 119:161), some copies of the first octavo of 1612 read 'printers have persecuted me without a cause'. Amusing variations include 'is there no blame in Gilead' (Jer. 8:22, 1613 quarto), and 'Darius the sting' (1 Esdras 4:47, 1612 quarto).

Development of the KJB text under Barker's aegis was limited. The smaller formats, each with its own peculiarities, were textual dead-ends, dying with their final printing.[21] The folios, for better and worse, made lasting changes. Mistakes in the first edition were corrected, readings that looked like – but probably were not – mistakes changed, and new mistakes were made. The second edition (the 'She' Bible), a page-for-page reprint of the first, was probably begun in 1611, the date on the NT title page, and some copies finished quite quickly. But then Judges 13 to Ezekiel 20 was destroyed in some way and had to be reset. Most copies have 1613 on the title page, and that is generally taken as the edition's date. Besides correcting obvious typographical errors, it created about thirty readings, some of them really spelling variations, that survive in standard KJBs. A few such as 'hooks' instead

---

[19] Sparke reports six printing houses being put to work by the King's Printer in 1629, producing a folio Bible in 1629 'on an instant' (*Scintilla*, p. 1).
[20] Plomer, 'The King's Printing House', p. 362; Norton, *Textual History*, p. 64.
[21] Norton, *Textual History*, p. 73.

of 'hoops' at Exodus 38:11 coincide with annotations in Bod 1602 and suggest that the translators' work was sometimes consulted; most are sensible corrections that did not need such consultation. Two of the readings, Ruth 3:15 and 'hewed' at Hosea 6:5, begin the process of introducing readings that go against the judgement of the translators. It also produced a crop of typographical errors, beginning with 'OE THE BIBLE' and 'Chkist' in the dedication.

Barker produced another folio in 1613 using smaller black letter and so cutting down the number of leaves needed from 732 to 508 and providing a cheaper alternative for churches. It played a minor role in the history of the text, introducing four readings that became standard, one of which, Matt. 6:3, goes against the evidence of Bod 1602. It also introduced a reading still occasionally found, 'fleshly' for 'fleshy' (2 Cor. 3:3). Its greatest interest lies in what it shows of Barker's (or his workers') attitude to the text. It used the first and second editions as copy, following one for long stretches, then moving to the other, and occasionally mixing the two. If two compositors or printing houses were used in the typesetting, one set Genesis to Judges from the first edition while the other set Ruth to 1 Kings from the second, and so on. Or it may be that a single compositor worked sometimes from the first edition, sometimes from the second. Either way, it seems that Barker's men had no particular sense of difference between the two editions. For them, one folio was as good as another.

A roman type small folio was printed in 1616 using the first edition as copy but adding a sprinkling of second edition readings. It brought in some twenty new readings, some of which involve a degree of scholarship and seem to draw particularly on older translations. Only a few of these were picked up in subsequent editions from the King's Printer, but the makers of the Cambridge edition of 1629 consulted this folio and so gave currency to some of its readings. As far as the King's Printer was concerned, the text became settled in 1617 in the third of the large folio editions. It mixed first and second edition readings, supplemented with a few new readings, and is a far from perfect form of the text.

Cambridge had printed a Geneva Bible and NT in the early 1590s. In the 1620s it sought to print the KJB, and finally had its original privilege from Henry VIII confirmed in 1628. The resulting Bibles of 1629 and 1638 were, after the first edition, the two most important folios in the development of the text. As noted above (p. 77), two of the original translators, Bois and Samuel Ward, as well as Joseph Mede and Thomas Goad, are said to have taken part in the work on the 1638 edition; though this report is uncertain, it is possible that they were also involved with the 1629 edition. Men of their calibre were needed.

This first Cambridge edition made, by my count, 356 changes to readings and spellings of names which became standard, and the 1638 edition a further 235. It also restored some fifty-nine variants from the first KJB. This is a sizeable number, more than one in every second chapter. It developed the cross-references and the italics, something that could only be done through examination of the text in the light of the Hebrew and the Greek. Painstaking scholarly care is the hallmark of these Cambridge editions. Whereas the King's Printer's editions had mostly dealt with typographical errors, they focussed on inaccuracies of translation.

Characteristic of this care is the change to 1 Maccabees 5:13. The 1629 editors noticed and corrected an error of punctuation, so saving the lives of wives and children. The 1611 text reads:

Yea all our brethren that were in the places of Tobie are put to death, their wives and their children; also they have carried away captives, and borne away their stuff.

This punctuation could not have been the creation of the translators because the Greek is unambiguous: the wives and children did not die. In all likelihood the KJB's manuscript change was unpunctuated, like most of the annotations in Bod 1602, and the printer made an incorrect decision as to how to punctuate it, perhaps not even noticing that the text was capable of two meanings. Reading the translation against the Greek, the 1629 editors saw the problem and, by changing the punctuation, made the text true to the Greek:

Yea all our brethren that were in the places of Tobie are put to death: their wives and their children also they have carried away captives, and borne away their stuff.

The 1629 edition's commonest changes are to number, and they do not always agree with the translators' original decisions. 1 Samuel 28:7 reads this way in 1611:

Then said Saul unto his servants, Seek me a woman that hath a familiar spirit, that I may go to her and inquire of her. And his servant said to him, Behold, there is a woman that hath a familiar spirit at Endor.

1629 restored the 1602 Bishops' Bible reading at the beginning of the second sentence, 'and his servants said'. This is literally what the Hebrew gives, but the translators deleted the 's' in Bod 1602, no doubt thinking that the servants did not reply in chorus. Literal fidelity is the 1629 editors' tendency; probably not knowing the translators' reasoning, they inserted the translation that, in their judgement, 1611 should have given. Such changes are the beginning of revision of the KJB towards a 'better' translation.

The work with names was of a similar sort. Often it made no difference to pronunciation but improved the fidelity to, usually, the Hebrew. 1611 had amended the Bishops' Bibles 'Kenezites' to 'Kenizites' (Gen. 15:19), but 1629 observed that the Hebrew doubled one of the letters, so gave the still more accurate 'Kenizzites'. 1638 made further changes of this sort. Sometimes pronunciation was involved. 1611 changed from 'Olofernes' to 'Holofernes' in Judith 3. 1629 followed the second edition in regularising to the Greek form, 'Olofernes', then 1638, following the spirit of instruction 2 to the translators, gave the commonly used form, 'Holofernes'.

Very occasionally there was some minor rewriting, 'I said' becoming 'said I' (Isa. 6:8), and, conversely, 'saw I' becoming 'I saw' (2 Esdras 13:12). One verse was rewritten. 1611's rendering of Job 4:6 comes straight from a Bod 1602 annotation, following the Hebrew words without making sense: 'is not this thy fear, thy confidence; the uprightness of thy ways and thy hope?' 1629 tweaked this into sense: 'is not thy fear, thy confidence; and the uprightness of thy ways, thy hope?', and 1638 had another go, creating the standard KJB reading, 'is not this thy fear, thy confidence, thy hope, and the uprightness of thy ways?'

The 1629 edition was also a significant step forward in the spelling of the Bible. Superfluous 'e's begin to be omitted, and other modern – and nearly always shorter – spellings appear. Coupled with the use of roman type, including 'v' and 'j', this makes the text look much more modern. Short forms were, of course, economical for a printer.

Sometimes, though, inconsistent compositorial practices produce inconsistent, antiquated results, notably where 'vv' is used instead of 'w' at the beginning of a word. 1638 made a few further changes, and introduced a very few apostrophes.

Just how much minute innovation went into the 1629 edition is apparent if it is compared with the specimen page from 1611, Genesis 16–17. There are seventy-four differences (including two which are typographical errors in 1629), most of them variations of spelling. Seven uses of italics are introduced, and there are nine changes of punctuation, seven of them semicolons. Names of all books in the marginal references are capitalised. 'Thy eyes' (16:6m) becomes 'thine eyes'.

Punctilious refinement of the text was matched by the accuracy and general quality of the printing in both editions. In these respects they were far better than anything the King's Printer produced, if not absolutely perfect. 1638's most famous mistake changed a verse read in relation to the appointment of deacons, Acts 6:3, from 'look ye out among you seven men of honest report...whom we may appoint' to 'whom ye may appoint', which so suited the puritans that it was later supposed to have been the result of bribery of £1,000 or even £1,500.[22] The 1638 edition became the standard text for over 100 years. A 1645 Dutch edition advertised itself on its title page as printed 'according to the copy printed by Roger Daniel, printer to the University of Cambridge'; 'according to the copy' is in especially tiny type on the NT title page, making it appear that the edition itself is printed by Daniel.[23] William Bentley, who challenged the monopoly-holders with several editions from 1646 on, printed a text 'corrected by the Cambridge Bible only'.[24]

Some critics still looked for a definitive text while printers, including the Universities, continued to produce Bibles with sometimes more than their fair share of errors at prices that were complained of. William Kilburne, enemy to the burgeoning collection of printing errors, unsuccessfully campaigned for the establishment of a master copy to which all editions could be referred. He proposed

---

[22] Herbert, *Historical Catalogue*, 520; McKitterick, *A History*, vol. I, pp. 326–7.
[23] Herbert, *Historical Catalogue*, 584.   [24] Anon., 'The case of the printery at Finsbury'.

Printing through to 1800   145

Abrams vision.   Chap.xv.xvi.xvii.   Hagar fleeth from Sarai.

CHAP. XV.

1 *God encourageth Abram.* 2 *Abram complaineth for want of an heire.* 4 *God promiseth him a sonne, and a multiplying of his seed.* 6 *Abram is justified by faith,* 7 *Canaan is promised againe, and confirmed by a signe,* 12 *and a vision.*

After these things the word of the LORD came unto Abram in a vision, saying, Feare not, Abram: I am thy shield, *and* thy exceeding * great reward.

2 And Abram said, Lord GOD, what wilt thou give me, seeing I go childlesse, and the steward of my house is this Eliezer of Damascus?

3 And Abram said, Behold, to me thou hast given no seed: and lo, one born in my house is mine heire.

4 And behold, the word of the LORD *came* unto him, saying, This shall not be thine heire, but he that shall come forth out of thine own bowels shall be thine heire.

5 And he brought him forth abroad, and said, Look now toward heaven, and tell the starres, if thou be able to number them: and he said unto him, * So shall thy seed be.

6 And he * beleeved in the LORD; and he counted it to him for righteousnesse.

7 And he said unto him, I am the LORD that brought thee out of Ur of the Chaldees, to give thee this land to inherit it.

8 And he said, Lord GOD, whereby shall I know that I shall inherit it?

9 And he said unto him, Take me an heifer of three yeares old, and a she-goat of three yeares old, and a ramme of three yeares old, and a turtle-dove, and a young pigeon.

10 And he took unto him all these, and divided them in the midst, and laid each piece one against another: but the birds divided he not.

11 And when the fowls came down upon the carcases, Abram drove them away.

12 And when the sunne was going down, a deep sleep fell upon Abram; and lo, an horrour of great darknesse fell upon him.

13 And he said unto Abram, Know of a suretie * that thy seed shall be a stranger in a land *that* is not theirs, and shall serve them, and they shall afflict them foure hundred yeares.

14 And also that nation whom they shall serve, will I judge: and afterward shall they come out with great substance.

15 And thou shalt go to thy fathers in peace; thou shalt be buried in a good old age.

16 But in the fourth generation they shall come hither again: for the iniquitie of the Amorites is not yet full.

17 And it came to passe, that when the sunne went down and it was dark, behold a smoking furnace, and † a burning lamp that passed between those pieces.

18 In that same day the LORD made a covenant with Abram, saying, *Unto thy seed have I given this land, from the river of Egypt unto the great river the river Euphrates:

19 The Kenites, and the Kenizzites, and the Kadmonites,

20 And the Hittites, and the Perizzites, and the Rephaims,

21 And the Amorites, and the Canaanites, and the Girgashites, and the Jebusites.

CHAP. XVI

1 *Sarai being barren giveth Hagar to Abram.* 6 *Hagar being afflicted for despising her mistresse, runneth away.* 9 *An angel sendeth her back to submit her selfe,* 11 *and telleth her of her childe.* 15 *Ishmael is born.*

Now Sarai Abrams wife bare him no children: and she had an handmaid an Egyptian, whose name *was* Hagar.

2 And Sarai said unto Abram, Behold now, the LORD hath restrained me from bearing: I pray thee go in unto my maid; it may be that I may † obtain children by her: and Abram hearkened to the voice of Sarai.

3 And Sarai Abrams wife took Hagar her maid, the Egyptian, after Abram had dwelt ten yeares in the land of Canaan, and gave her to her husband Abram to be his wife.

4 ¶ And he went in unto Hagar, and she conceived: And when she saw that she had conceived, her mistresse was despised in her eyes.

5 And Sarai said unto Abram, My wrong *be* upon thee: I have given my maid into thy bosome; and when she saw that she had conceived, I was despised in her eyes: the LORD judge between me and thee.

6 But Abram said unto Sarai, Behold, thy maid *is* in thy hand; do to her as it pleaseth thee. And when Sarai † dealt hardly with her, she fled from her face.

7 ¶ And the angel of the LORD found her by a fountain of water in the wildernesse, by the fountain in the way to Shur.

8 An he said, Hagar, Sarais maid, whence camest thou? and whither wilt thou go? And she said, I flee from the face of my mistresse Sarai.

9 And the angel of the LORD said unto her, Return to thy mistresse, and submit thy self under her hands.

10 And the angel of the LORD said unto her, I will multiply thy seed exceedingly, that it shall not be numbred for multitude.

11 And the angel of the LORD said unto her, Behold, thou *art* with childe, and shalt beare a sonne, and shalt call his name Ishmael; because the LORD hath heard thy affliction.

12 And he will be a wilde man; his hand *will be* against every man, and every mans hand against him: * and he shall dwell in the presence of all his brethren.

13 And she called the name of the LORD that spake unto her, Thou Godseest me: for she said, Have I also here looked after him that seeth me?

14 Wherefore the well was called, † Beer-lahai-roi; behold, *it is* between Cadesh and Bered.

15 ¶ And Hagar bare Abram a sonne: and Abram called his sonnes name, which Hagar bare, Ishmael.

16 ¶ And Abram *was* fourescore and six yeares old, when Hagar bare Ishmael to Abram.

CHAP. XVII.

1 *God reneweth the covenant of Abram: his name is changed in token of a greater blessing.* 10 *Circumcision is instituted.* 15 *Sarai her name is changed, and she blessed.* 16 *Isaac is promised.* 23 *Abraham and Ishmael are circumcised.*

And when Abram was ninetie yeares old and nine, the LORD appeared to Abram, and said unto him, I am the Almightie God; * walk before me, and be thou ‖ perfect.

2 And I will make my covenant between me and thee, and will multiply thee exceedingly.

3 And Abram fell on his face; and God talked with him, saying,

4 As for me, behold, my covenant *is* with thee, and thou shalt be a father of † many nations:

5 Neither shall thy name any more be called Abram, but thy name shall be Abraham; * for a father of many nations have I made thee.

6 And I will make thee exceeding fruitfull, & I will make nations of thee; & kings shall come out of thee.

7 And I will establish my covenant between me, and thee, and thy seed after thee, in their generations, for an everlasting covenant; to be a God unto thee, and to thy seed after thee.

8 And I will give unto thee, and to thy seed after thee, the land † wherein thou art a stranger, all the land

Side notes:
! Psal.16.5.

* Rom.4.18.

* Rom. 4.3.
Galat.3.6.
James 2.23.

‡ Acts 7.6.

† Heb. a lamp of fire.
* Chap. 12.7.
and 13.15.
and 26.4.
Deut.34.4.

† Heb. be builded by her.

† Heb. that which is sent into mine eyes. † Heb. afflicted her.

That is, God shall heare.

* Chap. 25.18.

* Chap. 24.62
† That is, the well of him that liveth and seeth me.

* Chap. 5.22.
‖ Or, upright, or, sincere.

† Heb. multitude of nations.
* Rom.4.17.

† Heb. of thy sojourning.

that there may be a fair copy of the last translation of the Bible, engrossed either in parchment or vellum, in a full character, which may be compared with the original, by four or five ministers, and so kept in Sion College, as an authentic record: for orthography so truly and critically written, that hereafter a letter shall not be altered: that so all people, upon any doubt, may have recourse to the original, to prove whether their printed copies vary, or not.[25]

He added that he thought that 'the Bible was never better printed' than in the Cambridge 1638 edition, and he seems to have envisaged this master copy as a completion and perfection of the Cambridge editors' work. In general terms, the idea was a good one, but it had an element of unreality in it: the readings might perhaps have been fixed, but English was far from having fixed standards of spelling. Had Kilburne's proposal succeeded, the KJB might have come to us in a form that, though revised, was closer to the translators' work, probably odder in spelling, and punctuated in a way that would have been somewhat easier for modern tastes.

Kilburne was right to inveigh against the printing standards of his time. English printing in general was poor, and, in the Bible, standards of book production and textual correctness were dropping. Some editions, he thought, had as many as 20,000 errors. Among the particular errors he cites are 'found rulers in the wilderness' for 'found the mules in the wilderness' (Gen. 36:24), 'the Lord gave her corruption' instead of 'conception' (Ruth 4:13), and, arguably as serious as the omission of 'not' from the seventh commandment, 'the unrighteous shall inherit the kingdom of God' for 'shall not inherit' (1 Cor. 6:9).[26] Poor standards, it should be added, continued. W.J. Loftie nominates the Edinburgh NT of 1694 (possibly printed overseas) as the worst, with good reason: 'But while he thought on these things, behold, the Augel of the Lord apppeared unto him in a dream, saying, Joseph thou son of Davih. fear not to take unto thee Mary thy wife: for that which is couceived in her, is of the holy Ghost' (Matt. 1:20; there is no final punctuation).[27]

---

[25] Given in McKitterick, *A History*, vol. 1, p. 388. 'In full character' probably means in a large hand and without abbreviations. Sion College, a body of London Anglican priests, was founded in 1630.

[26] Norton, *Textual History*, appendix 6, lists all the errors identified by Kilburne.

[27] Loftie, *A Century of Bibles*, p. 18; Herbert, *Historical Catalogue*, 836.

The declining standards had much to do with the monopoly system that controlled printing. As Sparke showed in 1641, high prices accompanied the low quality. Church Bibles had gone from £1 10s to £2. What became the commonest format, octavo, went from 3s 4d unbound to 4s, even though the text was cramped into fewer sheets. Octavo NTs similarly were 1s instead of 10d. Duodecimo Bibles imported from Holland in 1639 were better than the King's Printer's of the same year, and at 2s each unbound, were half the price – 'pity the manufactory should be carried thither by dear selling here'. Only once was the London price cheaper: the Cambridge edition of 1629 on cost 10s unbound, and was immediately undersold by a quarto from the King's Printer for 5s.[28]

Whether or not Kilburne was right that £10,000 a year could be made,[29] the monopoly was fiercely protected and coveted. In 1642, during the Civil War, the office of King's Printer lapsed and other printers entered the market.[30] Also in 1642, the KJBs with the Geneva/Tomson/Junius annotations began to be printed. The 1642 title page for the NT states that the notes were 'placed in due order by J. C.', probably John Canne, a leading Brownist, who from 1647 provided a different set of annotations to the KJB consisting largely of cross-references which eventually contributed substantially to the KJB margin (see below, p. 164). The Company of Stationers began printing Bibles, and William Bentley, with the authority of Parliament, produced octavo editions without the Apocrypha in 1646, 1648 and 1651.[31]

One of Bentley's editions, dated 1646 but probably later, is remarkable. Chapter summaries are revised and shortened, and end '&c.'. The notes are, after the beginning of Genesis, far fewer and almost completely independent, and the cross-references are greatly expanded and also independent. The marginal material commonly expands over the foot of the page, sometimes even between chapters. It also introduced dates as they are commonly found in KJBs after 1701: Genesis 1 is 'before Christ 4004'.[32]

[28] Sparke, *Scintilla*, pp. 1–4.   [29] McKitterick, *A History*, vol. 1, p. 389.   [30] Ibid., p. 319.
[31] Herbert, *Historical Catalogue*, 591, 607; Kilburne, *Dangerous Errors*, p. 6, adds 1651 etc.
[32] 1646 anticipates the publication of James Ussher's *Annales veteris testamenti* (1650), commonly held to be the source of the dates later found in the KJB. Bentley probably did use Ussher. The false date on the title page was probably an attempt to avoid harrassment by Field and Hills under legislation passed in 1649.

In 1648, John Field, who was to be the dominant figure in Bible printing for twenty years, issued his first Bible. As seen earlier (above, p. 109), he established his position as the new monopolist by his purchase of the translators' manuscript. In March 1656, with his partner Henry Hills, he registered his copyright with Oliver Cromwell's authority.[33] Bribery, strongarm tactics such as sending soldiers to seize Bentley's work on a New Testament in 1656, and his election in 1655 as 'Printer to the Uneversete of Cambrig'[34] all entrenched his power. With the Restoration, Bill and Barker's heirs returned as King's Printer, but Field and Hills bought off competition from Oxford for £80 a year, and Field remained the dominant figure in spite of the deservedly low reputation of his previous work.[35]

Save for two Amsterdam KJBs with Geneva notes, there had been no folio KJBs since the last edition in the original format in 1640. Field's ambition as one of the Cambridge printers was to produce a folio; he achieved this with such grandeur and size in 1659 that his reputation was considerably improved. An ambitious and enterprising publisher, John Ogilby took over most of the edition and gave it illustrations and a new title page. This 1660 version marked the beginning of illustrated Bibles for the high end of the market – or even the highest end: it was dedicated, and probably presented to Charles II, and Ogilby first presented a copy to the House of Commons, then extracted a payment of £50 for it.[36] It had one of the more extraordinary title pages ever seen on a KJB; though it represents Solomon enthroned (see 1 Kings 10:18–20), it is blatantly and flatteringly royalist, for it is difficult not to see the long-haired king as Charles II, and the twelve small lions as twelve apostolic spaniels. The contrast with Boel's 1611 original is stunning. Within, there are 100 double-page 'chorographical sculps by J[ohn] Ogilby', a very odd phrase for elaborate engravings, generally Dutch in origin, based on the works of artists such as Rubens (but the phrase does suggest two of Ogilby's other careers, dancing master and map-maker). Ogilby's investment in this Bible and other printing ventures was slow to bring in returns; one of his expedients to move it was to make it the star

[33] McKitterick, *A History*, vol. 1, p. 323.
[34] Title page of one of his 1664 Bibles, Herbert, *Historical Catalogue*, 686.
[35] McKitterick, *A History*, vol. 1, p. 326.
[36] Van Eerde, *John Ogilby and the Taste of his Times*, p. 46.

prize, worth £25, in a number of lotteries.[37] This seems a sad fate for so ambitious a project, but perhaps no more than it deserved for making the Bible at once a pulpit Bible and what we would now call a coffee-table book.

This was not the first illustrated KJB. A set of plates, also of Dutch origin, that first appeared in some copies of the first KJB printed in Scotland caused controversy. This 1633 Scottish Bible, an octavo by the newly appointed King's Printer for Scotland, Robert Young, was probably connected with the coronation of Charles I in Edinburgh. A letter of 1638 describes the plates as 'such abominable pictures that horrible impiety stares through them'.[38] Sparke, in a second *Scintilla*, saw them as part of a Popish plot, and it was one of the charges against Archbishop Laud that he approved of these 'Romanish images', and wanted them generally circulated as part of his attempt 'to seduce the people to popery and idolatry'.[39]

Illustrations, as an optional extra, gradually made their way into seventeenth-century Bibles for the middle of the market. A 1680 Bill and Barker octavo sometimes included, with a separate title page, 'The History of the Old and New Testament in Cuts'; in the NT there are 120 full-page cuts, in the OT fifty-three cuts, four pictures to a page, together with three full-page royalist cuts, the return of Charles II illustrating 2 Sam. 22:44, 51, the gunpowder plot (Pss. 9:16, 10:14), and the murder of Charles I (Ps. 31:13).[40]

Non-conformists objected to the Apocrypha in the Bible (and no doubt printers had no objection to omitting it);[41] it was first omitted from editions of English Bibles (as opposed to omission from binding at the request of the purchaser) in a Dutch-printed Geneva Bible of 1640. Prefaced to this is a translation of the decision of the Synod of Dort which argues in detail the non-canonical and uninspired nature of the Apocrypha. Bentley omitted the Apocrypha in 1646, and by 1673 editions of the KJB were being issued that gave the Apocrypha

---

[37] McKitterick, *A History*, vol. 1, pp. 327–8. A curiosity of the Cambridge University Library copy is that it has, at the beginning of Psalms, a single-page engraving of George I, dated 1715.

[38] Quoted in Herbert, *Historical Catalogue*, 475.

[39] Prynne, *Canterbury's Doom*, pp. 109–10.   [40] Herbert, *Historical Catalogue*, 755.

[41] Gell, who thought many of the KJB's marginal readings better than those in the text, complained that 'those marginal notes have been left out, together with the Apocrypha, to make the Bible portable and fit for the pocket' (fol. c4[v]).

6. Field and Ogilby's 1660 folio, title page. Cambridge University Library.

7. Cuts from Bill and Barker's octavo, 1680, with 'The History of the Old and New Testaments in Cuts'. Bible Society: BSS.201.C80.2. The first is located opposite the beginning of Genesis. The second is opposite 2 Samuel 22–23.

in the list of contents but foliated the pages without reference to the Apocrypha and are not found including it.

Cambridge declined then disappeared as a printer and publisher of Bibles, its last edition for more than half a century appearing in 1683. London, Scotland and Holland continued strong, and Oxford began its rise with quartos in 1675 and 1679. John Fell, Bishop of Oxford, Vice-Chancellor of the University and the driving force behind what became Oxford University Press, had proposed that Oxford should produce a newly annotated edition that might have 'advantages beyond any other design that we can think of', but his scheme probably failed because it was impractical.[42] Consequently the early Oxford Bibles offered little that was distinctive. Besides the re-introduction of dates in the 1679 edition, given as numbers in the margin beginning from zero, there was slightly odd spelling. Sometimes the 1675 edition uses 1611 spellings that had become generally disused in Bibles such as 'daies', sometimes innovations are introduced such as these from Matthew 4–5, 'temter', 'judg', 'bin' (for 'been') and 'neighbor'. These produced complaints such as this from Humphrey Prideaux: 'I must confess, since Mr Dean [Fell] hath taken the liberty of inventing a new way of spelling and using it therein, which I think will confound and alter the analogy of the English tongue, that I do not at all approve thereof'.[43] The innovations were unsuccessful: most were removed in the 1679 edition.

A significant development happened at this time. The 1679 edition was printed for four London booksellers who had been involved in importing cheaper and often better-printed Bibles from Holland. The Stationers' Company (and, within it, the King's Printer) had become more effective in blocking the often better-printed Bibles from Holland, seriously affecting the business of four London booksellers. The most famous of them, Thomas Guy, founder of Guy's Hospital in London, and a dissenter by background, was particularly keen to go on selling Bibles, so he and the three others contracted with Oxford in 1678 to create what became the Oxford Bible Press, an entity long distinct from the academic press at Oxford, and, especially in the nineteenth century, both larger and more profitable. Initially its work was to produce large numbers of cheap Bibles, thereby arousing

---

[42] Carter, *A History of Oxford University Press*, pp. 86–7.   [43] Quoted in ibid., p. 72.

years of costly legal opposition, underselling and disruption from the Kings' Printers.[44] Such competition and increase in supply led to a substantial fall in the price of Bibles: in a memorandum written in 1684, Fell noted that folios had fallen from £6 to £1 10s, and that the smallest formats were now sold at 1s 4d. Bulk purchases for charity contributed to this fall.[45]

In 1699 the Church of England Convocation asked William Lloyd (soon to be Bishop of Worcester) to produce an improved KJB, but little in his 1701 folio was new except for the reintroduction of dates as they had been given in Bentley's '1646' Bible, calculated *Anno Domini*.

One man dominated printing of the KJB in the first half of the eighteenth century, John Baskett. Between 1710 and 1712 he acquired successively part, then all of the office of Queen's Printer (as it was in 1710), part of the office of Queen's Printer in Scotland, and a monopoly on printing at Oxford. He survived bankruptcy and the destruction by fire of his Oxford printing office to leave a re-established empire to his children (they sold the office of King's Printer to Charles Eyre for £10,000, whence it came to be held by Eyre and Spottiswoode, who were taken over by Cambridge University Press, the present holders of what is now only a nominal office).[46] Baskett's 1717 Oxford folio is one of the most famous KJBs of the century, grandiose to a fault (there was a complaint that a crane was needed to lift it),[47] and eloquent of the continuing failure to attend to the text itself. Four years before the publication, Arthur Charlett described the work in progress:

We are here printing a most magnificent English Bible, some very few copies will be in vellum for a present to the Queen and my Lord Treasurer. You know Dr Wallis and Dr Gregory pronounced Mr Denison absolutely the best corrector they ever met with. If this work have not the advantage of his nice eye at least in giving the first directions, and settling the distances of lines and words and the great art in a beautiful and uniform division of syllables, with several other minute regulations, invisible to vulgar eyes, the work will want of its proposed splendour ... We shall throw out all

[44] *ODNB* Guy; Carter, *A History of Oxford University Press*, pp. xxviii–xxix, and chapter 8.
[45] Carter, *A History of Oxford University Press*, p. 98.
[46] *ODNB* Baskett; Herbert, *Historical Catalogue*, 910, 1219.
[47] Carter, *A History of Oxford University Press*, p. 172.

the vast numbers of references added by some late reformers and improvers of the Bible, reserving only those of the original translators themselves, as believing they who were at the pains of the version had good reasons for their references, though I fear by this omission we may incur the censure of some Right Reverends, but we have been so often and so long under them as to be almost insensible of their weight.[48]

'Proposed splendour' is the point: all the work described is to achieve perfection of typography. The work of the 'corrector' is really page design and inspection of the type: this is to be a printer's Bible – as such its only rival in this century was John Baskerville's Cambridge folio of 1763. The decision to revert to the 1611 margin is sensible – as is the fear about the response – but there appears to be no thought about the text.

Yet this Bible was – in the inevitable pun – 'a Baskettful of errors': its nickname, the 'Vinegar Bible', comes from 'the parable of the vinegar' instead of the 'the parable of the vineyard' in the header to Luke 20. Charlett was wrong not to anticipate that these would be what the 'Right Reverends' would object to: textual accuracy did matter to some Bible-purchasers. William Lowth wrote to him from Winchester:

I am desired by some of my brethren here to acquaint you that the great Church Bible... which they lately bought for the use of our Cathedral is very falsely printed. In the two lessons upon St Peter's Day we found two considerable mistakes... Finding two such faults in two successive chapters, we have reason to fear that the whole edition is faulty, and several others have been observed by those of our quire who read the daily lessons. One might expect, besides the dishonour done to religion by such careless editions of the Bible, the printer should have a little consulted his own reputation and the interest he has in the sale of the book, which we shall take all occasions to let the world know how unfit it is for public use.[49]

In this way, as Carter observes, 'fame has fastened on the errors: what might have been one of the glories of English printing is one of its curiosities'. It did not sell well, and the unbound price dropped from £4 4s to £3 5s in 1728; Carter thought it 'would not be worth much

---

[48] Quoted in ibid., p. 170.
[49] Quoted in ibid., p. 171. The two readings given were the omission of 'all' from 'and all the prophets' (Acts 3:24; Lowth himself misquotes the text), and 'when they had that' for 'when they heard that' (Acts 4:24).

more now',[50] but such grand curiosities of Bible printing now fetch a high price from collectors.

Lowth went on to make the old complaint against monopoly pricing:

And I must further beg leave to take notice to you that Mr Baskett, by reason of his interest in the King's and the University Printing House, has got the monopoly of Bibles, and so has of late raised the common Bibles that used to be for 4s to 4s 6d, and hereby has laid a vast tax upon the common people, as well as upon those that give away Bibles in charity.

Such complaints were effective. The Scottish General Assembly of 1717 issued instructions 'to get printing, vending and importing of the incorrect copies of the Holy Scriptures stopped and prevented', and in England a royal order of 1724 mandated:

I. That all Bibles printed by them [the patentees, i.e. Baskett] hereafter shall be printed upon as good paper at least as the specimens they had exhibited.

II. That they forthwith deliver *four* copies of the said specimens to be deposited and kept in the two secretaries' offices and in the Public Registries of the Archbishop of Canterbury and Bishop of London, to the end recourse may be had to them.

III. That they shall employ such correctors of the press, and allow them such salaries as shall be approved from time to time by the Archbishop of Canterbury and Bishop of London for the time being.

IV. That the said patentees for printing Bibles, etc., do print in the title-page of each book the exact price at which such book is by them to be sold to the booksellers.[51]

Errors did not disappear (in 1793 the Synod of Glasgow University complained of imperfect printing and poor paper producing almost illegible results),[52] but prices were printed on some title pages, beginning with Baskett's 1725 London octavo, which was 'price six shillings unbound', and his Oxford quarto of the same year, 'price 9s unbound'. Standard unbound prices settled at 2s for duodecimo, 6s (sometimes 3s) for octavos and 9s for quartos.

---

[50] Ibid., p. 172.
[51] Herbert, *Historical Catalogue*, 959, quoted in Lewis, *History of the Several Translations*, p. 351.
[52] Herbert, *Historical Catalogue*, 1383.

The major players in the story so far have been the King's Printers (including those in Scotland), the two Universities, the Stationers' Company and the Dutch printers, but Bible printing was spreading elsewhere. In 1714 Aaron Rhames, for William Binauld and Eliphal Dobson, printed the first extant Irish KJB, a folio, and he printed at least two other editions in smaller formats. Regular printing – about one edition every three years – in Ireland began in 1739, this time from the King's Printer in Ireland, the Edinburgh-born Dublin bookseller and printer, George Grierson. Most eighteenth-century Irish KJBs are the work of Grierson and his heirs. America, meanwhile, depended on imported Bibles, Genevas as well as KJBs, until 1777. There may have been American printings in the middle of the century, and there were several unsuccessful proposals for annotated editions before independence, but the first extant American printing is Robert Aitken's duodecimo NT, and the first complete Bible his 1782 duodecimo. There were a dozen NTs in the war period, then, in the last two decades of the century, twenty-four Bibles and forty-four NTs.

Printing was also spreading within England. Attempts to avoid the monopoly became commoner in the eighteenth century. From the time of Henry Hammond's *A Paraphrase and Annotations upon all the Books of the New Testament* (1653), some Bible paraphrases and annotations had included the KJB text. Hammond and some of his successors such as Richard Baxter (1685), Samuel Clark (1701, continued by Thomas Pyle), Daniel Whitby (1702), John Guyse (1739) and Philip Doddridge (1739) were producing substantial new work of which the KJB was a part, and this may have contributed to the view that annotated Bibles were not an infringement of the monopoly, which was held to be for the printing of the text only. In other hands such as J.W. Pasham's in his *Holy Bible... with Notes* (1776), token lines of annotation at the bottom of a page – with a goodly space between them and the text – became an excuse for flouting the monopoly, and such Bibles are more commonly found with the page cut off above the notes.

Family Bibles developed out of these commentaries (sometimes there is no way to tell them apart other than the use of 'family' on the title page). Baxter's NT paraphrase was 'by plainness and brevity fitted to the use of religious families in their daily reading of the Scriptures', and aimed at the development 'of family religion, and the Christian education of youth' (title, preface), Clark's title declared his work to be 'very useful for families', and Guyse's *Practical Expositor* was 'for the use of the family and closet'. The short title of Doddridge's highly popular work was *The Family Expositor*. The first Bible to style itself a family Bible was S. Smith's *The Complete History of the Old and New Testament: or, a Family Bible* (1735). Such Bibles tapped a market that the King's Printers and the Universities had scarcely touched. Often they were published in parts, a move that was economical for the printer since it required much less capital and produced an immediate return, and that made a large-scale Bible affordable to a new section of the population. A folio in sixty 6d parts, as advertised by William Rider in 1762, amounted to £1 10s, less than the cost of most folios from the monopolists, and offering considerably more in the way of annotation and illustrations – the latter not being an extra cost. *The Universal Family Bible: or Christian's Divine Library* (?1773) – to which Henry Southwell allowed his name to be attached for 100 guineas but which was the work of a hack-writer, Robert Sanders, who was paid £1 5s per sheet – was sold in 100 folio numbers, again 6d each, and the purchaser had the option of the whole, 'elegantly bound in calf and lettered', for £2 18s.[53] Nevertheless, such publications were not always profitable. One of the most highly reputed, Thomas Scott's *The Holy Bible... with original notes and practical observations* (1788–92), was a financial disaster. Thomas Bellamy contracted Scott to produce 100 weekly issues, payment a guinea each, borrowed money from him and went bankrupt, leaving Scott in debt and having to finance the project after the fifteenth issue. The projected 100 issues became 174, and Scott was not rescued from a tangle of litigation and debt until 1813.[54]

About forty different family Bibles appeared in the eighteenth century, three-quarters of them between 1760 and 1790. The majority were folios, most of the rest quartos, and there was a certain sameness to them which bespeaks a strong sense of what was saleable. Some were blatantly commercial, with no more than a gesture at annotation, most were genuine attempts to open the Scriptures and educate the people: these not only helped reinforce a sense of family but also placed the Bible even more firmly at the centre of the family.

[53] Ibid., 1225; Cook, *A New Catalogue*, p. 4.
[54] *ODNB* Scott; Herbert, *Historical Catalogue*, 1366.

Samuel Newton's folio, *The Complete Family Bible* (1771?), is representative. The title page describes it as containing both Testaments
'at large', and the Apocrypha, 'with a complete illustration of all the
difficult passages, wherein all the objections of the infidels are obvi-
ated, the obscure passages elucidated, and every seeming difficulty
explained. Together with notes historical and critical.' The reference
to 'objections of the infidels' invokes the rationalistic temper abroad,
manifest in atheistic or deistic attacks on the Bible. Rather than the
dedication to King James, there is a preface extolling the Scriptures
and Christianity, summarised in these terms: 'such is the lovely form
of revealed religion; such its benevolent principles; such its noble
precepts; and such the duties it enjoins the human race; and to
encourage them to listen to its dictates, and persevere in well-doing,
it offers the rewards of a glorious resurrection, and eternal happiness in the mansions of the heavenly Canaan'. The final paragraph,
more briefly than most, touches on the difficulties of the Scriptures,
the author's 'earnest desire to remove those difficulties' which 'has
furnished me with an abundant reason for engaging in this perfor-
mance', and an invitation to 'the impartial public' to judge how well
it is executed. There are brief summaries of the books but no chapter summaries; the text is clearly printed in two columns, and as
much as half the page is given to commentary. There are thirty-three
engravings illustrating the text (fewer than in many of the competi-
tors), notable more for their decorative borders than their intrinsic
quality.

Some family Bibles included miscellaneous information such as
tables of Jewish weights and measures. Thomas Bankes's *The Christian's New and Complete Family Bible: or Universal Library of Divine
Knowledge* (1790?) – a typical title – gave some statistics about the KJB
that were repeated more often than their trustworthiness deserves:

	OT	(Apoc.)	NT	Total
Books	39	–	27	66
Chapters	929	(183)	260	1,189
Verses	23,214	(6,081)	7,959	31,173
Words	592,439	(152,185)	181,253	773,692
Letters	2,728,100	–	838,380	3,566,480

THE

FIRST BOOK OF MOSES,

CALLED

G E N E S I S.

The ARGUMENT.

This book is called Bereschith, *in the beginning, by the Hebrews, and* Genesis, *generation, by the Greeks; because it begins with the history of the creation of the world. It includes a history of two thousand three hundred and sixty-nine years, from the beginning of the world to the death of the patriarch Joseph. Moses has here given us an authentic account of the creation of the world; the original innocence and fall of man; the propagation of the human species; the rise of religion; the invention of arts; the deluge; the restoration of the world; the division and peopling of the earth; the origin of nations and kingdoms; and the genealogy of the patriarchs from Adam to the sons and grandsons of Jacob.*

CHAP I.

IN the beginning God created the heaven and the earth.
2 And the earth was without form, and void; and darkness *was* upon the face of the deep: and the Spirit of God
moved upon the face of the waters.
3 ¶ And God said, Let there be light: and there was light.
4 And God saw the light, that it *was* good: and God divided the light from the darkness.
5 And God called the light Day, and the darkness he called
Night: and the evening and the morning were the first day.
6 ¶ And God said, Let there be a firmament in the
midst of the waters, and let it divide the waters from the
waters.
7 And God made the firmament; and divided the waters
which *were* under the firmament, from the waters which *were*
above the firmament: and it was so.
8 And God called the firmament Heaven: and the evening
and the morning were the second day.
9 ¶ And God said, Let the waters under the heaven be gathered together unto one place, and let the dry *land* appear:
and it was so.

10 And

Commentary on the First Chapter.

Ver. 1. *In the beginning, &c.*] Moses begins his account of the creation with asserting, that the world had a beginning, in opposition to those who held it to be eternal; laying at once, the foundation of religion in the belief of one supreme, self-existent Being, the Maker and absolute Lord of all other beings in the universe, in opposition to the polytheism of the adjacent nations. For it appears to have been the fatal error of the idolatrous unthinking world, in those early ages, to believe, that the heavens and heavenly bodies, especially the sun, moon, and planets, were a kind of independent beings, the sovereign disposers of good and evil, whose benign or malignant influence scattered blessings or calamities on mankind at pleasure; and consequently that they were the just objects of religious worship.

God created the heaven and the earth.] Though the Jews by *the heaven and earth* understood the universe, as appears from *Acts* xvii. 24. yet it is evident, that Moses in the subsequent part of this chapter confines himself to describe only the creation of the solar system, or this visible world; and though in this verse he asserts, that God is the creator of all things, yet it is used as a preface, not as an explanation of the remaining part of this chapter.

2 *And the earth was without form, and void.*] This terrestrial globe, which we now inhabit, was a confused indigested heap, having neither beasts, trees, herbs, or any thing else which now adorn it: a chaos, a heap of confusion, wherein the elements of things were all blended together. The words in the original are *Tohu Vabohu*, which signifies emptiness and confusion.

Darkness was upon the face of the deep.] To use the image of sacred poetry, thick darkness, like a swaddling-band, surrounded the infant world. Nothing was visible but to him with whom *the darkness and light are both alike.*

And the Spirit of God moved upon the face of the waters.] By the Spirit of God, the best commentators understand the divine power or energy, which exerted its influence in reducing and disposing the chaos into form and order. The Hebrew word, which we render *moved*, properly signifies *brooded*, as a hen does on her eggs; and therefore implies the communicating a vivifying spirit and virtue to the earth, for producing plants and animals in the proper time and order appointed by God.

3 *And God said, let there be light, and there was light.*] Longinus has justly admired the sublimity of this expression. What can give us a greater idea of the omnipotent power of the great Creator, than to conceive the starting of light into being, at his word. Light, of all material beings, most resembles its divine Creator in purity, power and brightness, and is therefore often considered in Scripture as an emblem of God himself. *God is light*, 1 John i. 15.

6 *And God said, Let there be a firmament, &c.*] The Hebrew word, which we render *firmament*, signifies an *expansion*, or *extension*; and in this sense the royal psalmist uses the word, when he represents the Almighty as spreading out the heavens like a curtain. As the waters under the firmament evidently signify those on the earth, so the waters above it are those suspended in the clouds; between which and the earth, the firmament or airy expansion is stretched out.

9 *Let the waters, &c.*] The air being thus formed, and the vapours and clouds suspended in the upper regions, the waters which covered the surface of the earth, were collected into seas and lakes, that the dry-land might appear. The original word rendered *gathered*, comes from *kav*, a square rule, or perpendicular line; and therefore denotes the wisdom displayed by our paternal creator, in proportioning the quantity, and in setting out the bounds of this raging element; for in the sublime expressions of scripture we may say, " He hath compassed the water with bounds"—*He hath shut up the sea with doors, and brake up for its decreed place, and set bars and doors, saying, Hitherto shalt thou come and no further; and here shall thy proud waves be stayed.* Job xxxviii. The two last verses are thus rendered in the Arabic; " And when from the night and day, the second day was passed; God willed, that the water under the heaven should be gathered together into one " place,

NUMB. 1. B

8. Samuel Newton's *The Complete Family Bible*, 1771. First page of Genesis. British Library.

'And' occurs 35,543 times in the OT, and 10,684 in the NT, while 'Jehovah' occurs 6,855 times. The middle and shortest chapter of the Bible is Psalm 117, the middle verse Psalm 118:8, and the middle time 2 Chronicles 4:16. Ezra 7:21 has all the letters of the alphabet (the capital 'I' of black-letter Bibles may be taken as a 'J', but they used 'u' for 'v').

The popularity and glut of these Bibles was such that the monopolists not only slashed prices but nearly abandoned printing folio Bibles.[55] Cambridge's last folio of the century was a printer's Bible *par excellence*, John Baskerville's of 1763. Though Baskerville could style himself 'Printer to the University', he had purchased this limited right in order to fulfil his ambitions to produce 'books of consequence, of intrinsic merit, or established reputation', especially the Book of Common Prayer and a folio Bible, in editions perfected 'with the greatest elegance and correctness', or, as he wrote elsewhere, 'a more correct and beautiful edition of the Sacred Writings than has hitherto appeared'.[56] The claim to beauty and elegance was achieved, but not that to correctness. Baskerville's design skills and his many innovations in printing technique, including his type, paper, ink and glossy finish to a page were all amply demonstrated – yet this was not a commercial success: limited to 1,250 copies, not much more than half had been sold after three years, and he sold the remainder to a London bookseller.

Baskerville was an interloper in Bible printing and at Cambridge, accommodated there because the University could profit from his work, but otherwise unhelped as the University's main printer, Joseph Bentham, under instruction from the Syndics (syndicate or committee running the Press), competed with him. One product of this competition was a folio that at last developed the work on the text accomplished in Cambridge's 1629 and 1638 Bibles.

Cambridge had made an unsuccessful attempt to return to Bible printing in 1731 when it leased its right to a group that proposed to stereotype the KJB, that is, to make plates of each page, thus removing the need for constant resetting and all the inevitable errors

---

[55] McKitterick, *A History*, vol. ii, p. 224. Oxford produced four after Blayney's 1769 edition, and the King's Printer, now Eyre and Strahan, only one, in 1772.

[56] Quoted in McKitterick, *A History*, vol. ii, p. 197; 'Proposals for printing by subscription the Holy Bible', reproduced in McKitterick, *A History*, vol. ii, p. 199.

and expense involved. Stereotyping had already been used in Holland, but it seems that the compositors, anticipating Luddism, made sure the plates were worthless; whatever the exact reason, this anticipation of the most important practical development in printing the KJB came to nothing. Cambridge then decided to make printing the Bible and the Prayer Book a part – as it turned out, the major part – of the Press's ordinary business; in 1740 a new printer, Bentham, was appointed, and work towards new editions of good quality was in hand. A contemporary account shows the commercial reasoning behind this decision:

The Syndics thought it would be advisable for them to undertake the printing a Bible of such a size as is of most general demand, and this they did, 1. in order to serve the public with a more beautiful and correct edition than can easily be found. 2. For the honour of the University, which would be advanced by such a work being well executed at their Press. 3. That, by their being secure of constant employment for them, they may be always able to retain a number of good hands ready for any work that shall be brought in. 4. Because they believe a considerable profit may accrue to the University by printing Bibles, though it cannot yet be estimated how great it will be, nor is expected to be equal to that of a private trader.[57]

The first outcome was a duodecimo in 1743. Since 1638 little had changed in the KJB text, by contrast with the margin where the cross-references were growing sevenfold from the original 8,990 (6,588 in the OT, 885 in the Apocrypha and 1,517 in the NT), and the original 8,357 marginal notes (6,610 in the OT, 996 in the Apocrypha and 751 in the NT) by 346, with a further seventy-three revised. The long-missing element of careful proof-reading and correction of the text was resumed in this 1743 Bible. The work was undertaken, with a fee of £40, by one of the Syndics, Francis Sawyer (F.S.) Parris of Sidney Sussex College, aided by Henry Therond of Trinity College.[58] Compared with Cambridge 1638's text of the specimen page from Genesis, there are thirty-five changes, the majority corresponding with what has become the standard text. Most concern spelling and punctuation, including the insertion of possessive apostrophes; save for the continued use of what to modern eyes looks like an 'f', the long 's', the text has a very familiar look. Unusually, the paragraphing is extended

[57] Quoted in ibid., p. 180.   [58] Ibid., p. 183.

to the end of Acts and revised elsewhere. The most important aspect of this Bible is the extent to which it anticipates Parris's 1762 edition, until now taken as the major eighteenth-century Cambridge edition. Setting aside the margin and the Apocrypha, which are not included in 1743, seventy-one of the later edition's eighty-seven new readings originate here, together with three found in other editions published between these two; a further thirteen anticipate the Oxford edition of 1769. There are five correct placements of possessive apostrophes, all involving grammatical decisions, that are not otherwise found until F.H.A. Scrivener's *Cambridge Paragraph Bible* of 1873. That there was work left to do, not just on the Apocrypha and the margins, but also on the spelling and, inevitably, on the typographical errors, should not detract from the importance of this unpretentious little Bible. Parris shows himself to have been a very perceptive editor, highly attentive to the relationship between the translation and the original, and sensitive to small details of language and punctuation. Though Cambridge gave no publicity to this massive labour of dedication, the result was in several ways a characteristic Cambridge production, scholarly and faithful, well produced, available on two different qualities of paper (the better quality available for a premium of 6d over the standard 2s), aimed at the largest market (this not always a Cambridge characteristic), and sold both to the general public and in bulk to a Christian charitable society, in this case the Society for Promoting Christian Knowledge, the SPCK, founded in 1698.

Parris's work culminated in the Cambridge 1762 quarto and folio (both printed from the same setting).[59] Much of it was adopted for the Oxford quarto and folio of 1769 (again both were printed from the same setting), and there, but for a very few changes, the generally printed text was settled. Oxford had become concerned about its Bible printing, no doubt partly in response to the developments at Cambridge, and in 1764 ordered a collation be made with 'the original or most authentic edition of the present translation', the result of which was to be used in correcting Oxford Bibles, 'making due allowance for modern variations in mere orthography'.[60] Not knowing what text to take, the delegates asked the Archbishop of

---

[59] Ibid., pp. 192, 441, n. 87.
[60] Quoted in Carter, *A History of Oxford University Press*, p. 356.

the most high God, the possessor of heaven and earth,

23 That I will not take from a thread even to a shoe latchet, and that I will not take any thing that is thine, lest thou shouldest say, I have made Abram rich:

24 Save only that which the young men have eaten, and the portion of the men which went with me, Aner, Eshcol, and Mamre; let them take their portion.

CHAP. XV.

1 *Abram is encouraged.* 4 *A son is promised.* 6 *He is justified by faith.* 7 *Canaan is promised again.*

After these things the word of the LORD came unto Abram in a vision, saying, Fear not, Abram: I am thy shield, and thy exceeding great reward.

2 And Abram said, Lord God, what wilt thou give me, seeing I go childless, and the steward of my house is this Eliezer of Damascus?

3 And Abram said, Behold, to me thou hast given no seed: and lo, one born in my house is mine heir.

4 ¶ And behold, the word of the LORD came unto him, saying, This shall not be thine heir; but he that shall come forth out of thy own bowels shall be thine heir.

5 And he brought him forth abroad, and said, Look now toward heaven, and tell the stars, if thou be able to number them: and he said unto him, So shall thy seed be.

6 ¶ And he believed in the LORD; and he counted it to him for righteousness.

7 ¶ And he said unto him, I am the LORD that brought thee out of Ur of the Chaldees, to give thee this land to inherit it.

8 And he said, Lord God, whereby shall I know that I shall inherit it?

9 And he said unto him, Take me an heifer of three years old, and a she-goat of three years old, and a ram of three years old, and a turtle dove, and a young pigeon.

10 And he took unto him all these, and divided them in the midst, and laid each piece one against another: but the birds divided he not.

11 And when the fowls came down upon the carcases, Abram drove them away.

12 And when the sun was going down, a deep sleep fell upon Abram; and lo, an horror of great darkness fell upon him.

13 And he said unto Abram, Know of a surety that thy seed shall be a stranger in a land that is not theirs, and shall serve them, and they shall afflict them four hundred years.

14 And also that nation whom they shall serve, will I judge: and afterward shall they come out with great substance.

15 And thou shalt go to thy fathers in peace; thou shalt be buried in a good old age.

16 But in the fourth generation they shall come hither again: for the iniquity of the Amorites is not yet full.

17 And it came to pass, that when the sun went down and it was dark, behold a smoking furnace, and a burning lamp that passed between those pieces.

18 In that same day the LORD made a covenant with Abram, saying, Unto thy seed have I given this land, from the river of Egypt unto the great river the river Euphrates:

19 The Kenites, and the Kenizzites, and the Kadmonites,

20 And the Hittites, and the Perizzites, and the Rephaims,

21 And the Amorites, and the Canaanites, and the Girgashites, and the Jebusites.

CHAP. XVI.

1 *Sarai giveth Hagar to Abram,* 6 *who flying from her mistress,* 9 *is sent back by an angel.* 15 *Ishmael is born.*

Now Sarai Abram's wife bare him no children: and she had an hand-maid, an Egyptian, whose name was Hagar.

2 And Sarai said unto Abram, Behold now, the LORD hath restrained me from bearing: I pray thee go in unto my maid; it may be that I may obtain children by her: and Abram hearkened to the voice of Sarai.

3 And Sarai Abram's wife took Hagar her maid the Egyptian, after Abram had dwelt ten years in the land of Canaan, and gave her to her husband Abram to be his wife.

4 And he went in unto Hagar, and she conceived: and when she saw that she had conceived, her mistress was despised in her eyes.

5 And Sarai said unto Abram, My wrong be upon thee: I have given my maid into thy bosom, and when she saw that she had conceived, I was despised in her eyes: the LORD judge between me and thee.

6 ¶ But Abram said unto Sarai, Behold, thy maid is in thy hand; do to her as it pleaseth thee. And when Sarai dealt hardly with her, she fled from her face.

7 And the angel of the LORD found her by a fountain of water in the wilderness, by the fountain in the way to Shur.

8 And he said, Hagar, Sarai's maid, whence camest thou? and whither wilt thou go? and she said, I flee from the face of my mistress Sarai.

9 ¶ And the angel of the LORD said unto her, Return to thy mistress, and submit thyself under her hands.

10 And the angel of the LORD said unto her, I will multiply thy seed exceedingly, that it shall not be numbered for multitude.

11 And the angel of the LORD said unto her, Behold, thou art with child, and shalt bear a son, and shalt call his name Ishmael; because the LORD hath heard thy affliction.

12 And he will be a wild man; his hand will be against every man, and every man's hand against him: and he shall dwell in the presence of all his brethren.

13 And she called the name of the LORD that spake unto her, Thou God seest me: for she said, Have I also here looked after him that seeth me?

14 Wherefore the well was called Beerlahai-roi; behold, it is between Kadesh and Bered.

15 ¶ And Hagar bare Abram a son: and Abram called his son's name, which Hagar bare, Ishmael.

16 And Abram was fourscore and six years old, when Hagar bare Ishmael to Abram.

CHAP.

9. Genesis 15–16, Parris's Cambridge 1743 duodecimo. BSS.201.D43.6.

Canterbury for a recommendation; he too did not know, but replied that he had heard that Parris 'took great pains in the same good work'.[61] The upshot was a collation of the first edition (whether this was correctly identified is unknown – uncertainty as to which was the first edition persisted into late Victorian times) with the Cambridge editions of 1743 and 1760, and Lloyd's 1701 folio. Benjamin Blayney, later Regius Professor of Hebrew at Oxford, edited the resultant edition which, for better and worse, became the standard. His report on his work, though it makes claims that were not met and does not mention either the indebtedness to Parris and Cambridge or the substantial use of Canne's cross-references,[62] gives some good sense of what he did. Spelling – 'mere orthography' – gets no attention, punctuation a passing comment, and all that he says of the readings is that the text was collated (as instructed), and 'reformed to such a standard of purity, as, it is presumed, is not to be met with in any other edition hitherto extant' – a claim too vague to be helpful. The one quasi-textual item that is commented on in some detail is the revision of the italics. For the rest he is concerned with extra-textual matters, the chapter summaries and running titles, the notes, cross-references and chronology. Finally he relates the care with which the work was seen through the press.[63] In spite of these claims to have given most attention to editorial aids to the understanding of the text (the italics are one such aid rather than a genuine matter of the text), his most significant contribution was to the spelling and, in some respects, the grammar of the text.

The effect of Parris and Blayney's work is best seen if they are discussed together. There are ninety-nine readings in most modern editions that come from Parris and fifty-eight from Blayney – figures that are rougher than they appear, since they depend on just what is taken as a reading and the fallibility necessarily involved in making such counts. Three-quarters of Parris's variants and three-fifths of Blayney's are matters of English. Most of the other variants – not

---

[61] Quoted in ibid., p. 358.
[62] Following the advice of the Archbishop of Canterbury, Blayney consulted and selected from references in Scottish Bibles, that is, Canne's references (ibid., p. 359).
[63] Originally published in *The Gentleman's Magazine* 39, November 1769, pp. 517–19; reproduced in Norton, *Textual History*, pp. 195–7.

a large number – make the KJB more literal, usually by inserting a definite article or changing the number of a noun in opposition to the decisions taken by the original translators; for example, Parris in 1743, exactly following the Hebrew and reflecting the translators' practice in the NT, changed 'of passover' to 'of the passover' (Exod. 34:25), and, becoming more sharp-eyed or pedantic in 1762 than he was in 1743, 'all thy coasts' to 'all thy coast' (Deut. 16:4). Both editors tended to be more literal than the translators judged appropriate.

The changes to the KJB's English are often just a matter of spelling as Parris and Blayney continued the gradual – and usually beneficial – modernisation found in earlier editions, but it has some peculiarities and leads to some changes of language. Where words have two different possible spellings, Blayney particularly attempted to create consistency. The translators used 'among' ten times more often than 'amongst', and Blayney decided to regularise to 'among' – but he missed two early examples, Genesis 3:8 and 23:9. It is noteworthy, and, I think, right, that he ignored the apparent difference in sound, and characteristic that he did not achieve full consistency. Some of the changes overstepped the line between change of spelling and change of word, as when Parris changed Susanna's 'I am straited on every side: for if I do this thing, it is death unto me: and if I do it not, I cannot escape your hands' (v. 22) to 'I am straitened'. The two words are closely related but different. She is obviously in dire straits, but she is not narrowed as 'the breadth of the waters is straitened' (Job 37:10). The danger in spelling changes is that the precision of the translators' language is sometimes obscured. Occasionally the changes amount to rewriting, as in Parris's change from 'the four hundred and fourscore year' to 'the four hundred and eightieth year' (1 Kings 6:1). One of the biggest problems Parris and Blayney tried to tackle was the use of 'ye' and 'you', a problem made particularly difficult because usage and grammatical prescription were at variance in their time. Usually the translators used 'ye' as subject and 'you' as object but sometimes, e.g., Deuteronomy 5:32–3, the two were mixed freely. Parris tried for a while to follow the translators' normal practice, then left well alone. Blayney made a nearly successful attempt to do the same, but still missed some examples. Consequently, nearly all 289 instances of what is now normal English, 'you' as subject, have disappeared from the KJB. Blayney was not averse to making the language of the KJB more archaic: there are five modern third-person singulars such as 'he sticks' (1 Esdras 4:21) in the Apocrypha; he changed four to the old form ('he sticketh', etc.), but missed one, so 'every man that takes' (Ecclus. 22:2) remains as the only modern third-person singular in standard KJBs.

Neither his folio nor his quarto is as free from errors as Blayney claimed; Scrivener thought them 'conspicuously deficient', and that 'the commonly estimated number of 116 such errata would seem below the truth'.[64] In spite of the blemishes, Blayney considered the folio 'somewhat the more perfect of the two, and therefore more fit to be recommended for a standard copy'.[65] Oxford University Press kept a copy which, inevitably, accumulated revisions. It

was for many years the standard by which Oxford Bibles were corrected; that is to say, Blayney's [folio] as corrected in manuscript by many hands in course of time. The folio volume kept for reference has hardly a page, except in the Apocrypha, without a corrector's mark carefully written in ink. All but a few of these amendments are of slight significance: a capital instead of a small letter in a reference, a comma added, an English spelling modernized.[66]

As well as Oxford, most other printers at home and abroad took Blayney as standard, so that the text as now generally found is not that of the first edition but something that evolved unevenly over a century and a half before becoming nearly fixed by the standards of the 1760s imperfectly applied.

One of the main reasons why Blayney's became the standard text is that it is a massive task to undertake such editing. Cambridge, not once but several times, and Oxford, the scholarly guardians of the text, had now each undertaken that task, and it is not to be expected that they would want to do it again immediately. That Blayney's rather than Parris's became the standard was not simply a matter of his offering it as such. Even without close scholarly scrutiny, it was clearly a step beyond Parris: in terms of scholarship it adopted and added

---

[64] Pp. 30–1; Scrivener gives substantial lists of errors in the following pages. Among the errors are 'ERZA' as the header to Ezra 10 (folio only), 'a sweetsmelling favour' for a 'sweetsmelling savour' (Eph. 5:2), and the omission of half of Rev. 18:22.

[65] Blayney's report; Norton, *Textual History*, p. 197.

[66] Carter, *A History of Oxford University Press*, p. 358.

to his work, and in terms of orthography, grammar and punctuation it was a large step beyond, achieving a reasonable approximation to eighteenth-century standards. Though it was not perfect, as any close examination would have revealed, it was clearly the best text so far. It is also probable that it became the standard because, by 1769, general opinion of the KJB had at last settled into reverence, and neophobia was beginning to dominate. Though the *Critical Review* was referring to alternative translations in 1787, its judgement reflects attitudes to the KJB itself: 'to reform the text of the Bible would have appeared to the ignorant little less than a change of a national religion'.[67] Such a spirit could attach itself to the smallest details of Blayney's text.

The specimen page from Genesis 17 and 18 shows one difference from modern editions in the text[68] and notes: Blayney's paragraph mark at 17:5, inherited from Parris, has been removed. The chapter summaries and cross-references are a different matter: these are rarely followed. Looking backwards, however, small differences from 1611 are visible everywhere. There is an extra note in the margin to 17:7, some fifty-seven spelling changes, including the scholarly change of 'Cadesh' to 'Kadesh' (16:14), twenty-one changes of punctuation, including the addition of apostrophes, seven additional uses of italics, and a few other miscellaneous changes to things like capitalisation.

Viewed as a whole, Blayney's Bible represents an accumulation of changed readings. Very few changes were subsequently introduced into the standard texts, six new readings, together with the reintro-duction of at least thirty old readings, twenty-two involving spellings of names.[69] Counts vary as to how many changed readings there are in Blayney, and are usually much higher than the nearly 700 that I list in appendix 8 of *A Textual History*, a list based on Scrivener's work, other collations and my own observations.[70] 201 of these changes make needed corrections to the 1611 text, but 420 go against the translators, changing readings they created that can be shown to have been deliberate or which may well have been deliberate. In addition,

---

[67] *Critical Review* 63 (January 1787): 46.
[68] I have used a 1992 copy of the Cambridge Concord edition as representative of the modern text.
[69] Norton, *Textual History*, p. 115.
[70] This list includes the Apocrypha, and omits changes in the italics, repeated changes, and corrections of the printer's errors in the first edition. It also omits sixty-eight variants where Blayney's reading is the same as 1611 and the current text.

10. Genesis 17–18, Blayney's 1769 folio, with annotations by Gilbert Buchanan, *c.* 1822, showing differences from the original text. UL Rare Books: Adv.bb.77.2.

seventy-three of the new readings need further revision. This is not to denigrate the work that went into all these changes – all are the product of close observation and thought – but to observe that the basis on which they were made, that the work of the translators is improvable, can easily be taken too far. Inevitably there are textual principles and questions of judgement involved here, and it is perhaps remarkable that the attention to the text demanded by its errors should have produced so few changes. But, if the text is allowed to be improvable in places where it is not demonstrably wrong, the process that led from Tyndale's work to the KJB can carry on until at last the KJB has become the Revised Version (to look no further forward).

If respect and reverence for the KJB translators' work is to be one's principle, then the revised text represented by the 1769 Bible and most subsequent KJBs is not as good as it should be. That said, if any differences in the text are allowed to be small, then most of the differences between 1611, 1769 and most current KJBs are small, and, given the size of the text, few. By contrast, the other differences in the text, those to the spelling and punctuation, are innumerable. And the spelling changes in particular have this in common with the changes to readings, that they are mostly, by standards that had developed through to 1769, well done.

Many of the superfluous letters that were characteristic of 1611 were removed by the first two Cambridge editions, editions which were early manifestations of new standards of spelling and had a significant influence in establishing them. This process was brought close to completion by 1769, though some words with extra letters remained, most commonly those ending in 'ck' such as 'musick'. Overall, current English texts (American texts and standards are not quite the same) have some 219 single words that do not conform to modern standards, words such as 'alway' (thirty-two times alongside eighty-four uses of 'always'), 'arrogancy' (one of a number of words that used to end '-ncy' but now end '-nce'), 'asswage', 'astonied' (ten times alongside forty-six uses of 'astonished'), 'bason', 'clift', 'cuckow' and 'ensample'.[71] All of these are obviously obsolete and easy to modernise. Sometimes, though, there are stories behind the spellings

---

[71] See Norton, *Textual History*, appendix 9, for a list of obsolete spellings in the KJB.

that show the fine line that there can be between modernising spelling and changing language. 'Ensample' and 'example', for instance, were alternative spellings of one word in 1611, but 'bewray' and 'betray' were different words with different meanings. Overall, the spelling of the current text has inherited a significant amount of obsolete and inconsistent spelling, some of it reflecting eighteenth-century standards, some older, from Blayney.

Punctuation in the KJB has always been erratic. The first edition shows the same variety, even in successive examples of the same structure, that also characterises the spelling, though it is often less easy to see reasons for the differences other than a lack of accepted standards and, even for an age when consistency was not a fetish, human frailty. A significant element in the variety is that the punctuation is sometimes grammatical, sometimes rhetorical. We are accustomed to punctuation that marks grammatical relationships, but the KJB quite often uses punctuation to mark what we might call the rhythms of the text. In the second half of Psalms, for instance, colons become increasingly common in the middle of a verse, effectively marking the break between the two parts of a parallelism. This is something we are accustomed to as a line break in poetry. So in the first edition's 'He hath not dealt with us after our sins: nor rewarded us according to our iniquities' (Ps. 103:10), we, punctuating grammatically, would probably put a comma where the colon is. But the effect 1611 achieves is fittingly like that of poetry:

He hath not dealt with us after our sins:
Nor rewarded us according to our iniquities.

Current editions, following Blayney, characteristically fall half-way between rhetorical and grammatical punctuation by using a semi-colon in such places.

Printers and editors treated the original punctuation freely, making the current text relatively consistent according to eighteenth-century standards. But it is only relative: one of the most striking inconsistencies, partly inherited from 1611, is the use of a semicolon instead of a comma before speech; this becomes increasingly common from about Jeremiah 21 onwards. About one-fifth of the punctuation is revised. The first Cambridge edition made a quarter of these changes, Parris another quarter, and Blayney half. Ruth provides a small sample of what was done. There are seventy-nine changes, twenty-three from the first Cambridge edition, one from the second, seven from Paris and forty-eight from Blayney. The commonest is the removal of commas, and several times full stops are substituted for colons. These changes give a lighter, more modern feel. Others have the opposite effect. Blayney sometimes adds commas (one of his commonest changes throughout the Bible is to make 'and behold' into 'and, behold'), and he makes fourteen commas into semicolons and seven semicolons into colons.

Some things were never done in the KJB. We should be grateful that the habit of capitalising nouns – and a few other words – was not adopted. Perhaps we should regret that the work on punctuation did not extend to the inclusion of speech marks, a much more efficient way of identifying speech than relying on context and the use of a capital letter to begin the speech. More importantly, the basic format of the KJB remained essentially unchanged from 1611 through to most modern editions, something that we should be grateful for with reservations. Typographically, the KJB (and many other Bibles before and since) is different from other books: one has only to see a page without reading a single word to know that one is looking at a Bible. The layout declares it different from secular books, immediately evoking feelings appropriate to the sacred book. It is also highly efficient, allowing a great deal of text to be included on a page while keeping to a minimum the difficulties of keeping one's place. Finding a particular place could not be easier because of the numbered and visually separate verses. Moreover, the student is encouraged to take a holistic view of the inspired word, moving from one place in the text to related places sometimes at the other end of the Bible by way of the cross-references, for example from Deuteronomy 4:2 to Revelation 22:18 by way of Deuteronomy 12:32, Joshua 1:7 and Proverbs 30:6 (1611 references). In short, it feels right, suits the student of the text, encourages a sense of the Bible as united and inspired, and, in the larger editions, is easy to read aloud from.

The format also has its shortcomings. Setting aside the cross-references, it shows two kinds of structure in the writing, the small units represented by verses and the larger units represented by chapters, but both these are primarily designed for ease of reference rather than as a way of showing how the text is constructed. There are of course the paragraph marks, but they compete weakly with the visual presentation of the verses as paragraphs. The philosopher John Locke, struggling to understand Paul's Epistles (which lack even the paragraph marks), put the problem forcefully. To him, a major difficulty in the Epistles is

the dividing of them into chapters and verses... whereby they are so chopped and minced, and, as they are now printed, stand so broken and divided that not only the common people take the verses usually for distinct aphorisms, but even men of more advanced knowledge in reading them lose very much of the strength and force of the coherence, and the light that depends on it. Our minds are so weak and narrow that they have need of all the helps and assistances [that] can be procured to lay before them undisturbedly the thread and coherence of any discourse, by which alone they are truly improved and led into the genuine sense of the author. When the eye is constantly disturbed with loose sentences that by their standing and separation appear as so many distinct fragments, the mind will have much ado to take in and carry on in its memory an uniform discourse of dependent reasonings, especially having from the cradle been used to wrong impressions concerning them, and constantly accustomed to hear them quoted as distinct sentences, without any limitation or explication of their precise meaning from the place they stand in and the relation they bear to what goes before or follows. These divisions also have given occasion to the reading these Epistles by parcels and in scraps, which has further confirmed the evil arising from such partitions.[72]

Though this is especially true for the Epistles, it applies to the Bible as a whole. In traditional presentation, the Bible is a pile of precious bricks instead of a temple. The kind of presentation Locke was looking for is that which Tyndale (working before the creation of numbered verses) had given his NT, continuous prose ordered only by paragraph breaks and chapter divisions, with poetry such as the Magnificat given in poetic lines. Tyndale's reason for translating was 'because I had perceived by experience how that it was impossible to establish the lay people in any truth, except the Scripture were plainly laid before their eyes in their mother tongue, that they might see the process, order and meaning of the text'.[73] His NT modelled how to present the text for such plain, contextual reading.

The traditional format makes no distinction between prose and poetry. There are grounds for thinking this a good thing: sometimes there is no clear distinction between the two, and the translators did not set out to make a poetic translation of the poetic parts.

---

[72] Locke, *Essay for the Understanding of St Paul's Epistles*, p. vii.
[73] Preface to the Pentateuch (1530), unfoliated.

Against this, some parts of the KJB, especially the Psalms and parts of Isaiah, work remarkably well as poetry, and it is useful to have a visual reminder of the nature of what one is reading, especially if that reminder helps to bring out the way the words work. Tyndale, making a prose translation, certainly thought so. Some eighteenth-century critics in their turn realised that sometimes the KJB had a kind of poetic form that could be revealed through the use of poetic lines. The non-conformist clergyman Samuel Say presented some verses of the Bible as poetry in the course of a general argument about the power of rhythm in prose and poetry. He gives Genesis 49:7 in this way (incidentally illustrating some of the eighteenth century's habits of capitalisation and spelling):

Cursed be their Anger! for it was fierce,
And their Wrath! for it was Cruël.
I will divide 'em in Jacob; and scatter 'em in Isräel.[74]

But for this presentation, one might not realise how powerful the cadences of the KJB are in this verse; the exclamation marks bring out the high points of the first two lines. At much the same time, Robert Lowth, Oxford Professor of Poetry and future Bishop of London, was developing his insights into Hebrew poetry, including his theory of parallelism; he argued that 'a poem translated literally from the Hebrew into the prose of any other language, whilst the same forms of the sentences remain, will still retain, even as far as relates to versification, much of its native dignity, and a faint appearance of versification'.[75] The KJB is just such a literal translation, and Say shows that the appearance of versification might be more than faint.

SOME LATER DEVELOPMENTS

How and when the few changes to Blayney's text were made cannot be fixed precisely. Publishers have generally not kept good records of their work, and there are no complete collections of the multi-tudinous editions of the KJB published since 1769. On occasions a

---

[74] Say, 'Essay . . . on the harmony, variety and power of numbers in general, whether in prose or verse', in *Poems on Several Occasions*, p. 103.
[75] Lowth, *Lectures on the Sacred Poetry of the Hebrews*, vol. I, p. 71.

great deal of work was done on the text with no fanfare at all. By 1805, for instance, Cambridge had revised its text, restoring a number of 1611 readings, but it is not clear what principles lay behind this work, nor who did it. Less than twenty years later Cambridge itself had no idea what had happened, as became apparent during a new campaign against the monopolists and for a reliable text. This was the work of a committee of dissenting ministers led by Thomas Curtis, whose *The Existing Monopoly, an Inadequate Protection of the Authorised Version of Scripture* (1833) gives insights into the workings of the Universities and had a decided effect on the printed text, though not the one Curtis had hoped for: it settled the use of Blayney's text (but not its margin, summaries and headers) as the standard. The use of 'Authorised Version' in this title is striking. He believed that the KJB was authorised by the Hampton Court conference, and that this authority was fulfilled by the translators' delivery of their work to the King's Printer; at that point it ceased, so that even 'the translators themselves possessed no right whatever to make in future a single critical alteration without a renewed authority' (p. 51). Cambridge and Oxford therefore had no right to make 'material critical alterations'; their sole duty was 'to preserve the public and authorised, a settled and uniform version' (p. 2). Nevertheless, according to his observations of about a quarter of the text, margin, chapter summaries and headers, there are more than 11,000 changes from the 1611 text, not including small details of spelling and punctuation.

Having further discovered that 'there was no common system, nor common concord between the Universities' in discharging their responsibilities to the text, he inquired of Cambridge 'what were the methods which the University had taken . . . to secure future correctness?' The answer was 'that the Cambridge authorities would print the Bible correctly – if they "did but know the standard to be followed"'; further, evidently ignorant of Parris's work and what they had subsequently done around the turn of the century, they asked the Bishop of London for information on a standard (shades of the question the Archbishop of Canterbury was unable to answer seventy years earlier), and 'professed, on these subjects an utter want of confidence in "the Oxford men"' (pp. 4–5). Nevertheless, Cambridge was sympathetic to proposals to rectify the situation, and Curtis embarked on a substantial collation as part of the University's effort to produce 'an edition which may be considered as a standard' (p. 22), a phrase which translated into the Syndics' wish 'that the new edition should be an exact reprint of that of 1611, with the exception of typographical errors' (p. 28). However, the Syndics changed their mind and the edition was aborted.

Curtis also approached Oxford. 'Can you,' he asked the Regius Professor of Divinity, Edward Burton, 'be fairly said to have a standard (certainly you have not an authorised one) at Oxford?' (p. 37). The question was double-edged, for he knew the answer, that they generally followed Blayney, and he also knew how to undermine it. Not only was Blayney full of errors, but Oxford's own prestigious 1817 folio, edited by George D'Oyly and Richard Mant, had not followed Blayney for the whole text, instead returning to the margin and summaries of the first edition because, as they say of the added marginal references, 'they do not rest on the same authority as the references of the translators'.[76] Burton replied that all the mistakes listed by Curtis had been corrected, and took this as evidence that Oxford did refer to the first edition: 'the fact is, that Mr. Collingwood has introduced a system of accuracy which is perhaps not to be found in any other Press; he constantly refers to the original edition, a copy of which is lodged in the Press, and your own letter is a convincing proof that he makes good use of it' (p. 39). However, he would be obliged to Curtis if he acquainted the Press with mistakes in the latest edition.

This invitation led to Curtis visiting Oxford, where Samuel Collingwood, the Printer, kindly sent the Press's copy of the first edition to Curtis's inn for inspection. As well as inspecting other copies, Curtis 'found at the Bodleian . . . a folio Bible of 1602, originally Selden's; with many MS suggestions, as they are thought to be, of one of King James's Translators' – that is, he found Bod 1602. He adds prophetically that 'in a rigid collation, for the sake of perfectly returning to the standard, I saw reason to suppose this book would be useful' (p. 42n).

At this time Curtis's involvement with Cambridge came to light, leading, he supposes, both to the breakdown of the Cambridge project and, very importantly, to something that was also

---

[76] Oxford, 1817, 3 vols. 'General Introduction to the Bible', vol. 1, unpaginated.

becoming a commercial necessity, renewed cooperation between the Universities.[77] Curtis meanwhile was left on the outside, still campaigning.

The chief consequence of this episode was that, with the necessity of standardisation brought home to the Universities, the Oxford standard, essentially Blayney's text, now ruled. Another consequence was an exact reprint of the first edition, published by Oxford in 1833, a truly remarkable piece of work that reproduces all the quirks of the first edition, even inverted letters, with scarcely an error. This was judged by the Delegates to be 'the most effectual method for enabling themselves and others to judge how far the complaints were well-founded'.[78] Scrivener comments that this edition 'virtually settled the whole debate, by showing to the general reader the obvious impossibility of returning to the Bible of 1611, with all the defects which those who superintended the press had been engaged, for more than two centuries, in reducing to a more consistent and presentable shape' (p. 35). One might add in qualification that many of Curtis's complaints had been justified, and that the studious general reader might still want to see exactly what the translators and their printer produced.[79]

American texts also aligned themselves closely to Blayney. By the 1830s the American Bible Society's text was serving as the model for other American publishers,[80] but almost from its foundation in 1816 the Society had been concerned over the accuracy of its text. In 1847 its Board of Managers established a Committee on Versions to create its own standard text. After four years work the Committee recommended 'that the Octavo Reference Bible, now in the course of preparation . . . be adopted as the Standard Copy of the Society; to which all future editions published by the Society shall be conformed', and presented a report giving some occasionally inaccurate history

---

[77] See McKitterick, *A History*, vol. ii, pp. 254–5.

[78] *The Holy Bible, an Exact Reprint*, statement bound in at the beginning.

[79] In recent times this has been possible through the Nelson 1990 (and Hendrickson 2010) 'word-for-word reprint of the First Edition of the Authorized Version presented in roman letters for easy reading and comparison with subsequent editions' (title page); save for some of the introductory material, this is a photographic reproduction of the Oxford edition.

[80] Herbert, *Historical Catalogue*, p. 397; I am indebted to Herbert for some of the information here.

of the text and detailing the ongoing work.[81] The Society's 'royal octavo edition' was collated with 'copies of the four leading British editions, viz. those of London, Oxford, Cambridge, and Edinburgh; and also with the original edition of 1611' (p. 16); the Oxford edition was Blayney's, which 'has been regarded, ever since its publication, as the standard copy' (p. 10). Though this collation yielded nearly 24,000 variations in text and punctuation (not including the margin, summaries or headers), the Committee declared there was 'not one which mars the integrity of the text, or affects any doctrine or precept of the Bible' (p. 31). Curtis would have been astonished at this, and his apoplexy can only be imagined at the further declaration that 'the English Bible, as left by the translators, has come down to us unaltered in respect to its *text*; except in the changes of orthography which the whole English language has undergone' (p. 7), and, similarly, that the lesson of the 1833 reprint of the first edition was that, typographical errors and orthography excepted, 'the text of our present Bibles remains unchanged, and is without variation from the original copy as left by the translators' (p. 11).

Having collated its six texts without considering that its four modern texts might be Blayney's and three close representations of his work, the Committee treated this unscholarly sample in a still more unscholarly way, that is, it treated them democratically. The rule it adopted for variations in punctuation, that 'the uniform usage of any *three* of the copies shall be followed', appears to reflect its general practice, which resulted 'in the great majority of instances [in] conformity with the [modern] English copies' (pp. 17, 25). If this is an unkind reflection on a huge project, the Committee brought it on itself by obliterating almost all signs of scholarly consideration of the actual merits of readings: only five readings settled with reference to the original are noted, under the innocent heading, 'WORDS'.[82] As far as the readings are concerned what the Committee offered was Blayney with his own 116 typographical errors removed. With

---

[81] Anon, *Report on the History*, p. 32.

[82] Pp. 19–20. Josh. 19:2, Ruth 3:15, Song 2:7, Isa. 1:16 ('wash yee', 1611), and Matt. 12:41. In this last, which the *Report* misquotes, the definite article is inserted, giving 'in the judgment', because the Greek has the definite article and the same phrase is so translated in the next verse. The Committee does not record how it reconciled this change with its principles.

its 'great and leading object [being] *uniformity*' (p. 19), it helped to entrench the Oxford standard.[83]

The policy of following the punctuation of the majority of their copies prevented innovation, and also worked against uniformity with any one of their copies: the result was an eclectic version of eighteenth-century punctuation. Nevertheless, the committee did good work in other areas such as the chapter summaries, the regularisation of names (something that now makes the American Bible Society's Apocrypha strikingly different from the British editions), and the spelling. This last is what catches the eye because it contains a significant number of the changes that still need making to the British editions, including regularising the use of 'a' and 'an'.[84] Subsequent American editions followed this example, but with no great thoroughness, although the policy of the American Bible Society continued to be that spelling should be conformed to modern standards.[85]

The result of this work was a fine quarto Bible published, without the Apocrypha, in 1856, and intended to be the standard American Bible Society text. The *Report* itself was initially accepted then rejected 'on the ground of alleged want of constitutional authority, and popular dissatisfaction with a number of the changes made'.[86] Similarly, the 1856 Bible ran into trouble, mainly because of its work on the chapter summaries. A new committee was formed, changes were reconsidered, and new editions were produced which did become standard for seventy years. Blayney's text had become, with some variations of spelling and punctuation, the American text.

Another revision of the text was published in 1873 by Cambridge, F.H.A. Scrivener's *The Cambridge Paragraph Bible of the Authorized English Version, with the text revised by a collation of its early and other principal editions, the use of the italic type made uniform, the marginal references remodelled, and a critical introduction prefixed*. Its considerable historical importance turned out to be in Scrivener's account of the work, the 'critical introduction', later published separately as *The Authorized Edition of the English Bible (1611): its subsequent reprints*

[83] Scrivener's view of this edition is the same, though he expresses himself more harshly, pp. 37–8.
[84] Fifty-nine changed spellings are listed in Norton, *Textual History*, pp. 121–2.
[85] Herbert, *Historical Catalogue*, p. 399.
[86] Lightfoot *et al.*, *Revision of the English Version of the New Testament*, p. xxx.

and modern representatives (1884). *The Cambridge Paragraph Bible* itself was never reissued in the form Scrivener created; rather, its text was used for a 500-copy fine edition, the Doves Press Bible (1905), its NT text for Bagster's NT Octapla (1962), and its text again in Zondervan's 'KJV Gift & Award Bible, Revised' (2002). None of these used either Scrivener's paragraphed presentation or his extensively revised margin. Yet Scrivener had done an immense amount of work: the collation of texts was far more substantial than any previously attempted, even extending to minute work on the KJB's sources, and the work on the italics and the margin, especially the cross-references, was exhaustive and in many ways admirable. If Cambridge, which must have invested significantly in the project, did not deem it a failure, it nevertheless doomed it by not issuing further editions in an attempt to make it the new standard. The reality of continued demand for the accepted standard may have made it too risky to push something different.

The Cambridge Paragraph Bible, as its title suggests, pioneered new methods of presentation. It moved the chapter and verse numbers to the margin, leaving an 'unbroken text [arranged] in paragraphs accommodated to the sense', re-paragraphed the whole and presented the poetic parts in poetic form.[87] In this way it anticipated many modern translations though, sadly, its crammed page layout makes it painful to read. Regrettably (rather than sadly), only a few editions of the KJB such as *The Reader's Bible*, jointly published by the three guardians of the text in 1951, followed the attempt to create an unbroken text, presumably because of the conservative pressures already remarked on, and because such editions appeared as literary editions.

Scrivener's primary concern was to prepare 'a critical edition of the Authorized Version' that would represent it, 'as far as may be, in the precise shape that it would have assumed, if its venerable translators had shown themselves more exempt than they were from the failings incident to human infirmity; or if the same severe accuracy, which is now demanded in carrying so important a volume through the press, had been deemed requisite or was at all usual in their age'

---

[87] *Cambridge Paragraph Bible*, p. ix. I have followed Scrivener's book except in this case where there is a significant difference between the original introduction and the book.

(pp. 1, 2). Implicit here and throughout is the idea that an editor's duty is to perfect the text in the light of the originals. By highlighting the translators' human infirmity, Scrivener opened the way to changing the text even where there is no printing error involved. This aligns him with most previous editors, feeling himself able to correct the text where he judges the translators to have erred as translators. So, aiming to give the text 'in the precise shape that it *would* have assumed', Scrivener is giving it in the shape he thinks it *should* have assumed. He tests the variants not by the evidence for the translators' judgements but by his view of how the original texts should have been translated. The result is more conservative than Blayney's text, for he restores about a third of the original readings (listed in his appendix C), but the reader of *The Cambridge Paragraph Bible* can never be certain that the text is that of the translators because Scrivener is at heart a reviser.

Shortly after this failed but fascinating reform of the KJB text, a much more radical reform of the KJB appeared, the Revised Version (NT 1881, OT 1885, Apocrypha 1895). This marked the resumption of the kind of scholarly and creative effort that had produced the KJB out of the work of Tyndale and his successors. Still continuing in fractured ways, this effort is usually characterised by a desire to keep something like the KJB's language, now absolutely established as religious English, while improving its scholarship in the light of modern discoveries and understanding. Versions such as the American Standard Version (1901), the New American Standard Bible (1971), the Revised Standard Version (1952), the New Revised Standard Version (1989), the New King James Version (1982) and the 21st Century King James Version (1994) appeal to the heritage of the KJB while being manifestly different. Together with the ever increasing number of translations and paraphrases into modern English, they are part of a large movement that has entirely destabilised the English text of the Bible. Consequently the KJB has gone from being the only Bible in England to being one of a multitude spread round the world. In this context, the stability of its text is like a hallmark. Whatever the qualities of the other versions – modern scholarship, simple, accessible English, political correctness, contemporary presentation – they are all pretenders to its throne, while it remains, apparently what it always was, the authentic, elderly, increasingly disregarded but still revered monarch among Bibles.

Despite the risks involved in deviating from the accepted standard, Cambridge produced one more revision of the KJB text. History was repeating itself. The text needed resetting because the images were losing quality, and Cambridge did not know the basis of its own text, other than that 'it was prepared/edited by someone from Oxford and an opposite number from Cambridge after the second War, and it is supposed to incorporate "modern" spelling and good editorial practice'.[88] This, the Concord edition, was indeed a thoroughly well produced standard text, essentially Blayney's with no further modernisation of spelling and a different set of cross-references, and it was the same as the Oxford text (though the 'concord' did not extend to the Apocrypha, which was by then only occasionally printed). After consultation and thought, Cambridge decided that the spelling needed work and that the Concord edition should be collated with Scrivener's text as the one distinctive edition with a good scholarly reputation and, through Scrivener's book, a full justification for its readings. As work progressed, it became clear that more than spelling needed attending to. As with the spelling, so the punctuation was neither right by current standards nor that of the translators. It too had to be revised. Scrivener's list of variant readings suggested that some of the changes, including some of his decisions, were questionable and that all the variants needed to be examined. In due course the importance of the manuscript annotations in Bod 1602, especially in the OT, were realised, and their evidence along with that of MS 98 was incorporated into the examination. Presentation also, we agreed, could be improved. The aim became to present the text that the translators had decided on as closely as it could be established, and to make the whole as accessible as possible to the reader and student by using modern spelling, revised punctuation and the best possible modern presentation.

The specimen page from Genesis shows a text very little changed from standard texts: the words and the grammatical forms are the same. Differences in spelling are 1611 and the *OED*'s 'man-child' for Blayney's 'man child' (17:10, 12), 'spoke' for 'spake' (16:13) and 'bore' for 'bare' (16:15–16). These latter two are how we would now spell and pronounce them. Six changes of punctuation are visible in chapter 17, all of them a return to 1611's punctuation and all involving

---

[88] Bible Publishing Manager to myself; quoted in Norton, *Textual History*, p. 132.

the eighteenth-century taste for semicolons. Three revert to commas (vv. 1, 3 and 8), and three revert to colons (vv. 5, 10 and 14), showing the logical relationship involved. One of Blayney's innovations, the use of a capital letter to begin a command, is removed from 17:10 (Blayney and the standard text read, 'This is my covenant . . . ; Every man child . . . ').

The appearance of the page is the most striking difference from traditional KJBs, though similar presentation can be found in some Bibles, including Tyndale's NT and Pentateuch. The units of the text are immediately visible because of the paragraphing and the use of speech marks.[89] Yet this is not how one would present a normal prose text: new paragraphs are not used for dialogue in places where this might be possible such as the last paragraph of chapter 16. The reference system is retained through the clearly-marked chapter numbers and the unobtrusive verse numbers, making it both a study text and a reading text. The original annotations (plus one that has become a part of standard KJBs at 17:5, marked by square brackets to indicate it is not from 1611) are placed in the margin as in 1611 but without the use of reference marks. This gives the student everything that the translators included as an aid to understanding.

There are also noticeable omissions. It might have been a nice touch, at the cost of interrupting the text, to have included the original chapter summaries, but new headers fitting the new pagination would have had to have been invented. No attempt was made either to revise the cross-references or restore those of 1611, which as noted earlier, were substantially derived from copies of the Vulgate and often inaccurate, so they are omitted for the time being. Finally, italics are omitted, not just because most readers do not understand their purpose but because they are, even in their most revised form, a quite inadequate guide to the relationship between the translation and the original. Much better guides have been created, notably Strong's numbers, which correlate each word with the word it translates, interlinear and digital Bibles. Only in the marginal notes where the translators offer a literal rendering of the original is such marking retained, for in these it is part of noting what was literally in the original, as in the note to 16:14.

---

[89] One fussy element I now regret is the placing of punctuation after the final speech mark where the speech is only part of the sentence.

16 Now Sarai Abram's wife bore him no children: and she had a handmaid, an Egyptian, whose name was Hagar. [2]And Sarai said unto Abram, 'Behold now, the LORD hath restrained me from bearing: I pray thee, go in unto my maid: it may be that I may obtain children by her'. And Abram hearkened to the voice of Sarai. [3]And Sarai Abram's wife took Hagar her maid the Egyptian, after Abram had dwelt ten years in the land of Canaan, and gave her to her husband Abram to be his wife. [4]And he went in unto Hagar, and she conceived: and she saw that she had conceived, her mistress was despised in her eyes. [5]And Sarai said unto Abram, 'My wrong be upon thee: I have given my maid into thy bosom, and when she saw that she had conceived, I was despised in her eyes: the LORD judge between me and thee'. [6]And Abram

[2]obtain: Heb. *be built by her*

said unto Sarai, 'Behold, thy maid is in thy hand; do to her as it pleaseth thee'. And when Sarai dealt hardly with her, she fled from her face.

[6]as: Heb. *that which is good in thy eyes*
[6]dealt: Heb. *afflicted her*

[7]And the angel of the LORD found her by a fountain of water in the wilderness, by the fountain in the way to Shur. [8]And he said, 'Hagar, Sarai's maid, whence camest thou? and whither wilt thou go?' And she said, 'I flee from the face of my mistress Sarai'. [9]And the angel of the LORD said unto her, 'Return to thy mistress, and submit thyself under her hands'. [10]And the angel of the LORD said unto her, 'I will multiply thy seed exceedingly, that it shall not be numbered for multitude'. [11]And the angel of the LORD said unto her, 'Behold, thou art with child, and shalt bear a son, and shalt call his name Ishmael; because the LORD hath heard thy affliction. [12]And he will be a wild man; his hand will be against every man, and every man's hand against him; and he shall dwell in the presence of all his brethren.' [13]And she called the name of the LORD that spoke unto her, 'Thou God seest me': for she said, 'Have I also here looked after him that seeth me?' [14]Wherefore the well was called Beer-lahai-roi; behold, it is between Kadesh and Bered. [15]And Hagar bore Abram a son: and Abram called his son's name, which Hagar bore, Ishmael. [16]And Abram was fourscore and six years old, when Hagar bore Ishmael to Abram.

[11]Ishmael: that is, *God shall hear*

[14]Beer-lahai-roi: that is, *the well of him that liveth and seeth me*

17 And when Abram was ninety years old and nine, the LORD appeared to Abram, and said unto him, 'I am the Almighty God, walk before me, and be thou perfect. [2]And I will make my covenant between me and thee, and will multiply thee exceedingly.' [3]And Abram fell on his face, and God talked with him, saying, [4]'As for me, behold, my covenant is with thee, and thou shalt be a father of many nations. [5]Neither shall thy name any more be called Abram, but thy name shall be Abraham: for a father of many nations have I made thee. [6]And I will make thee exceeding fruitful, and I will make nations of thee, and kings shall come out of thee. [7]And I will establish my covenant between me and thee and thy seed after thee in their generations for an everlasting covenant, to be a God unto thee, and to thy seed after thee. [8]And I will give unto thee, and to thy seed after thee, the land wherein thou art a stranger, all the land of Canaan, for an everlasting possession, and I will be their God.'

[1]perfect: or, *upright,* or *sincere*

[4]many: Heb. *multitude of nations*

[5][Abraham: that is, *father of a great multitude*]

[8]wherein: Heb. *of thy sojournings*

11. Genesis 16–17, *The New Cambridge Paragraph Bible.* Cambridge University Press.

The *New Cambridge Paragraph Bible* is essentially a work of restoration. As far as is possible, using the evidence of the translators' work found in Bod 1602, MS 98 and the first edition, it gives the text the translators themselves decided on. But perhaps its most obvious quality is restoration of the sort applied to an old master, making it newly vivid. The paragraphed presentation of the prose parts makes their structure clearer and, as Samuel Say's re-presentation of Genesis 49:7 showed (above, p. 173), poetic lines help the reader to a better sense of the poetry. The modern spelling is a particular help for the way it removes the dust and dirt of time. It sometimes involves an apparent change of sound but it never goes as far as changing words or grammatical forms, as sometimes happened in the development of the KJB. Two examples show that the value of this goes beyond what might sometimes look like antiquarianism. In modern KJBs Paul desires 'that women adorn themselves in modest apparel, with shamefacedness and sobriety; not with broided hair, or gold, or pearls, or costly array' (1 Tim. 2:9). 'Broided' is one of the specks of dust that impedes understanding and turns out to be a matter of sound: it is a variant of 'braided' (used in 1611 at Judith 10:3). But 'shamefacedness' is the most interesting word. Paul seems to want women to be ashamed of being women, but the Greek means 'with modesty' rather than 'ashamed'. 'Shamefacedness' entered the text in 1674, but the word the translators used was 'shamefastness', meaning 'modesty, sobriety of behaviour, decency, propriety' (*OED*). A modern reader probably has to work at the meaning of 'shamefastness', but that is better than being misled into a wrong understanding by an apparently easy similar word. 'Instead' would seem to be a much more innocent modernisation of 1611's 'in stead', especially as 'stead' is now rarely used as a single word. In 1611's English 'stead' meant place, and 'in stead' in place, rather than the abstract modern meaning of 'instead', as an alternative to. Consequently the KJB's meaning is lost in standard KJB's 'he took one of his ribs and closed up the flesh instead thereof' (Gen. 2:21). The KJB's meaning is not always easy, but changing one word (or two, as with 'in stead') for a similar word, as happens in the standard texts, almost always misleads.

CHAPTER 7

Reputation and future

REPUTATION

Hugh Broughton's infamous first review of the KJB was all about its failure of scholarship, that is, its failure to adopt Broughton's view of chronological relationships: 'the late Bible,' he begins, addressing a courtier, 'was sent me to censure, which bred in me a sadness that will grieve me while I breathe. It is so ill done. Tell his Majesty that I had rather be rent in pieces with wild horses than any such translation by my consent should be urged upon poor churches.'[1] Criticism of the KJB's scholarship has gone on ever since, but no one was as intransigent as Broughton. The earliest reported comment on its language comes from a man famous for his knowledge of Hebrew and translations, John Selden. After averring that the KJB (together with the Bishops' Bible) 'is the best translation in the world and renders the sense of the original best', he turns to its style:

There is no book so translated as the Bible for the purpose. If I translate a French book into English, I turn it into English phrase and not into French English. 'Il fait froid': I say 'tis cold, not it makes cold, but the Bible is rather translated into English words than into English phrase. The Hebraisms are kept and the phrase of that language is kept: as for example, 'he uncovered her shame', which is well enough so long as scholars have to do with it, but when it comes among the common people, Lord what gear [mockery] do they make of it![2]

Literal translation had used language fit 'for the purpose', but the people mocked it for its unnaturalness. This negative view of the KJB as English writing prevailed for roughly a century and a half,

---

[1] Broughton, 'Censure', unpaginated.   [2] Selden, *Table Talk*, p. 3.

absolutely at odds with later admiration for the KJB as great, in some eyes the greatest, work of English literature.

Scholarship and English, the intelligentsia and the common people: these four elements, sometimes separate, sometimes indistinguishable, are key to the KJB's reputation. For the half century until the Restoration, scholarship was the primary issue. John Lightfoot, editor of Broughton's works, at the end of a 1645 sermon to the House of Commons, encouraged the House 'to think of a review and survey of the translation of the Bible' so that 'the three nations... might come to understand the proper and genuine reading of the Scripture by an exact, vigorous, and lively translation'.[3] Two attempts at revision, possibly connected, were made in Commonwealth times. In 1652 or 1653 a group of revisers was appointed, led by the Baptist Henry Jessey: chief among his principles of translation was literalness leading to a version 'as exactly agreeing with the original as we can attain'.[4] Indicative of Jessey's priorities is his preference for the KJB's margin 'which in above 800 places is righter than the line', that is, more literal than the text (pp. 59–60). The work was nearly completed but, for reasons unknown, no commissioners were appointed to examine and approve it, and it disappeared without trace.[5] In January 1657 a sub-committee of the Grand Committee for Religion was set up 'to consider of the translations and impressions of the Bible, and to offer their opinions therein to this committee'. Leading oriental scholars were consulted, and the committee made 'divers excellent and learned observations of some mistakes in the translations of the Bible in English; which yet was agreed to be the best of any translation in the world; great pains was taken in it, but it became fruitless by the Parliament's dissolution'.[6] The KJB was admirable but improvable as an accurate translation, yet the failed attempts to improve it led to affirmations of its virtues as a translation.

The century's last attack on the KJB's accuracy was published in 1659, Robert Gell's *An Essay toward the Amendment of the Last English Translation of the Bible. Or, a proof, by many instances, that the last translation of the Bible may be* improved. Gell too was an

---

[3] Lightfoot, *A Sermon Preached before the Honourable House of Commons*, p. 30.
[4] E. W. [Edward Whiston], *The Life and Death of Mr Henry Jessey*, p. 45.
[5] Norton, *History of the English Bible as Literature*, pp. 98–102.
[6] Both quotations from Bulstrode Whitelocke, *Memorials of the English Affairs* (1682), p. 645.

advocate of literal translation, but the will to revise had passed with the Commonwealth, and the view that he wrote against, that the KJB is 'so exact... that it needs no essay toward the amendment of it' prevailed for a century.[7]

From the Restoration into Augustan times, 1660 to the middle of the eighteenth century, discussion moved from scholarship to the literary merits of the Bible, and was for much of this time especially concerned with the originals rather than the KJB. It became common to argue, as Milton's Jesus did to Satan in book IV of *Paradise Regained*, that the Bible was superior to the classics as literature. This was another battle of the books, rarely recognised alongside the well-known battle between the ancients and the moderns. Some writers followed a perennial line of thought, that the book of God, having the divine author, is the perfectly written book. While the rhetorical idea of literary excellence dominated, they showed how the Bible contained flowers of eloquence – more prosaically, how all the figures of speech could be found excellently used in it – and then, as Longinian ideas of sublimity in literature became the new fashion around the beginning of the eighteenth century, how the Bible possessed this affective power.

Such interest and ideas began to rub off on the KJB as the English representative of the admired originals: some writers simply generalised, some transcribed little bits from the originals as examples, some paraphrased, but more and more used the KJB. They might not have thought that the KJB itself was good English writing, but the effect of seeing literary quality demonstrated through the KJB became inescapable. The earliest handbook of rhetoric to use the KJB, John Smith's fairly popular *The Mystery of Rhetoric Unveiled* (1656; last printed 1688), shows this effect beginning. Smith demonstrated his Greek-derived figures of speech with Latin, English and scriptural examples, these last 'conducing very much to the right understanding of the sense of the letter of the Scripture' (from the title). Characteristic is his treatment of 'synonymia', 'a commodious heaping together of divers words of one signification' that, as he nicely puts it, 'adorneth and garnisheth speech as a rich wardrobe, wherein are many and sundry changes of garments to adorn one and the same person' (p. 160). The majority of the examples are scriptural, more

---

[7] Preface, fol. a2[r].

often than not verbatim from the KJB, so the reader begins to learn to appreciate what we would call parallelism through this description of synonymy and verses such as 'the Lord also thundered in the heavens, and the highest gave his voice, etc.' (Ps. 18:13). Amidst the classical figures, Smith includes a section on Hebraisms. He finishes with 'pathopoeia', which designates not a device but an effect, so looking forward to ideas of the sublime. It is 'a form of speech whereby the speaker moves the mind of his hearers to some vehemency of affection, as of love, hatred, gladness, sorrow, etc.' (p. 266); he illustrates it only from the Bible, including this striking image: 'can a woman forget her sucking child? yea, they may forget, yet will I not forget thee: behold, I have graven thee upon the palms of my hands, etc.' (Isa. 49:15–16, abbreviated). Thus he both demonstrates and teaches literary appreciation of the KJB.

But it took time for this kind of awareness to take hold. Appreciation of the originals did not transfer easily to the KJB because it had, as far as the Augustans were concerned, 'all the disadvantages of an old prose translation'.[8] Translation was necessarily inferior to the originals – but how much more so when it was literal, when prose was inferior to poetry, and when, as Dryden, thinking of himself as Horace before Augustus, put it in 1679,

it must be allowed to the present age that the tongue in general is so much refined since Shakespeare's time that many of his words and more of his phrases are scarce intelligible. And of those which we understand, some are ungrammatical, others coarse, and his whole style is so pestered with figurative expressions that it is as affected as it is obscure.[9]

Augustan pride in classical refinement led in 1724 to this declaration:

it is not, unless I mistake, much more than a century since England first recovered out of something like barbarism with respect to its state of letters and politeness . . . we have laid aside all our harsh antique words and retained only those of good sound and energy; the most beautiful polish is at length given to our tongue, and its Teutonic rust quite worn away.[10]

With irony in the image, one of the literati described himself and his peers as 'so full of Homer and Virgil, and . . . so bigoted to the Greek

[8] Husbands, *A Miscellany of Poems*, fol. d4ᵛ.
[9] *Troilus and Cressida*, dedication to the Earl of Sunderland; preface, fol. A4ᵛ.
[10] Welsted, *Epistles, Odes, etc.*, pp. vi–viii.

and Latin sects, that we are ready to account all authors heretical that are without the pale of the classics'.[11] In short, Augustan England was most unpropitious for appreciation of the KJB as a piece of English writing.

Yet the Augustans, while belittling the KJB, were beginning to appreciate it. Here is the phrase, 'all the disadvantages of an old prose translation' in context: 'yet how beautiful do the holy writings appear, under all the disadvantages of an old prose translation? So beautiful that, with a charming and elegant simplicity, they ravish and transport the learned reader, so intelligible that the most unlearned are capable of understanding the greater part of them.' It is a curious combination of praise and dispraise that was much repeated between 1690 and 1731, and even resurfaced in mid-eighteenth-century America: 'there is no stronger proof of the indestructible character of the poetry of the Bible, and of its inherent sublimity and beauty, than this fact, that through all the disadvantages and disguises of a literal prose translation, many passages of the poetical books, and nearly all the Psalms, still retain the spirit and rhythm and very music of the bard'.[12]

The change needed to turn these ideas – and some genuine appreciation of the KJB – into explicit admiration was slow coming. The people got there more quickly than the intelligentsia. From the time of Tyndale onwards, the Bible and literacy went hand in hand. People learnt to read in order to read the Bible; in due course the Bible became the chief book in teaching children to read. The KJB, as it became the only Bible in England, assumed a unique place not just in religious consciousness but in linguistic and literary consciousness. It was nursery story, primer, adolescent and adult reading, present from the alpha to the omega of verbal consciousness. Its faith, its language, imagery, story and poetry, heard, read and quoted, was the highest common factor in the mental environment of millions over many generations. It was a part of home and loved (or occasionally reacted against) like home. Regardless of the literary standards of the intelligentsia, regardless of what they thought the best standards of writing, such love created a sentimental basis for admiration of the KJB, and it made the KJB the most familiar standard of English.

[11] Blackmore, *Paraphrase on the Book of Job*, fol. ii[r–v].
[12] Halsey, *Literary Attractions of the Bible*, p. 74.

Jonathan Swift made the point in 1712, responding to the 'observation
that if [it] were not for the Bible and Common Prayer Book
in the vulgar tongue, we should hardly be able to understand anything
that was written among us an hundred years ago: which is certainly
true: for those books, being perpetually read in churches, have proved
a kind of standard for language, especially to the common people'.[13]

Besides creating that special form of English, religious English,
the Bible and the Prayer Book acted as a conservative force, keeping
current – or even, over a long period, returning to currency – older
forms of English and older English words that otherwise probably
would have disappeared. When the KJB translators wrote of their
varied choice of words, 'if we should say, as it were, unto certain
words, "Stand up higher, have a place in the Bible always", and to
others of like quality, "Get ye hence, be banished for ever"', they
wrote prophetically.[14] Words chosen lived, words unchosen might
have died. An eighteenth-century Bible translator who grew up in
Augustan times, the Quaker Anthony Purver, testified to the familiar power of the KJB's English: 'the obsolete words and uncouth
ungrammatical expressions in the sacred text pass more unheeded
as being oftener read and heard, especially when the mind is filled
with an imagination that a translation of the Scripture must be so
expressed'.[15] He went further and made detailed criticisms of the
KJB's English from an Augustan viewpoint which show that some
words that we are accustomed to were obsolete in the mid-eighteenth
century. To give one example: 'unwittingly', which Purver is not alone
in citing, was common until about 1630 and again from about 1815
(*OED*). The KJB was a kind of Noah's ark for English words and
expressions.

Admiration for the eloquence of the originals, pride in the century's
refinement of language and writing, and scorn for the antiquated
coarseness of the KJB's language, to say nothing of the ongoing sense
of faults of translation in the KJB, led to translations of a new kind
in the eighteenth century. All of them reflected the time in having an
explicit linguistic purpose, improvement of the KJB's English, and

[13] Swift, *A Proposal for Correcting, Improving and Ascertaining the English Tongue*, p. 32.
[14] 'Translators to the Reader', *NCPB*, p. xxxiv.
[15] Purver, *A New and Liberal Translation of All the Books of the Old and New Testament*, vol. 1,
    p. v.

most went further: without forgetting that it was sacred, they treated the Bible as a literary work and attempted to match the eloquence of the originals.

The first of these new versions, though it has more of a scholarly element to it than some, gives a fair taste of what was to come. It was a diglot Greek and English NT by Daniel Mace, a Presbyterian, published in 1729. Mace's work on the Greek text had some value but made no headway against contemporary respect for the Received Text. His translation is notable for the way it revises the KJB with touches of grandiose vocabulary and an element of chatty paraphrase, as in 'blessed are the pacific: for they shall be the children of God' (Matt. 5:9), and 'when ye fast, don't put on a dismal air' (Matt. 6:16). Some of these versions, such as Robert Lowth's *Isaiah* (1778), earned deserved respect, most, like Edward Harwood's much mocked *Liberal Translation of the New Testament* (1768), were one-edition wonders. Harwood gives testimony to the growing reverence for the KJB at the same time as condemning it, writing of his consciousness 'that the bald and barbarous language of the old vulgar version hath acquired a venerable sacredness from length of time and custom' (p. v). The hirsute and refined results of his attempt to 'clothe the genuine ideas and doctrines of the apostles with that propriety and perspicuity in which they themselves, I apprehend, would have exhibited them had they *now* lived and written in our language' (p. iii) speak for themselves:

Survey with attention the lilies of the field, and learn from them how unbecoming it is for rational creatures to cherish a solicitous passion for gaiety and dress – for they sustain no labour, they employ no cares to adorn themselves: and yet are clothed with such inimitable beauty as the richest monarch in the richest dress never equalled. Since then God lavishes such a variety of striking colours upon a transient, short-lived flower; ought ye, who are creatures so highly exalted in the scale of being, to distrust divine providence? (Matt. 6:28–30)

Not even his contemporaries admired this.

The general (but not universal) mediocrity of these versions made a strong contribution to the reputation of the KJB. The changing tone of reviews tells the story as they swing away from sympathy and encouragement to outright admiration for the KJB. In 1764, reviewing Richard Wynne's NT in lukewarm terms, *The Critical*

Review encouraged further effort to produce 'an accurate and elegant translation':

> these divine writings should be translated with accuracy and spirit. Our common version is, indeed, a valuable work, and deserves the highest esteem; but it is by no means free from imperfection. It certainly contains many false interpretations, ambiguous phrases, obsolete words and indelicate expressions which deform the beauty of the sacred pages, perplex the unlearned reader, offend the fastidious ear, confirm the prejudices of the unbeliever and excite the derision of the scorner. An accurate and elegant translation would therefore be of infinite service to religion, would obviate a thousand difficulties and exceptions, prevent a multitude of chimerical tenets and controversial questions, give a proper dignity and lustre to divine revelation, and convince the world that whatever appears confused, coarse or ridiculous in the Holy Scriptures ought to be imputed to the *translator*.[16]

In 1784 *The Critical Review* was still sympathetic to new versions, but in 1787 its position had reversed. Reviewing Alexander Geddes's *Prospectus of a New Translation of the Holy Bible* (1786), it claimed that 'to reform the text of the Bible would have appeared to the ignorant little less than a change of a national religion'.[17] What makes this startling is that the reviewer shares the feeling of 'the ignorant'. The literati and the people come together in a passage of real warmth:

> [The KJB's] faults are said to be a defect in the idiom, as English, a want of uniformity of style, mistake in the meaning of some words, too great precision, which has introduced the italic explanations, and a slight warping in the favour of the translator's peculiar sentiments. The defect in idiom we cannot allow to be a fault: it raised the language above common use and has almost sanctified it; nor would we lose the noble simplicity, the energetic bravery, for all the idiomatic elegance which a polished age can bestow. Dr Geddes objects to a translation too literal, but we wish not to see the present text changed unless where real errors render it necessary. The venerable tree which we have always regarded with a religious respect cannot be pruned to modern fashions without our feeling the most poignant regret. Our attachment to this venerable relic has involuntarily made our language warm. (p. 48)

Still a contrast is maintained between the standards of the KJB and the elegance of a polished age, but the judgement between the two has shifted decisively. Instead of the achievement of a polished Bible

---

[16] *The Critical Review* 18 (Sept. 1764): 189.   [17] *The Critical Review* 63 (Jan. 1787): 46.

being looked forward to, now the KJB is looked back to as the literary standard: it is not merely a relic but a 'venerable relic' that has beneficially influenced the language. Its age is still recognised but no longer disliked.

Insofar as one can locate this large change in the reputation of the KJB, it belongs to the 1760s. It was in this decade that Swift's observation that the Bible and the Prayer Book 'have proved a kind of standard for language, especially to the common people' turned into a general, frequently repeated rule. Robert Lowth's *Short Introduction to English Grammar* (1762) began this by observing that 'the vulgar translation of the Bible . . . is the best standard of our language' (p. 89). The general change in taste was neatly portrayed by Oliver Goldsmith in 1766 in *The Vicar of Wakefield*. An actor tells the aging Vicar, '"Dryden and Rowe's manner, Sir, are quite out of fashion; our taste has gone back a whole century, Fletcher, Ben Jonson, and all the plays of Shakespeare are the only things that go down."' The Vicar's puzzled response articulates the passing age: '"How," cried I, "is it possible the present age can be pleased with that antiquated dialect, that obsolete humour, those over-charged characters, which abound in the works you mention?"' (ch. 18). It was the decade when love for Shakespeare became idolatry: "Tis he! 'Tis he! / "The god of our idolatry!"', exclaimed David Garrick in 1769 – a convenient moment from which to date what has become known as bardolatry.[18] The taste for antiquity was taking hold, and is visible in works like James Macpherson's *Fragments of Ancient Poetry* (1760) which in some parts uses a quasi-biblical way of writing, and, most famously, in Thomas Percy's *Reliques of Ancient English Poetry* (1765). The change in the KJB's reputation was part of a more general change in taste, a change that now seems inevitable given the achievements of pre-Augustan literature and the effete excesses of the later Augustans, and the history sketched here shows that the KJB played a significant role in creating the change.

Criticism of the KJB's scholarship did not disappear. Lowth, the century's most important English critic of the Bible, believed that more progress had been made in the knowledge of the Scriptures

---

[18] Garrick, *Ode upon dedicating a building, and erecting a statue, to Shakespeare, at Stratford upon Avon*, p. 1; see also Daniell, *The Bible in English*, p. 620.

in the 150 years since the publication of the KJB than in the fifteen centuries preceding. He therefore advocated 'an accurate revisal of our vulgar translation by public authority' in order

to confirm and illustrate these holy writings, to evince their truth, to show their consistency, to explain their meaning, to make them more generally known and studied, more easily and perfectly understood by all; to remove the difficulties that discourage the honest endeavours of the unlearned, and provoke the malicious cavils of the half-learned.[19]

On the other hand, defending the closeness with which he followed the language of the KJB in his *Isaiah*, he observed that 'the style of [our vulgar] translation is not only excellent in itself, but has taken possession of our ear, and of our taste'. A revision was therefore more advisable than a new translation, 'for as to the style and language, it admits but of little improvement; but in respect of the sense and the accuracy of interpretation, the improvements of which it is capable are great and numberless'.[20] This became the dominant opinion. The KJB's scholarship could and should be improved, but its language could not and should not be tampered with. 'Revisal by public authority' was still a century away, but the parameters for the Revised Version had been set.

The new-found admiration for the KJB's language and its literary qualities combined with a sense that the century's attempt at literary revision had been a failure to create the idea that the KJB was a literary revision of its predecessors. One of the many works arguing for a new translation alleged that improvement of the language was one of the main motives which led King James to order a new translation, for the earlier translators (either the Geneva translators or the Bishops) 'appeared so well to have understood the Scriptures that little more than the language of it was altered by the translators in King James's time'.[21] Moreover, as admiration became customary so the travails of the KJB and even the persistent criticism of it through the first half of the century were forgotten, and people began to believe that the KJB's merits were immediately perceived and caused it to

---

[19] Lowth, *A sermon preached at the visitation of the Honourable and Right Reverend Richard Lord Bishop of Durham*, p. 15.
[20] Lowth, *Isaiah* (1778), pp. lxxii–lxxiii.
[21] Pilkington, *Remarks upon Several Passages of Scripture*, p. 114.

be an instant success; in the words of another advocate of revision, 'it was a happy consequence of this acknowledged excellence [of the KJB] that the other versions fell immediately into disrepute, are no longer known to the generality of the people, and are only sought after by the curious'.[22] All these ideas have proved tenacious, and sometimes the argument that the KJB was a literary revision has been powerfully made.

Much of the story of the KJB's reputation after the 1760s is taken up with praise, sometimes judicious, sometimes taken to rhetorical excess. Along with bardolatry what I have called AVolatry (Authorised Version-olatry) became the norm. One of its finest expressions came from a man who had experienced and seen the power of the KJB before converting to Catholicism (whence the accusation of heresy), Father Frederick William Faber:

If the Aryan heresy was propagated and rooted by means of beautiful ver-nacular hymns, so who will say that the uncommon beauty and marvellous English of the Protestant Bible is not one of the great strongholds of heresy in this country? It lives on in the ear like a music that never can be forgotten, like the sound of church bells which the convert hardly knows how he can forego. Its felicities seem often to be things rather than mere words. It is part of the national mind and the anchor of the national seriousness. Nay, it is worshipped with a positive idolatry, in extenuation of whose grotesque fanaticism its intrinsic beauty pleads availingly with the man of letters and the scholar. The memory of the dead passes into it. The potent traditions of childhood are stereotyped in its verses. The power of all the griefs and trials of a man is hidden beneath its words. It is the representative of his best moments, and all that there has been about him of soft, and gentle, and pure, and penitent, and good, speaks to him forever out of his English Bible. It is his sacred thing which doubt never dimmed and controversy never soiled. It has been to him all along as the silent, but O how intelligible voice, of his guardian angel; and in the length and breadth of the land there is not a Protestant, with one spark of religiousness about him, whose spiritual biography is not in his Saxon Bible.[23]

The unique place of the KJB in the hearts of many over more than 200 years is well captured.

A chorus of claims and phrases expressed faith in the excel-lence of the KJB. Thomas Babington Macaulay proclaimed of 'that

[22] White, *A Revisal of the English Translation*, p. 9.
[23] Faber, 'An essay on the interest and characteristics of the Lives of the Saints', pp. 116–17.

stupendous work' that it was 'a book which, if everything else in our
language should perish, would alone suffice to show the whole extent
of its beauty and power'.[24] Among many others, Richard Chenevix
Trench, Archbishop, philologist and one of the makers of the Revised
Version, and the American scholar George P. Marsh thought it 'the
first English classic', Marsh adding that it was 'the highest exemplar
of purity and beauty of language existing in our speech'.[25] J.G. Frazer,
author of *The Golden Bough*, recognised how much this had become
a cliché: 'that our English version of the Bible is one of the greatest
classics in the language is admitted by all in theory, but few people
appear to treat it as such in practice'.[26] Others including three of
the makers of the Revised Version liked the phrase from Spenser's
The Faerie Queen, 'well of English undefiled'. Another favourite with
a lengthy history was Lowes's essay title, 'the noblest monument of
English prose'.[27]

Inevitably some thought of the KJB as inspired. The first biographer of the KJB translators, the American evangelist Alexander
McClure, held 'that the translators enjoyed the highest degree of that
special guidance which is ever granted to God's true servants in exi-
gencies of deep concernment to his kingdom on earth'.[28] Eventually,
enlisting the historical position of the KJB that Faber described so
well, this became the fundamentalist position that Edward F. Hills
put this way:

the King James Version is the historic Bible of English-speaking Protestants.
Upon it God, working providentially, has placed the stamp of His approval
through the usage of many generations of Bible-believing Christians. Hence,
if we believe in God's providential preservation of the Scriptures, we will
retain the King James Version, for in so doing we will be following the clear
leading of the Almighty.[29]

To some, like Benjamin Jowett, Regius Professor of Greek at Oxford,
reflecting on the Revised Version NT, it seemed 'that, in a certain
sense, the Authorised Version is more inspired than the original'.[30]

[24] Macauley, 'John Dryden', *The Edinburgh Review* 47, 93 (January 1828): 18.
[25] Trench, *On the Authorised Version of the New Testament* (1858), p. 24, Marsh, ed. Smith,
Lectures on the English Language, p. 441.
[26] Frazer, *Passages of the Bible Chosen for their Literary Beauty and Interest* (1895), p. v.
[27] In Lowes, *Of Reading Books*, pp. 47–77.   [28] McClure, *The Translators Revived*, p. 248.
[29] Hills, *The King James Version Defended!*, p. 214.
[30] As reported in Abbott and Campbell, *The Life and Letters of Benjamin Jowett*, vol. I, p. 406.

Across the Atlantic, George P. Eckman understood Jowett to be putting forward a cumulative idea of inspiration:

It is to be presumed that the translators in 1611, being very devout men, constantly invoked the blessing of God upon their work, and that infinite wisdom was pleased to grant their request, so that upon the inspiration originally given to the Bible writers there was added the inspiration which God gave to the revered translators of the ancient tongues into the English vernacular.[31]

Alongside the acclaim for the KJB there were dissenting voices, though they had little effect on the KJB's general reputation. In the first years of Queen Victoria's reign the literary historian Henry Hallam protested that 'the style of this translation is in general so enthusiastically praised that no one is permitted either to qualify or even explain the grounds of his approbation'.[32] In terms of the KJB's literary and linguistic reputations, it was an ineffective protest. But while these reputations remained unassailable, other things were beginning to work against the KJB. Its perceived limitations of scholarship, especially in the light of modern knowledge of the Greek text of the NT, led slowly but inevitably to the Revised Version and its successors. From 1881 when the Revised Version NT appeared, the KJB was no longer the only Bible in the English-speaking world, but its language remained the only English for biblical translation.

Then, particularly after the Second World War, in spite of the chorus of admiration, the KJB's language as well as modern scholarship began to tell against it. There had been notable alternative versions earlier in the century such as James Moffatt's (1913 etc.), but the war was a decisive factor in the first of the major contemporary English versions, the New English Bible (NT 1961, OT 1970). Finding the KJB's language too archaic to be generally understood, some churches agitated for a translation in contemporary English. Geoffrey Hunt puts the situation clearly:

The experience of many British pastors, chaplains, teachers and youth leaders in the War of 1939–45, when they were trying under difficult conditions to expound and convey the message of the Bible, was that very frequently the

---

[31] Eckman, *The Literary Primacy of the Bible*, p. 197.
[32] Hallam, *Introduction to the Literature of Europe in the Fifteenth, Sixteenth, and Seventeenth Centuries*, vol. II, p. 464.

language of the Authorised Version was not a help but a hindrance. It was beautiful and solemn, but it put a veil of unreality between the scriptural writers and the people of the mid-twentieth century who needed something that would speak to them immediately. 'Whenever we have a certain time to teach a particular Bible passage', was the complaint, 'we have to spend half that time giving an English lesson, "translating" the Bible English into the current language of today. We need a Bible translation in which this is already done for us; then we can start from where people actually are and give them the Bible message in language they understand.'[33]

As one of the New English Bible translators somewhat unkindly put it, the language of the KJB had become a 'numinous rumble',[34] a medium that obscured the meaning in the Bible while yet giving those who loved it an experience of 'the beauty of holiness' that the Psalmist enjoins his hearers and readers to worship the Lord in (Ps. 29:2). Whatever critics thought of the New English Bible, the usefulness of having the Bible in contemporary language was inescapable. As people became accustomed to the idea that the Bible could be in contemporary language, so many also became unaccustomed to the KJB. However high the KJB's reputation might be, not only had it ceased to be the only Bible in England, it had ceased to be the only way of translating the Bible. Its monopoly on the English Protestant consciousness was broken.[35]

FUTURE

The KJB is not what it was because language has changed, because scholarship has changed and because we have changed. One of the most fundamental of these changes happened in the twentieth century as Christianity loosened its grip on the English-speaking world: it is no longer possible to think of the Bible, in whatever form, as a common part of everybody's life in the way Faber described it as being in Victorian times. In these circumstances, one must wonder whether the KJB has a future.

It would be sad if it lived on only because it was for about three centuries the central book of English-speaking Protestant Christianity,

---

[33] Hunt, *About the New English Bible* (1970), pp. 9–10.
[34] Willey, 'On translating the Bible into modern English', p. 5.
[35] The story sketched here is given at length in my *History of the Bible as Literature* and its shorter version, *History of the English Bible as Literature*.

and not because it is a living book. As is inevitable with a book so read and written about, its qualities have sometimes been understated, sometimes overstated. In particular, I think its scholarship – that is, its knowledge of and fidelity to the original texts – is underestimated. Setting aside the quality of the texts it translated, especially the Greek Received Text, it is remarkably sensitive in its awareness of how English may represent the originals. It is a triumph of judicious – rather than slavish – literal translation. So often when one puts a particularly meaningful or resonant phrase, verse or passage against the originals, the quality appears to stem directly from them. Something of this has, I hope, been apparent in Chapter 2. Equally what may appear bad through incomprehensibility or sheer ugliness often comes from its earnest fidelity to the originals. There are times when one may prefer renderings found elsewhere – Tyndale's imaginative engagement with the originals and his ability to turn obscurity into sense, or, say, the Revised Version's punctilious attention to prepositions[36] – but, taken as a whole, the KJB is startlingly faithful. William Blake's experience, related in connection with his beginning to learn Hebrew, is one that can still be shared by those able and willing to make the effort: 'astonishing indeed is the English translation, it is almost word for word, and if the Hebrew Bible is as well translated, which I do not doubt it is, we need not doubt of its having been translated as well as written by the Holy Ghost'.[37]

Its language may one day become as removed from modern English as Latin is from romance languages, and the KJB may become like the Vulgate, comprehensible to the select few but a magical mystery to most people. As the restoration work undertaken in *The New Cambridge Paragraph Bible* shows, the language is not as difficult as it often appears. So much based in the Anglo-Saxon roots of English, it has more in common with modern English than many English classics, including Shakespeare, and this puts the possible day of its death as comprehensible English further in the future. Moreover, it is a powerful form of English where there is often a strong sense of connection

---

[36] I have in mind Westcott's discussion of the theological significance of 'into' in Matt. 28:19, and 'in' in Rom. 6:23, *Some Lessons of the Revised Version of the New Testament* (1897), pp. 62–3.

[37] To James Blake, 30 Jan. 1803; Keynes (ed.), *The Complete Writings of William Blake*, pp. 821–2.

with realities that is diminished in the greater abstraction of modern English, as the difference between 'in stead' and 'instead' (above p. 184) showed. Nevertheless, it is language that makes demands of a modern reader. Some of its grammar is unfamiliar, notably the verb forms, but not unfamiliar enough to be a real difficulty. The vocabulary is the bigger challenge because some words are archaic and some look familiar but are used in unfamiliar senses (a publican does not serve drinks but gathers taxes). Glossaries as found in some editions, Bible word-books[38] or a historical dictionary are useful here, and there is obviously a case for putting glosses in the margin as in many editions of Shakespeare. One might say with Gregory the Great, the sixth-century Church Father, 'that even in the Scriptures there are parts where the elephant must swim, as well as others which the lamb may ford'.[39] Much of the KJB's English is easy, some not. Gregory of course had in mind the mixture of simplicity and difficulty in what the Scripture says, and this should never be forgotten in reading the Bible. Some of it speaks directly to soul and heart, some speaks with a complexity or even obscurity that has exercised two millennia of commentators. The reader may sometimes find the difficulties of the KJB's language unnecessary, but it is as well to be reminded that what is being read requires earnest engagement, and better still to have a version that so richly rewards this engagement.

---

[38] E.g. Bridges and Weigle, *The King James Bible Word Book*, Vance, *Archaic Words and the Authorized Version*.

[39] *Moralia in Job, Epistola ad Leandrum*, 4; *Corpus Christianorum, Series Latina* CXLIII, p. 6; as given by Samuel Taylor Coleridge, *The Friend, Collected Works*, vol. IV (1971 etc.), vol. II, p. 61n.

Select bibliography

BIBLES

1516	Desiderius Erasmus. *Novum Instrumentum.*
1525	William Tyndale. New Testament (incomplete).
1526	William Tyndale. New Testament. Facsimile. Intro. David Daniell. 2008.
1530	William Tyndale. Pentateuch. *Tyndale's Old Testament* (modern spelling edition). Ed. David Daniell. 1992.
1534	William Tyndale. New Testament (revised). *Tyndale's New Testament* (modern spelling edition). Ed. David Daniell. 1989.
1534	Martin Luther. *Biblia.* Intro. Stephan Füssel. 2003.
1535	Myles Coverdale. *Biblia, the Bible.*
1537	John Rogers, ed. The Matthew Bible. Facsimile. Intro. Joseph W. Johnson. 2009.
1539	Richard Taverner. *The Most Sacred Bible.*
1539	The Great Bible.
1557	Geneva New Testament.
1560	The Geneva Bible. Facsimile. Intro. Lloyd E. Berry. (1969) 2007.
1568	The Bishops' Bible.
1576	Laurence Tomson. *The New Testament . . . translated out of Greek by Theod. Beza.*
1582	Gregory Martin. Rheims New Testament.
1587	Geneva with Tomson NT.
1589	William Fulke. *The Text of the New Testament of Jesus Christ.*
1599	Geneva with Tomson NT and Junius's annotations to Revelation.
1602	Bishops' Bible with KJB translators' annotations. Bodleian Library: Bibl. Eng. 1602 b. 1.
1609–10	Douai Old Testament.
1611	King James Bible. Facsimile. Intro. A.W. Pollard. 1911.
1613	King James Bible. Second edition.

1629, 1638   King James Bible. First and second Cambridge editions.

1642   King James Bible with Geneva annotations. Broerss, Amsterdam.

1646 (?)   King James Bible with dates. Bentley, Finsbury.

1653   Henry Hammond. *A Paraphrase and Annotations upon all the Books of the New Testament.*

1657   Theodore Haak. *The Dutch Annotations upon the whole Bible.*

1660   King James Bible 'illustrated with chorographical sculps by J. Ogilby'. Cambridge.

1680   King James Bible with 'The History of the Old and New Testament in Cuts'. Bill and Barker.

1675, 1679   King James Bible. First and second Oxford editions.

1717   King James Bible. Baskett, Oxford.

1729   Daniel Mace. *The New Testament in Greek and English.* 2 vols.

1743   King James Bible. Ed. F.S. Parris, Cambridge.

1762   King James Bible. Ed. F.S. Parris, Cambridge.

1763   King James Bible. Baskerville, Cambridge.

1764   Anthony Purver. *A New and Liberal Translation of all the Books of the Old and New Testament.* 2 vols.

1768   Edward Harwood. *A Liberal Translation of the New Testament.* 2 vols.

1769   King James Bible. Ed. Benjamin Blayney, Oxford.

1771 (?)   *The Complete Family Bible.* Ed. Samuel Newton.

1790 (?)   *The Christian's New and Complete Family Bible: or Universal Library of Divine Knowledge.* Ed. Thomas Bankes.

1833   King James Bible. Exact reprint in roman type of the first edition.

1873   *The Cambridge Paragraph Bible of the Authorized English Version, with the text revised by a collation of its early and other principal editions, the use of the italic type made uniform, the marginal references remodelled, and a critical introduction prefixed.* Ed. F.H.A. Scrivener, Cambridge.

1885   The Revised Version. (NT 1881, Apocrypha 1895).

1898   Robert Young. *Literal Translation of the Holy Bible.* 1863; rev. edn.

2005   *The New Cambridge Paragraph Bible.* Ed. David Norton.

OTHER WORKS

Abbott, Evelyn, and Lewis Campbell. *The Life and Letters of Benjamin Jowett.* 2 vols. 3rd edn. London. 1897.

Allen, Ward S. (trans. and ed.). *Translating for King James.* Nashville: Vanderbilt University Press. 1969.

(ed.) *Translating the New Testament Epistles 1604–1611: A Manuscript from King James's Westminster Company*. Ann Arbor: Vanderbilt University Press. 1977.

Allen, Ward S., and Edward C. Jacobs. *The Coming of the King James Gospels: A Collation of the Translators' Work-in-Progress*. Fayetteville: University of Arkansas Press. 1995.

Anon. (perhaps William Bentley). 'The case of the printery at Finsbury'. 1659.

Anon. 'An essay upon the English translation of the Bible'. *Bibliotheca Literaria* 4 (1723): 1–23.

Anon. *Report on the History and Recent Collation of the English Version of the Bible: Presented by the Committee on Versions to the Board of Managers of the American Bible Society*. New York. 1857.

Anon. 'A true state of the case of John Field and Henry Hills'. 1659.

Arber, Edward (ed.). *A Transcript of the Registers of the Company of Stationers of London, 1554–1640 A.D.* 5 vols. Gloucester, Mass.: P. Smith. (1875–94) 1967.

Babbage, Stuart Barton. *Puritanism and Richard Bancroft*. London: SPCK. 1962.

Ball, William. *A Brief Treatise Concerning the Regulating of Printing*. London. 1651.

Barlow, William. *The Sum and Substance of the Conference . . . at Hampton Court*. London. 1604.

Barnard, John. 'The financing of the Authorized Version 1610–1612: Robert Barker and "combining" and "sleeping" stationers'. *Publishing History* 57 (2005): 5–52.

Blackmore, Richard. *Paraphrase on the Book of Job*. London. 1700.

Blake, William. *The Complete Writings of William Blake*. Ed. Geoffrey Keynes. London: Oxford University Press. 1966.

Bois, John. Diary. Cambridge University Library. MS Add 3856. Copy of parts of the diary by Miss Howes of Norwich. MS Add 3857.

Bridges, Ronald, and Luther A. Weigle. *The King James Bible Word Book* (1960). Nashville: Thomas Nelson. 1994.

Broughton, Hugh. *An Advertisement of Corruption in our Handling of Religion*. Middleburg. 1604.

'A Censure of the Late Translation'. Middleburg. ?1612.

Works. Ed. John Lightfoot. London. 1662.

Budaeus (Guillaume Budé). *Commentarii Linguae Graecae*. Paris. 1529.

Bush, Sargent, Jr, and Carl J. Rasmussen. *The Library of Emmanuel College, Cambridge, 1584–1637*. Cambridge University Press. 1986.

Carter, Harry. *A History of Oxford University Press*. Vol. 1: *To the Year 1780*. Oxford: Clarendon Press. 1975.

Cook, John. *A New Catalogue of Useful, Important, Instructive and Entertaining Books . . .* No. 17. 1784?

Corbett, Margery, and Ronald Lightbown. *The Comely Frontispiece.* London: Routledge and Kegan Paul. 1979.

Critical Review 63. January 1787.

Curtis, Thomas. *The Existing Monopoly, an Inadequate Protection of the Authorised Version of Scripture.* London. 1833.

Daiches, David. *The King James Version of the English Bible.* University of Chicago Press. 1941.

Daniell, David. *William Tyndale: A Biography.* New Haven: Yale University Press. 1994.

The Bible in English. New Haven: Yale University Press. 2003.

Dillingham, William. *Vita Laurentii Chadertoni.* Cambridge. 1700.

Downame, John (?). *Annotations upon all the Books of the Old and New Testament.* London. 1645.

Dryden, John. *Troilus and Cressida.* London. 1679.

Eckman, George P. *The Literary Primacy of the Bible.* New York: Methodist Book Concern. 1915.

Faber, Frederick William. 'An essay on the interest and characteristics of the Lives of the Saints'. In L.F.C. Chalippe, *The Life of S. Francis of Assisi.* London. 1853.

Foxe, John. *Acts and Monuments.* London. 1563.

Frazer, James George. *Passages of the Bible Chosen for their Literary Beauty and Interest.* London. 1895.

Fuller, Thomas. *The Church History of Britain.* London. 1656.

The History of the Worthies of England. London. 1662.

Garrick, David. *Ode upon dedicating a building, and erecting a statue, to Shakespeare, at Stratford upon Avon.* London. 1769.

Gaskell, Philip. *Trinity College Library: The First 150 Years.* Cambridge University Press. 1980.

Gell, Robert. *An Essay toward the Amendment of the last English Translation of the Bible.* London. 1659.

Goldsmith, Oliver. *The Vicar of Wakefield.* Salisbury. 1766.

Greenslade, S. L. (ed.). *The Cambridge History of the Bible.* Vol. III: *The West from the Reformation to the Present Day.* Cambridge University Press. 1963.

Greetham, D.C. *Textual Scholarship: An Introduction.* London: Garland. 1994.

Gutjahr, Paul C. 'Four centuries of typography in the King James Bible'. In Paul C. Gutjahr and Megan L. Benton (eds.), *Illuminating Letters: Typography and Literary Interpretation.* Amherst: University of Massachusetts Press. 2001. Pp. 1–44.

Hallam, Henry. *Introduction to the Literature of Europe in the Fifteenth, Sixteenth, and Seventeenth Centuries*. 4 vols. (1837–9). 6th edn. London. 1860.

Halsey, Le Roy J. *The Literary Attractions of the Bible*. Philadelphia. (1858) 1860.

Hammond, Gerald. *The Making of the English Bible*. Manchester: Carcanet Press. 1982.

'William Tyndale's Pentateuch: its relation to Luther's German Bible and the Hebrew original'. *Renaissance Quarterly* 33 (1980): 351–85.

Handover, P.M. *Printing in London from 1476 to Modern Times*. London: Allen & Unwin. 1960.

Happé, Peter (ed.). *English Mystery Plays*. Harmondsworth: Penguin. 1975.

Herbert, A.S. *Historical Catalogue of Printed Editions of the English Bible, 1525–1961*. London: British and Foreign Bible Society. 1968.

Hills, Edward F. *The King James Version Defended!* Des Moines: Christian Research Press. 1956.

Hoare, H.W. *The Evolution of the English Bible*. London: John Murray. 1901.

Hughes, Lewes. *Certain Grievances*. London. 1640.

Humphry, W. G. *A Commentary on the Revised Version of the New Testament*. London. 1882.

Hunt, Geoffrey. *About the New English Bible*. London: Oxford University Press. 1970.

Husbands, John. *A Miscellany of Poems*. Oxford. 1731.

James, Thomas. *Catalogus Librorum Bibliothecae Publicae . . . Thomas Bodleius*. Oxford. 1605.

Catalogus universalis librorum in bibliotheca Bodleiana. Oxford. 1620.

Johnson, Anthony. *An Historical Account of the Several English Translations of the Bible, and the opposition they met with from the Church of Rome*. London. 1730.

Kilburne, William. *Dangerous Errors in several late printed Bibles*. Finsbury. 1659.

Knappen, M.M. (ed.). *Two Elizabethan Puritan Diaries* by Richard Rogers and Samuel Ward. Chicago: American Society of Church History; London: SPCK. 1933.

Laud, William. *The Works*. 7 vols. Oxford. 1847–57.

Leedham-Green, E.S. *Books in Cambridge Inventories*. 2 vols. Cambridge University Press. 1986.

Lewis, C.S. 'The literary impact of the Authorised Version'. In C.S. Lewis, *They Asked for a Paper*. London: Bles. 1962.

Lewis, John. *History of the Several Translations of the Holy Bible*. 1731, prefixed to *The New Testament . . . by John Wiclif*. 2nd edn. London. 1739.

Lightfoot, John. *A Sermon Preached before the Honourable House of Commons*. London. 1645.

Lightfoot, John B., Richard Chenevix Trench and C. J. Ellicott, intro. Philip Schaff. *The Revision of the English Version of the New Testament*. New York: Harper and Brothers. 1873.

Lloyd Jones, G. *The Discovery of Hebrew in Tudor England: A Third Language*. Manchester University Press. 1983.

Locke, John. *An Essay for the Understanding of St Paul's Epistles*. London. 1707.

Loftie, W. J. *A Century of Bibles, or the Authorised Version from 1611 to 1711*. London. 1872.

Lowes, John Livingston. 'The noblest monument of English prose'. In *Of Reading Books*. London: Constable. 1930. Pp. 47–77.

Lowth, Robert. *A sermon preached at the visitation of the Honourable and Right Reverend Richard Lord Bishop of Durham*. London. 1758.
Short Introduction to English Grammar. London. 1762.
Isaiah. London. 1778.
Lectures on the Sacred Poetry of the Hebrews. Trans. George Gregory. 2 vols. London. 1787.

Lysons, Daniel. *The Environs of London*. London. 1795.

Macaulay, Thomas Babington. 'John Dryden'. *The Edinburgh Review* 47 (January 1828): 93.

MacCulloch, Diarmaid. *Thomas Cranmer: A Life*. New Haven and London: Yale University Press. 1996.

Marsh, George P. *Lectures on the English Language*. Ed. William Smith. New York. 1862.

McClure, Alexander. *The Translators Revived*. New York. 1853.

McKitterick, David. *A History of Cambridge University Press*. 3 vols. Cambridge University Press. 1992–2004.

Metzger, Bruce M. *The Text of the New Testament: Its Transmission, Corruption and Restoration*. Oxford: Clarendon Press. 1964.

Mombert, J.I. *English Versions of the Bible*. London and New York. 1883.

More, Thomas. *The Confutation of Tyndale's Answer* (1532, 1533); *The Complete Works of St. Thomas More*, vol. VIII. New Haven and London: Yale University Press. 1973.

Morgan, Paul. 'A King's Printer at work'. *Bodleian Library Record*, 13:5 (October 1990): 370–4.

Mozley, J.F. *Coverdale and his Bibles*. London: Lutterworth Press. 1953.

Nicolson, Adam. *Power and Glory: Jacobean England and the Making of the King James Bible*. London: HarperCollins. 2003.

Norton, David. *A History of the Bible as Literature*. 2 vols. Cambridge University Press. 1993.
A History of the English Bible as Literature. Cambridge University Press. 2000.
A Textual History of the King James Bible. Cambridge University Press. 2005.

'John Bois's notes on the revision of the King James Bible New Testament: a new manuscript'. *The Library*, sixth series 18 (Dec. 1996): 328–46.

'John Bois, Bible translator, in old age'. In *Still Shines When You Think of It: A Festschrift for Vincent O'Sullivan*. Ed. Bill Manhire and Peter Whiteford. Wellington: Victoria University Press. 2007. Pp. 318–42.

Opfell, Olga S. *The King James Bible Translators*. London: McFarland. 1982.

Oxford Dictionary of National Biography (online version).

Oxford English Dictionary (online version).

Paine, Gustavus S. *The Men Behind the King James Version*. Grand Rapids: Baker Book House. (1959) 1977.

Pettie, George. *The Civil Conversation of M. Stephen Guazzo*. London. 1581.

Pilkington, Matthew. *Remarks upon Several Passages of Scripture*. Cambridge. 1759.

Plomer, Henry R. 'The King's Printing House under the Stuarts'. *The Library*, n.s. 2 (1901): 353–75.

Pollard, Alfred W. (ed.). *Records of the English Bible*. London: Oxford University Press. 1911.

Prynne, William. *Canterbury's Doom*. London. 1646.

Rosenthal, Erwin I.J. 'Edward Lively: Cambridge Hebraist'. In D. Winton Thomas (ed.). *Essays and Studies Presented to Stanley Arthur Cook*. London: Taylor's Foreign Press. 1950. Pp. 95–112.

Saintsbury, George. *A History of English Prose Rhythm*. London: Macmillan. 1912.

Say, Samuel. 'Essay . . . on the harmony, variety and power of numbers in general, whether in prose or verse'. In *Poems on Several Occasions*. London. 1745.

Scragg, D.C. *A History of English Spelling*. Manchester University Press. 1974.

Scrivener, F.H.A. *The Authorized Edition of the English Bible (1611): Its Subsequent Reprints and Modern Representatives*. Cambridge University Press. (1884) 1910.

Selden, John. *Table Talk*. London. 1689.

Simpson, Percy. *Proof-reading in the Sixteenth, Seventeenth and Eighteenth Centuries*. London: Oxford University Press. 1935.

Smith, John. *The Mystery of Rhetoric Unveiled*. London. 1656.

Smith, Miles. *Sermons of . . . Miles Smith*. London. 1632.

Sparke, Michael. *Scintilla*. London. 1641.

Sperber, Alexander (ed.). *The Bible in Aramaic*. Vol. III: *The Latter Prophets According to Targum Jonathan*. Leiden: Brill. 1992.

Spottiswoode (Spotswood), John. *History of the Church of Scotland*. London. 1655.

Strype, John. *The Life and Acts of Matthew Parker*. London. 1711.

Stubbings, Frank, compiler. *Forty-Nine Lives: An Anthology of Portraits of Emmanuel Men*. Cambridge University Press. 1983.

Swift, Jonathan. *A Proposal for Correcting, Improving and Ascertaining the English Tongue*. 2nd edn. London. 1712.

Trench, Richard Chenevix. *On the Authorised Version of the New Testament*. London. 1858.

Tyndale, William, *The Obedience of a Christian Man*. Marlborow [Antwerp]. 1528.

Van Eerde, Katherine S. *John Ogilby and the Taste of his Times*. Folkestone: Dawson. 1976.

Vance, Laurence M. *Archaic Words and the Authorized Version* (1996). Pensacola: Vance Publications. 1999.

Venn, John. *Biographical History of Gonville and Caius College*. 3 vols. Cambridge University Press. 1901.

Voet, Leon. *The Plantin Press (1555–1589). A Bibliography*. 3 vols. Amsterdam: Van Hoeve. 1980.

W., E. (Edward Whiston). *The Life and Death of Mr Henry Jessey*. London. 1671.

Walker, Anthony. 'The Life of that Famous Grecian Mr John Bois'. Originally published in Francis Peck, *Desideria Curiosa* (1779). Reprinted in Allen, *Translating for King James*. 18th-century manuscript copy. British Library. MS Harley 7053.

Walton, Izaak. *The Life of Dr Sanderson*. London. 1678.

Ward, Samuel. *Diary*. Sidney Sussex College archives. MS 45.
  Thomas Baker, selections from Ward's manuscripts. Cambridge University Library. Baker Mss, Mm 2 25. Pp. 308–26 (fols. 159^r–168^r).

Welsted, Leonard. *Epistles, Odes, etc*. London. 1724.

Westbrook, Vivienne. 'Translators of the Authorised Version of the Bible'. *Oxford Dictionary of National Biography*.

Westcott, Brooke Foss. *A General View of the History of the English Bible* (1868). 3rd edn, rev. William Aldis Wright. London: Macmillan. 1905.

Wheeler, G.W. (ed.). *The Letters of Sir Thomas Bodley to Thomas James*. Oxford: Clarendon Press. 1926.

White, Joseph. *A Revisal of the English Translation of the Old Testament Recommended*. Oxford. 1779.

Whitelocke, Bulstrode. *Memorials of the English Affairs*. London. 1682.

Willey, Basil. 'On translating the Bible into modern English'. *Essays and Studies*, n.s. 23 (1970): 1–17.

Wood, Anthony à. *Athenae Oxonienses*. London. 1691.
  The History and Antiquities of the University of Oxford. 2 vols. Oxford. 1792.

Wright, William Aldis. *The Authorised Version of the English Bible 1611*. 5 vols. Cambridge University Press. 1909.

Index

Printed in the United States
By Bookmasters